Holding Stone Hands

On the Trail of the Cheyenne Exodus

ALAN BOYE

University of Nebraska Press : Lincoln and London

The following publishers have generously given permission to quote from copyrighted works: Excerpt from "Golden Feather," by Robbie Robertson © WB Music Corp. (ASCAP) & Medicine Hat Music (ASCAP). All Rights administered by WB Music Corp. All Rights Reserved. Used by permission Warner Bros. Publications U.S. Inc., Miami FL 33014.

Excerpt from *And as I Rode Out on the Morning*, by Buck Ramsey, copyright 1993, reprinted by permission of the publisher, Texas Tech University Press.

Excerpts from "East Coker" and "Little Gidding" in *Four Quartets*, copyright 1943 by T. S. Eliot and renewed 1971 by Esme Valerie Eliot, reprinted by permission of Harcourt Brace & Company, and Faber and Faber Ltd. Acknowledgments for other previously published materials appear on page xii.

LIBRARY OF CONGRESS CATALOGING-IN-PUBLICATION DATA
Boye, Alan, 1950–
Holding stone hands: on the trail of the Cheyenne exodus / Alan Boye. p. cm. Includes bibliographical references. ISBN 0-8032-1294-1 (cloth: alkaline paper).
1. Cheyenne Indians – History – 19th century. 2. Cheyenne Indians – Relocation. 3. Cheyenne Indians – Government relations. 4. Dull Knife, ca. 1828–1879 or 1883. 5. Little Wolf, d. 1904. I. Title.
E99C53B68 1999 978'.004973 – dc21 98-49783 CIP

For Linda Wacholder & to the memory of Matilda Jean Boye

The great trouble with the world was
that that which survived was
held in hard evidence as to past events.

CORMAC MCCARTHY, *The Crossing*

Contents

Illustrations

Acknowledgments

This book owes its existence to the encouragement and support of the Northern Cheyenne people. Without their graceful tolerance of my intrusions and their uncomplaining assistance at every step, this project would not have been possible.

Sadly, Ted Risingsun did not live to see the book's completion, but it is his encouragement, support, and strength that give this book its life.

My research simply would not have been possible without the help of the following folks, and I am thankful they are in the world: David and Carol Wilson, Wayne Leman, Cathy One Bear, Lillian and Dewayne Hodgson, Rex Myers, Peggy Williams, Carey O'Brien, Gail Montany, Marla Sawyer, John Boye, and Benjamin Boye.

In the dark, quiet hours of writing, these offered their crucial encouragement and boundless inspiration: Richard Moye, Omar Johnson, Jeff Briggs, Buck Beliles, Mel Mann, Dr. Rob Hoppe, Kris Fritz-Hoppe, W. Clark Whitehorn, and Andrew Boye.

For their tireless help in research I am grateful for the assistance of Fonda Farr, Director of the Last Indian Raid Museum, Oberlin, Kansas; Craig Cox, Director of the Atwood, Kansas, Museum; Darrell Rice and Mrs. Olson of Waynoka, Oklahoma; Rosalie Seeman, County Clerk of Thomas County, Kansas; Marilyn Carder of the Sheridan County, Kansas, Historical Society; Robert Richter of Ogallala, Nebraska; Angie Bowman of Trenton, Nebraska; Vyrtis Thomas and David Burgevin, Museum Specialist, Smithsonian Institution; and Tom Buecker, Curator, Fort Robinson State Park. In addition, numerous others along the route provided me with detailed maps and suggestions, and I thank them for their patient and prompt assistance. I am indebted to the staffs at the various special collections where I did my research, and especially to those at the Mari Sandoz Collection at the University of Nebraska, the National Archives, the Nebraska State Historical Society, the Kansas State Historical Society, the Oklahoma State

Historical Society, and the Colorado State Historical Society, and to the public library staff in Hardin and Billings, Montana. Special thanks are due to the staff at the Samuel Read Library at Vermont's Lyndon State College for their assistance. For many others who are not mentioned here, and on whose help I depended, your gifts of time and effort are in my heart.

For medical advice and assistance, my thanks to Dr. John Ajamie and Meri Simon.

To Caroline Sandoz Pifer, Margot Liberty, the Ron Harris family, Yolando "Cowboy" Fisher, Jeanne Eder, Lee Lone Bear, Orlan Svingen, William Tall Bull, Randolph Lewis, Amy Erlich, Kathy Bales, David Boye, and Bill Price, my thanks for essential help with everything from contacts, rides, steak dinners, encouragement, and prayers to a welcomed place to sleep.

My main traveling companions, Andrew Sooktis and Samuel Spotted Elk Jr., tolerated my eccentricities with grace and good humor and have sealed a place in my heart with their ongoing friendship. I owe a special thanks to those whose support was critical to the successful completion of this project: Rubie Sooktis, Barbara One Bear Spang, the Vermont State College's Advanced Study Program, and Linda Wacholder.

And thanks too to these others, here and gone on, for their gift of inspiration and courage: Colin Fletcher, Edward Abbey, Eileen Andrews, and Ken Kesey.

Some portions of this book have been published previously, in slightly different form. "Coming to See Bear Butte" appeared in *South Dakota Review* 33, 1 (Spring 1995), p.57. "By Cheyenne Campfires" was published in *Twin Towers* 9, 2 (Winter 1996), p.2. "The Divide" first appeared in *Lyndon Review* (Spring 1997), p.75. "The Barren Wastes" was published in *North Dakota Quarterly* 65, 2 (Spring 1998), p.146. "Kit Drums and the Wild Dogs of Fonda" appeared in *Southern Humanities Review* (1998). "Oh Kom Ha Ka" and "Morning Star" will appear in *Wild West* (1999). And "Henry Ford and Mr. Goodnight" will be published in *Heritage of the Plains* (1999).

Holding Stone Hands

Prologue

The camp was moving at night.

The story catchers could not weave their stories, and there would be no waiting while they lit their pipes, glanced about the circle, and said, "I will tie another story to the one just told," and begin anew, story after glorious story, on and on again until the dawn light came pink on the east.

The camp was moving at night.

There would be no great circle of lodges to be set up, no callers to go out inviting guests to feasts, no stick games for the warriors, no bead games for the women, no sweat lodge, no sacrifice ceremonies, and no sleep, for the camp was moving at night.

They were moving north, back to a place that no longer existed. Exiled from a homeland others now called Wyoming, Nebraska, Montana. Escapees from a refugee camp known as Indian Territory. Oklahoma.

American refugees.

At the moment of night's deepest darkness, on the knife edge of the turning of an age, the passing of an era, approximately three hundred Northern Cheyenne slipped so silently away from their standing tepees that one hundred soldiers, camped nearby and positioned to prevent their escape out of Indian Territory, continued to sleep unaware. It was September 9, 1878. They were leaving the bad place; they were going back home.

The fabric of that story, and of stories since, are tied here together so that — despite everything — we might know it remains a single tale we hear.

PART ONE

Kit Fox Drums and the Wild Dogs of Fonda

When you find a golden feather it means
you'll never lose your way back home.
ROBBIE ROBERTSON, "Golden Feather"

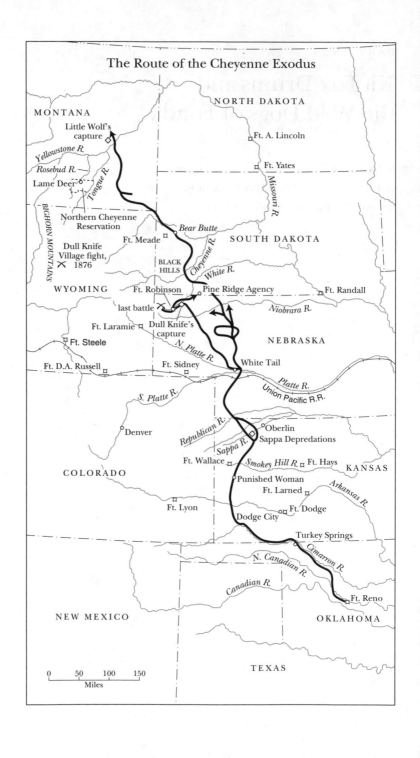

The Route of the Cheyenne Exodus

NORTH DAKOTA

MONTANA

Little Wolf's capture

Ft. A. Lincoln

Yellowstone R.

Rosebud R.

Ft. Yates

Lame Deer

Tongue R.

Missouri R.

Northern Cheyenne Reservation

Bear Butte

Ft. Meade

SOUTH DAKOTA

Cheyenne R.

Dull Knife Village fight, 1876

BLACK HILLS

White R.

WYOMING

Ft. Robinson

Pine Ridge Agency

Ft. Randall

last battle

Niobrara R.

Ft. Laramie

Dull Knife's capture

NEBRASKA

Ft. Steele

N. Platte R.

Ft. D.A. Russell

Ft. Sidney

White Tail

Platte R.

Union Pacific R.R.

S. Platte R.

Denver

Republican R.

Oberlin

Sappa Depredations

Sappa R.

Ft. Wallace

Smokey Hill R.

Ft. Hays

KANSAS

COLORADO

Punished Woman

Ft. Larned

Arkansas R.

Ft. Lyon

Ft. Dodge

Dodge City

Turkey Springs

N. Canadian R.

Cimarron R.

Canadian R.

Ft. Reno

NEW MEXICO

OKLAHOMA

TEXAS

0   50   100   150

Miles

1. The Leaving

I have not slept all night. Not even changed clothes. Instead, I have busied myself with the countless items left to do before I can leave. At 3 A.M. I realize that the strange sorrow that has overcome me and the frenetic, nearly psychotic, activity of the long night have only tried to mask a simple fact: I don't want to leave.

To leave the boys, Linda, the comfort of the familiar.

Earlier, the four of us danced about the house, an evening of tears and laughter and loving. Every emotion was near the surface for everyone; everyone was full aware of the coming changes. We all saw the creature that lurked in our home: the leaving. My leaving for two months was an uninvited guest whose intentions were far from clear.

The night before departing to prison, or to war, must be much like tonight was for us.

My backpacking journey has neither the ever-present specter of death nor the horror of war; nor does it have the isolation and subjugation of prison. My purpose is simply to retrace a bit of history. I am going to try to walk the trailless route of a handful of desperate Indians who had fled across America.

In 1878 about three hundred Northern Cheyenne men, women, and children fled to escape the starvation and disease of a prison known as Indian Territory: Oklahoma. Their journey turned into a thousand-mile running battle of pain and sorrow.

The reason for their journey was far too complex ever to fully comprehend. But at the heart of all such journeys is the longing for home. What I was leaving, by choice, they died trying to regain. The same specter who haunted my family this evening came down on them like the black clouds of raging spring storms that sweep the prairies of Oklahoma. Such longings can press down on your chest like stones, brought on by the sweet smell of the prairie grasses, the pale yellow of flowers blooming on the soap plant yucca, the touch of the wind, the rains of Montana. It is the same for anyone: either lift them away or be crushed.

I have not slept all night because of this weight, this longing, this uninvited guest. By 5 A.M. I demand a change, some way of disinviting it, of lifting away the sorrow of my leaving.

So I take an hour's walk into the cool, brightening dawn and am transformed. On a hill above my Vermont home I stop at the expansive view to the east. The dawn is arriving. An arch of arrow-straight rays shoot from the unseen sun below the horizon. Behind me, to the west, deep yellow and gold clouds glimmer in the reflected light. Below, gray steeples and dark rooftops: the town sleeps peacefully still in the shadow of night. My home.

In the morning time passes quickly, and the boys seem less concerned about my leaving and more directed at the excitement of their own trip to the Maine coast that Linda had planned as a diversion to my leaving. This hike would never have come to pass had it not been for her support and encouragement, and even now as I stammer my apologies for such a harebrained idea, she silences me. "We'll be fine," she says. "Stop talking like that." She takes my hand in hers. "I love you."

We leave three sets of greasy marks where our lips have pressed on either side of the window glass, and they drive away, three white arms waving until they are gone.

At eight sharp I hoist the backpack. I am shocked at its weight. My first thought is: I will never be able to carry this eight hundred miles or more. But I take a deep breath, pause a second for a prayer, and step outside.

That step sends me around the far side of the house in order to stay in the yard as long as possible. I pass the garden and at its edge is a broken Frisbee the boys use to mark home plate. The lilac leaves are half out, the still-dormant blossoms of apples are pink, wax balls on barely green twigs. In the grass at the edge of the yard is a small piece of a blue egg, speckled with flecks of white. Undoubtedly someone's nest was robbed.

Then I am away from home.

At the end of the block I turn back for last a look. A solitary sunbeam has broken from a white cloud and shines across the sky. Every hill surrounding our home is about to bloom. Spring is being born.

In a half mile I am on the bridge over the Passumpsic River –

my first river crossing. From the top of the bridge I can see down the Passumpsic Valley. A light fog clings to the path the river takes through my home, which I am leaving, which is a good home, a peaceful, hidden home, in this valley in New England hills and history. Like the Cheyennes, I too am going away to Oklahoma, and will have a long journey back to my home, this sunny-bright Saturday town.

"That's quite a load," a woman says at the convenience store, which doubles as the town's bus station. She is buying a quart of whole milk. "Where are you going?"

"Oklahoma."

"Oklahoma?" She inspects me closer now, suspicious. "Why would you want to go there?" Two weeks earlier a bomb at the Federal Building in Oklahoma City had taken the lives of 168 people.

"I'm going to try to walk from Oklahoma to the Black Hills," I say.

"Are you following some kind of trail?" she asks.

"Well, I'm going to try and follow the route of a historic incident. Cowboys and Indians."

She nods. In the weeks leading up to my leaving people had been responding to my plans in one of two ways. Either they have smiled and said, "Have a great time," or have been somber and whispered, "Be careful." This woman does both; she says, "Good luck."

As she leaves, the bus pulls up in a cloud of black diesel smoke. The driver winces as he throws the pack into the luggage compartment. I take a last look at my town, then step onboard. I sit down and flip open the newspaper I bought. The news is still all of the Oklahoma City tragedy. The injured, the bereaved, the motives, the suspect. I read that the only man arrested so far was just transported to a federal penitentiary at El Reno, Oklahoma.

I sit bolt upright. El Reno is within a stone's throw of the old Cheyenne-Arapahoe Indian Agency, the headquarters for the military. The Northern Cheyennes had escaped from that very place.

The bus roars westward, but a specter rides with me. It has reached out and placed the recent tragedy side by side with the long-ago suffering of the Cheyenne people. For a moment it has lifted them both above the haze of time. I must be quick and watchful in order to best understand the truths it may reveal.

Three days later I will stand in the gray rain at the old Fort Reno cemetery on a grassy hill above the federal penitentiary about to begin walking in the footsteps of the Cheyennes.

2. Black Kettles in the Land of Roman Nose

Above the darkened downtown of Oklahoma City an exploding lightning bolt scatters its sizzling incandescence across the black sky. It is ten o'clock at night and we have been driving all day from our boyhood home of Lincoln, Nebraska. My brother is driving, but he has not spoken in some time, concentrating instead on the gigantic storm that is pounding down on the city. He is driving me to where I will start my hike. All day long our talk has been animated and cheerful, but since entering the Oklahoma City limits, we have been silent.

I squint through the bullets of rain on the window, but there is nothing to see of the recent bombing. From the interstate, the downtown sparkles banally in artificial and storm light. Earlier today the city detonated carefully placed sticks of dynamite to demolish the shell of the devastated Federal Building, more dust falling on the memory of the sudden, violent deaths of so many.

The deaths came of a violence not of nature but of a nurtured hatred. Once the shock passes that such terror can happen here in the ordinary bustling of a midwestern spring morning, comes the harder truth that such malice can happen at all. In the faces of the murderers who brought such death lies hidden the dark and abhorrent features of a larger truth. Its hideous visage appears in the smoke and blood of such a tragedy, a face all the more frightening because we suddenly recognize its features as familiar, even commonplace. In the blood and tears and twisted architecture of human remains is the snarling profile of common, ordinary hatred.

We pass a billboard thanking the nation for support and prayers during the tragedy. The radio reports tornadoes to the east of the city. We are headed west, toward El Reno.

In thirty minutes we are standing in the lobby of some nameless motel just off Interstate 40. A young, very pregnant woman sits behind the desk, but she does not look up at us. Instead, she is staring at a television set. The 10 P.M. news is on. She watches, transfixed. We do not speak but stare with her as video of a blast fills the screen. The final explosion leveling the bombed-out Alfred P. Murrah Federal Building is shown and reshown from a dozen different angles. For the full ten seconds it takes to reduce the building to dust, the roar of the blast is the only sound.

The newscaster says, "Barricades were set up by authorities to prevent anything being taken as souvenirs."

The pregnant clerk turns to us, her eyes downcast. "Souvenirs? What monster would ever want a souvenir?"

It is an overcast morning and a light rain is falling. We drive a short distance to the old fort grounds just west of El Reno. The fort is on a long, low hill in the tree-lined valley of the North Canadian River. The Cheyenne-Arapahoe Indian Agency was on the riverbank opposite the fort. Although only a few tattered clapboard buildings remain of the fort, one brick building still houses busy governmental offices. The building is locked up tight, and I have to pound on the door to get someone's attention. The cheerful woman who comes to open the door shrugs when I ask her about the locked doors. "Everyone's being cautious since the bombing," she explains. At my request she directs us to the cemetery.

The cemetery is just west of the building. We wander around the old, uniform white markers, reading the names. It looks as if no one has been buried here for decades, and most of the markers are from the days when Oklahoma was Indian Territory. Against the rear stone wall, which now functions largely to keep out range cattle, a single, isolated marker is the final resting place of Chalk, an Arapaho scout for the army who was killed in the first battle against the fleeing Cheyennes at a place seventy or eighty miles from here known as Turkey Springs. I stand at this marker and call to my brother, who is in a far corner of the cemetery. "Here. Here's something from that time," I say.

A mile to the southwest, in its own shelter of tiny trees, the pink walls of the federal penitentiary are glistening in the gray rain where the suspect in the bombing sits, perhaps staring up at this very hill.

We leave the cemetery, then drive back through the fort and on a few miles to the northwest looking for the place I am to start. I know what the place should look like: a solitary bluff, just north of Geary, where the Cheyennes had camped the night they escaped. The landscape is flat, deep green fields and red soil in the skinny rain.

I am fidgeting and babbling, trying not very successfully to hide my fear. I am no stunning physical specimen, and despite my months of training, I realize that I may not make it.

My brother notices my agitation. "Tell me again why you want to do this?" he says.

I had first heard of the story of Little Wolf and Dull Knife and their long flight toward home while growing up in Nebraska, and I had always been drawn to it. Initially it seemed like a perfect metaphor for the history of white and Indian relations, and later not a metaphor at all, but a heart-wrenching tale of courage, desire, and strength. But in the end neither of those reasons were what had brought me here.

Because of its antiquity, the human history of almost every place in the world has faded to nothing more than fables, dead stories whose characters seem but remote fictions. When I was a boy, many of the elderly men and women who walked the streets of Lincoln had been brought to the state in covered wagons, had been boys and girls in the time of Dull Knife and Little Wolf. Here was a part of the human history: this faded tragedy was a part of the explanation of who we had come to be, something that might explain us to ourselves and how we had come to live here in the high, open prairies of America.

And it all had happened but a heartbeat ago.

"There's got to be an easier way to get a feel for history than walking a thousand miles," my brother says.

I shake my head. "I guess I just was attracted to the Cheyennes' desire for home, and why so many people risked their lives to return there." This is what I say, but I am thinking more selfish thoughts. Even with the best of luck, I have less than half my life remaining, and I am dulled into believing that the safety of my modern life will insulate me from the enormity of time. "I want to truly understand," I say out loud, "that once, long ago, these people were as alive as we are. They were breathing and laughing and crying human beings – then they died out here somewhere. If I can really picture that, then I think I may understand some simple truth in my own life."

"Well," he says with a laugh, "it isn't hard to see who has the most common sense in the family."

In a moment he points ahead and to the west side of the road. In the distance the landmark is unmistakable, even in the gray rain. A large horseshoe-shaped hill rises above the flat, plain landscape. He pulls over onto a wide stretch of shoulder. We look at the bluff in silence.

Here it began, and it began because of the children.

On Sunday morning, September 8, 1878, the Indian Agency doctor, a man by the name of Robert Hodge, came from Fort Reno to this bluff, where several hundred Northern Cheyennes had set up their camp. The Cheyennes had paid no attention to an order from the commander at the fort that all children had to report to the Indian school at the agency. Hodge had been sent to ascertain if the children were too sick to come into the fort school, as the Cheyennes claimed. Two companies of troops had accompanied him and were camped a mile away to help move the children into the fort school. The military command at the fort believed that a show of force would convince the Cheyennes to send their children in.

The doctor moved from tepee to tepee and found much distrust and suspicion. He was not allowed to go anywhere in the camp without someone accompanying him. "They were camped upon a small, level piece of bottom land that was surrounded on all but the south side with sand hills from one to two hundred feet high," he later wrote.

Only later did he realize the advantage of the location. "The Indians had been prepared to massacre the troops had they attempted to encircle the camp, for they would have been subjected to an infuriating fire from all sides and probably would have been killed to a man." The Northern Cheyennes had protected themselves perfectly and commanded every square inch of the bluff.

At sundown the next night the commanding officer of Fort Reno, in the company of the Indian agent, visited the camp. They told the Cheyenne leaders that before rations would be issued to feed the hungry, their members had to be counted, and the children had to enroll in the school. Until then troops would guard the camp and food would be withheld. According to the officer in charge, the Cheyennes seemed friendly when the party left the camp at dusk.

That night two hundred soldiers camped near the horseshoe-shaped bluff. The Cheyennes held a dance that lasted late into the warm, star-filled night. A few guards stood at the fringe of the soldier's camp, squinting into the flecks of light from the Cheyenne campfires, watching the shadows dance and flicker.

In the middle of that dark, moonless night, with their campfires still burning, their tepees left standing, about three hundred Northern Cheyenne men, women, and children silently slipped over the back side of the bluff and mounted the horses that waited there. The troops nearby did not know they were gone until dawn.

"Oh, oh," my brother says. He is looking up and into the car's rearview mirror.

A police car has pulled in behind us, its lights flashing. The young state patrolman gets out and walks up to us, cautiously.

"You lost?" he says.

We explain, briefly, about my hike, and the last camp at the bluff in the distance.

"Is that right?" the patrolman says, excited now. "I grew up a mile from here. I always knew that bluff had some history, but I didn't know what." He points to a distant ranch house, visible near the base of the bluff. "That's my house. We've found arrowheads and such on that bluff for years, but I never knew what had happened there. Cheyennes, you say?"

"Northern Cheyennes," I say.

The patrolman climbs in his car and drives away with a slow, western wave of his hand. His departure is a sign, and I open the car door. "No more delaying," I say.

Ten minutes later I have put on my rain suit, hoisted the backpack, checked and rechecked my gear. I am ready.

A pure white cattle egret flies across a neighboring field. The pack is incredibly heavy. I shake hands with my brother and watch his car disappear. I begin.

Almost immediately everything changes. For one thing, I actually see what is around me. My eyes chance upon a tall clump of big bluestem grass, and I notice how the spreading turkey-foot pattern of flowers stand blue in the steel rain. I note the pattern of rocks and stones on the red soil, the shape of low clouds against the Cheyennes' bluff, the tick of rain against the hood of my raincoat.

My body shifts. The months of long walks preparing for this day have taught my body to fall quickly into the rhythmic, equal pace best suited for great distances.

And my mind alters, too. The self-doubt and fear that has characterized the last week I forcefully push away. For a second I begin to imagine how incredible the distance I want to cross, how unlikely my chance of success. I am stabbed by an overwhelming sorrow of missing my wife and children. I know enough of myself to understand that such thoughts will grow and fester in the weeks to come if I let them dominate. To combat this I try not to think about the countless future miles, nor on the past happiness of my sweet home, but only on the single day in front of me, the ten or twelve miles and path to camp.

My projected trip encompasses twenty-seven county maps, which I have numbered and packed in sets that Linda will mail to me along my route. I remove Map Number One and study the day's projected route. I have planned an easy first day; my destination is a state park, ten miles distant.

A car slows and stops.

"You've made two miles in forty-five minutes." My brother has followed my route after getting gas. "Are you sure you don't want a ride?"

We laugh and wave. He does a U-turn in the middle of the wet highway and drives away for good.

It is still raining when I walk through my first town, Watonga. Cars pass, their wipers slapping at the cold spring rain, but I am dry inside my rain suit. There are no people on the streets. My view of the town is limited: a short mile of houses and gas stations, a grain elevator, and a set of railroad tracks. North of town I leave the U.S. highway and take a smaller, paved road that rises slowly to a low ridge. There are more trees than I had imagined there would be; most hilltops and valleys are lined with them. A pickup truck passes by. The rancher inside eyes me suspiciously. I wave. He brightens, waves back, and dismisses me.

It is still raining an hour later. A school bus passes me and stops a quarter mile ahead. Three kids whirlwind out of the bus, across the wet highway, and up to a house set behind some trees. When I come up to the house there is a young man about twenty-five playing tag with the three children in the soft rain. He has long black hair and a straight, angular face. An Indian. He is so occupied with the game that he does not notice me until he nearly runs into me on the highway. He sees me and then does a double take.

"Hey, you guys, come!" he calls to the children. "A hiker!"

They gather around me, the children cautiously inspecting my pack and rain suit while the young man asks me why I am walking. I tell him, prepared to explain how Little Wolf and Dull Knife and others led the Northern Cheyennes north, but he cuts me off. He knows all about the story.

"I'm a Southern Cheyenne," he says. "I have relatives in Montana. Are you going to Sturgis? They say Little Wolf went there on his way north."

"I hope to," I say. "I want to go to Bear Butte."

"That's the Sioux name for it," he says. "We Cheyennes call it Noahvose: it means 'Teaching hill' or 'Place where people were taught.'" He holds out a big hand. "My name is Cecil Black. I'm a descendant of Black Kettle." He is nearly hopping around with energy, his dark eyes full of excitement and promise. "You gotta meet my mom," he says suddenly and darts away into the house, the three children following him.

I stand on the highway, dripping and staring at the comfortable house in disbelief. On the first day of my hike the first person I meet is Cheyenne – a descendant of Black Kettle, no less.

Black Kettle was one of the most significant chiefs in Cheyenne history. He was a Southern Cheyenne leader who had signed the Treaty of Fort Wise in 1861, reducing a vast territory originally ceded to the Cheyennes to a small reservation in southeastern Colorado. Three years later, however, fear of the Indians was high, and rumors were spreading among the pioneers of Colorado that the Cheyennes planned to rejoin their northern relatives and start a war against the whites. That spring a number of incidents between whites and Cheyennes intensified the fears. An order was issued by the leader of the Colorado Volunteers, Colonel John M. Chivington, to "kill Cheyenne whenever and wherever found."

On November 29, 1864, Black Kettle was one of the leaders of a band of five hundred Cheyennes who were camped on Sand Creek at the edge of their Colorado reservation. Two-thirds of the group were women and children. They had chosen the spot because Black Kettle had been assured by army officers that here they would be safe. At dawn the women were awake and starting the breakfast fires when they heard what they assumed was a large herd of buffalo moving toward them. It was Chivington and seven hundred Colorado Volunteers. Chivington's last order before he sounded the charge was to take no prisoners.

At the first gunshot, Black Kettle ran from his tepee, past the white flag of truce and the American flag he always flew. Years later an eyewitness told a writer:

> Children were brained and hacked to pieces, pregnant women were ripped open, stiffened corpses of men, women and children the next day were scalped, dismembered and indecently mutilated, and the bloody scalps and members hung at saddle bows and hatbands and carried into Denver and there paraded in a public theater.

Of the 137 Cheyennes who were killed, 28 were men and 109 were women and children. Black Kettle survived Sand Creek only to be killed a few years later in another battle with whites, this one on the banks of the Washita River in Oklahoma. His village was attacked again, this time by George Armstrong Custer, who had followed the trail of a war party to the Washita, even though most of the people there were Black Kettle's peaceful followers.

To the Cheyennes, Black Kettle is considered one of the most powerful and spiritual men to have ever walked this earth. A report in the *Wichita Eagle* said his hand had never been raised against any human being. His life had been spent in trying to preserve peace between his people and his oppressors.

In a moment Cecil returns, followed by a small, older woman wearing a shawl draped over her shoulders.

"Mom, this guy is walking to South Dakota. He's following Little Wolf and Dull Knife's route."

Roberta Black nods at me and as I speak, but she politely makes no eye contact. She asks if I have talked to anyone from the Northern Cheyenne Reservation in Montana, and when I tell her yes she nods again, gently correcting my pronunciation of names. She seems to know them all, though they are a thousand miles distant.

"Cecil tells me you are related to Black Kettle," I say.

She nods matter-of-factly, and a hint of a smile flashes over her face. "Where are you spending the night?" she asks.

"Roman Nose State Park," I tell her, and add, "but my legs are so tired I don't know if I can make it these last couple of miles, much less all the way to South Dakota."

"Oh, you'll make it." She is staring off over the hills in the distance. "I'll say a prayer. You'll make it."

We part, and I walk down the road, buoyed by this chance meeting on the empty high plains of Oklahoma.

With two miles to go I stop and remove the pack for the first time. My shoulders, back, and legs ache, but what is most fascinating is how my body is absolutely drained. It isn't even how every part of me is fatigued but the wholeness of the exhaustion that intrigues me. I eat a snack and hoist the backpack once more for the final trek to camp.

Roman Nose State Park is invisible. To see it you must approach across the low, flat, largely featureless plains of north central Oklahoma until, unannounced and sudden, the land drops away into a series of canyons and coulees, thick with oak and willow and pine.

I walk down into the canyon, past the deserted park headquarters and nearly empty resort building perched between a golf course and a reservoir. I walk into the resort to call my family. The phone rings and rings, and when it answers I hear nothing but my own voice on the answering machine. My heart falls, but I try to make my voice sound upbeat and carefree. I hang up and walk on. At the bottom of the canyon, along a shallow, flat creek, I set up camp in the small group of cottonwoods. Tomorrow's route, out of the canyon, is up a steep road to the west, but I do not think of that as I set up camp and prepare my first meal: freeze-dried lasagna.

Just as I finish eating, a car winds down the canyon road, slows, then pulls into my camp. A tall, serious-faced man about forty climbs out. "I'm Daryl Rice," he says, shaking my hand. "I'm a reporter for the Watonga paper. I heard you were in the area, and thought I'd check here."

Although he moved away for twenty years, Rice is a Watonga native. He's lived back home for the last eleven years, where he is the only reporter for the Watonga paper. He knows a lot about the Cheyennes and the Arapahos who populate the area.

"Oh, there are several people you should meet," he says, telling me the names of local people who could tell me about the Cheyennes. He asks if I visited the tribal headquarters in El Reno. He says I should meet an important tribal historian, although "he might not be worthwhile, since he's had troubles in recent years with alcohol." It turns out that another important person works for the stables right here in the park. "Let's go see if he's here," Rice says, and we shove aside the notebooks, gum wrappers, camera supplies, and cassette tapes of country music on the seat of his vintage 1980s car and drive up a shallow dirt road to the stables. There is a sprig of blue-green sage on the dashboard.

At the stables a lanky handlebar-mustachioed wrangler strolls over to chat. Rice leans on a wooden fence post. "I was hoping to introduce this guy to Ralph," he says, after introducing me and my hike. But the wrangler tells us that Ralph is gone for the day. On the drive back to my campsite, I turn to Rice. "Who was this guy you wanted me to meet?" I ask.

"Ralph Black," Rice says. "His family lives just a ways outside the park entrance."

"I met some Blacks, Cecil and Roberta." I say.

"That's his aunt, I believe," Rice says. "Well, too bad you missed him, but Roberta was a good person to meet. She'll watch after you in her prayers." We reach my tent, and Rice rests his wrists over the edge of the wheel while the car idles.

"This land was the allotment for the Henry Roman Nose family," Rice says. "His family settled on this land." He nods just upstream from my tent. "You picked a special place to camp. His cabin was just over there in those trees." He leans across the seat to shake my hand. "Well," Rice says, "good luck on your walk." He glances at his reporter's notebook. "This worked out just right," he says. "Just right."

I shut the door and wave as he pulls away. A vague fear and apprehension that had been with me since driving through Oklahoma City the night before has briefly lifted, and I am asleep in my tent before the sound of his car has crested the distant canyon top. In the morning, though, the sky is black with dark storms.

3. Oh Kom Ha Ka

His story started with horses. It grew with medicine and men and war. Not until 1904 on an isolated Montana riverbank, shamed and removed from the companionship of others, did his story end. An American story. An American tragedy.

He was known as Two Tails when he was born, sometime in the early 1820s, but as a young man was given the name Oh Kom Ha Ka: Little Coyote. The first white man to translate his name got it wrong, but from then on he was known by the mistaken name: Little Wolf.

As a small boy he wore the string that would later hold a breechclout, a sign of masculinity. It was said that long after the Cheyennes had come to live on the reservation, most men still wore breechclouts under their trousers. By then, however, Little Wolf would be a shamed outcast who had lost the respect he so nobly earned earlier in life. He gave up wearing the masculine breechclout under his white man pants.

Little Wolf had grown up early in the nineteenth century, when horses were still rare on the plains. Because of their usefulness in chasing buffalo they were very valuable currency when Little Wolf was a young man. Since he had always been fast, courageous, and one of the best with horses, Little Wolf was frequently selected to accompany the dangerous horse-stealing raids on the Crow, Shoshone, and Pawnee camps. On one such raid the Pawnees discovered the intruders, and dozens of them took out after the Cheyennes. Little Wolf, who was involved in the aborted raid, was forced to hide in a ravine while angry Pawnees trailed the marauders. He stayed motionless as their horses passed within inches. He did not move through the long, cold night, then at dawn he walked the long distance back to the Cheyenne camp.

In 1856 Little Wolf's fondness for horses led him to his first face-to-face encounter with the *veho* – the Cheyenne word for trickster, which soon came to be the word for white man as well. In the expansive Nebraska Territory a horse found wandering the prairies was an ownerless horse. To the Cheyennes the large, crude U.S. Army brands meant nothing.

On one spring day runners came into camp to say that *veho* blue coats were demanding the return of four such horses. The *veho* were ordering the Cheyennes to bring the horses to the fort at Upper Platte Bridge immediately. A few Cheyennes decided to go to the fort to talk about the problem. Once there, the blue coat soldiers demanded that the four horses be given up. It was a new and unheard of thing to simply give up a horse, but the *veho* owners would give the Indians a reward for having found and cared for the animals. When the Cheyennes returned to camp they were able to convince the owners of three of the horses to go along with the request, but there was a problem with getting the fourth horse.

The fourth belonged to Little Wolf.

He said he had found the horse with the strange, large "us" mark on its side long before, and it did not belong with the other three. People in the Cheyenne camp argued whether his refusal to surrender the horse would bring war with these new men. It didn't matter: Little Wolf would not give up the horse.

A few days later a small group of Cheyenne men returned to the fort with only three of the four horses the *veho* had demanded.

According to the report of the commissioner of Indian affairs, what happened next was a combination of bad timing, stupidity, and misguided judgment. The commanding officer at the fort ordered the Cheyennes who had come with the horses to be arrested. The Cheyennes fled. Shots were fired and a Cheyenne man was killed. Another, Wolf Fire, was captured. Although he had committed no crimes, Wolf Fire was held in the fort barracks, where he eventually died. Little Wolf himself was wounded in the disturbance. A few days later Little Wolf retaliated by killing and dismembering a herder who was working for a local rancher. The rest of the Cheyennes returned to camp, where preparations for war were made. Eventually, however, the tensions over this incident cooled, but his actions had helped to establish Little Wolf as a leader against the *veho*.

As his reputation grew, Little Wolf gained more and more leadership responsibilities. Soon he was chosen to be a headman, or leader, of the Elk Society. As in many cultures, the Cheyennes have a tradition of tribal societies. These societies serve different cultural functions, but historically the groups were composed of men who were warriors, or tribal police. Each society had its own rituals and traditions. These societies were critical for establishing unity and providing defense during times of war. Because the leaders of the soldier societies were considered the most fearless of all members, it was assumed that they would soon die in battle. The selection of Little Wolf as the chief of the Elk Society at such a young age was an indication not only of his bravery but also of his abilities as a military commander. "He was never afraid to speak the truth," a fellow Cheyenne, Wooden Leg, said. "He was a gentle and a charitable man, but if insulted to anger he was likely to hurt somebody."

George Bird Grinnell, an early anthropologist who lived with the Cheyennes at the turn of the twentieth century, had a personal friendship with Little Wolf in Little Wolf's late years. Grinnell claimed that Little Wolf was one of the great military leaders of all time, a meticulous strategist who planned each military encounter with precision and forethought. Little Wolf liked to consider all possibilities and plan for every eventuality. During battles he would ride about on one of his fine horses, shouting encouragement and directions to his warriors. He always was at the front in battle and would never let anyone ride ahead of him. It was said that if someone questioned his decision on the battlefield, Little Wolf would simply strike the man down with his fist.

It was precisely this quickness to anger, his ready, violent streak, and his careful attention to strategy that made him a great leader, and that also caused his downfall.

Little Wolf's stature in the Cheyenne tribe continued to grow. Soon he was one of the only four men presiding over the Council of Forty-four. The Council of Forty-four was a gathering composed of four men from each of the ten bands of Cheyennes, and four "old man chiefs," as they are sometimes called, who – although they had no greater authority than the other forty – were selected because of their special influence and importance. Since a chief was required to renounce warfare and no longer participate in his society's military actions, he had to relinquish his position as headman of his society. For some unknown reason Little Wolf was the only old man chief who was ever allowed to retain his position in the Elk Society. It was a great honor. The problem was that the honor meant his tendency toward quick anger and rash actions had to be curtailed. Being an old man chief also meant he had to be quick to forgive.

By the time he was thirty he was so esteemed in the tribe that he was entrusted with the care of one of the most sacred items of the tribe, the chief's bundle. This sacred bundle had been obtained from the ancestral prophet of the Cheyennes and handed down from generation to generation. This high honor indicated that Little Wolf was a direct link to the one who brought life to all people on earth: Sweet Medicine. The honor meant that a great war chief had now been made the most important peace chief of the Cheyennes.

Because of his position in the tribe, Little Wolf was among those who were chosen to represent the tribe in Washington DC in 1873, when several leaders went to the capital to sign an agreement that redefined the boundaries of the Cheyenne lands. During their stay in Washington the Southern and Northern Cheyenne leaders were ushered into a photographer's studio in sets of two and posed in front of a flowered curtain. All of the photographs are arranged in identical fashion: one leader stands and the other is seated on a stiff wooden stool placed on the tiled floor. Little Wolf entered the studio with his friend and fellow old man chief Dull Knife. Five years later the two men in this photo would be united during the trek northward as leaders trying to bring their people back from the hot, starving land of Indian Territory to Montana. Dull Knife sat on the stool and Little Wolf stood, and the shutter opened. Little Wolf's left hand clutched a white blanket that billowed around him like a skirt. Just above that hand, and at his waist, was a round leather pouch. He wore a hide shirt, draped with fur, or scalps, and beadwork. A large cross and horseshoe-shaped ornaments dangled on his chest, and a pillbox-shaped fur hat adorned his head. His jaw was taut, his cheeks sunken, his lips in a thin, long line. It is clearly an antiquated photograph from a time and a tribal culture now long past. Everything about the photograph is cold, dead, and ancient, everything, that is, except for Little Wolf's eyes.

Nearly all pupil and clear and bright as a living man's, his eyes stare straight into the present.

The fruitless trip to Washington in 1873 marked the beginning of the end of the old ways for the Cheyennes. Still able to travel freely across their homeland at the start of the 1870s, the Cheyennes would be confined to small government-designated areas by the decade's close. The suffering the Cheyennes endured during those ten years was among the most profound of the injustices shouldered by all native peoples of the plains. The wars of those days not only affected warriors and soldiers but inflicted a serious blow to Cheyenne culture as well. Often through willful intent, but just as often through nothing more diabolical than chance, the battles against the Cheyennes almost always drew a heavy casualty of children. They were killed on the Sappa, on the Washita, at Sand Creek, and on the frozen banks of Dull Knife's village at the foot of the Bighorns, at Punished Woman canyon, at Fort Robinson, and on a high, lonely Nebraska ridge where a dozen children helped to fight a last battle for survival. Certainly there were many whites – notably General George Crook – who passionately argued for the civilized treatment of the native population, but when the smoke of the decade cleared it was as if the Cheyenne future had vanished. Many of what few children were left were herded to Indian Territory only to have their food withheld until they agreed to be enrolled in government sponsored schools.

Through much of the 1870s Little Wolf led his warriors in battles for survival. It was Little Wolf, in fact, who inadvertently caused the Plains Indians' greatest triumph: the victory at Little Bighorn.

On June 24 and 25, 1876, Little Wolf had been traveling in a small band of seven or eight lodges on the divide between Davis and Reno creeks, about eighteen miles east of the Little Bighorn River, when Custer's men came upon them. The troops fired on the Cheyennes, resulting in a minor skirmish, but Custer, believing his presence was now discovered, elected to attack the villages on the Little Bighorn a day earlier then planned. And although Little Wolf and his band did not participate in the Battle of Little Bighorn, their presence made Custer decide to attack before reinforcements arrived.

After Custer's death the government was determined to solve the Indian "problem" completely and finally. An unprecedented winter campaign was launched, intent on striking a fatal blow to the "savages." As seemed their fate, it was the Cheyenne children who suffered most under the snowy boots of war.

Following their normal seasonal habits, for the remainder of the summer after Custer's defeat, smaller bands of Cheyennes, Sioux, and other Indians broke away from the large band that had defeated the Seventh Cavalry and sought out the few remaining herds of buffalo to store up provisions for the coming winter. In November Little Wolf and his people had joined with many other Cheyennes at Dull Knife's camp on a fork of the Powder River. Many Cheyennes were together in the winter camp. Many sacred items were there. Storytellers and elders were there. And, of course, children were there. Although scouts had reported that the soldiers were nearby, the warrior society leaders ordered the dances to be held against others' judgment. Few people expected a winter battle.

When the attack on Dull Knife's village came, at a snowy dawn on November 26, it came strong and swift. People ran from lodges half dressed or naked and grabbed what weapons were nearby.

Over a thousand mounted troops, under the command of General Ranald Mackenzie, stormed down on the village and went straight for the lodges. The battle raged all day amid snowbanks, in small, frozen streambeds, and scattered itself among the surrounding trees. There were many stories of bravery that day. Little Wolf himself was wounded six times but managed to lead his warriors in forming a defensive line for the surviving women and children to make an escape. Many fought bravely. By nightfall, however, the Cheyennes' camp was lost, the village was captured, and the Cheyenne horses were rounded up. By dawn the next morning nothing remained of the Cheyenne possessions but lingering smoke and frozen bodies. With centuries of cultural artifacts and all of their winter provisions destroyed, some say the old way met its end that day in the ashes and blood on the cold, snowy riverbank. The destitute Cheyennes who escaped spent the remainder of the winter with Crazy Horse's village of the Oglala Sioux, who took them in and shared their meager provisions.

In January 1877 Colonel Nelson A. Miles caught up with Crazy Horse's winter-weary band, and another battle in frigid winter conditions again signaled the coming end.

In the spring of 1877 the Northern Cheyenne survivors of this long, bloody winter divided into four main groups. One of those groups, under the leadership of Two Moon, surrendered at Fort Keogh. Another group fled south to Indian Territory, while a third group joined with the Northern Arapahos in Wyoming. Having survived the harsh, bloody winter of 1876–77, the starving and destitute members of the largest group – which included Little Wolf, Dull Knife, Standing Elk, Spotted Elk, Black Wolf, and others – surrendered at Red Cloud Agency in northwestern Nebraska in April.

The government's plan was to concentrate as many Indians as possible into a single area – Indian Territory – so as to segregate all tribes of Indians from the whites. In addition, controlling and feeding them would be made easier if they were grouped together. Little Wolf, Dull Knife, and others said they wanted to remain in the north, but despite their long history there and the terms of the 1868 Fort Keogh Treaty (which promised an unspecified reservation in the north), Mackenzie said the government insisted they go south. During a period of indecision and confusion among the Cheyennes, Mackenzie made arrangements for an escort and that spring removed nearly a thousand Cheyennes to the south.

During the next year in Indian Territory the Northern Cheyennes found nothing but meager rations, strained relationships with their southern kinsmen, and outright neglect by the government.

"The people were raised in the far north among the pines and the mountains," Little Wolf told his captors in Indian Territory. "In that country we were always healthy. Now, since we are in this country we are dying everyday. No one will speak our names when we are dead. If you do not give us the power to go back home we will all be dead in a year. If we die in battle our names will be remembered and cherished by our people."

Permission was denied.

"I do not wish the ground about this agency to be made bloody, but now listen to what I say to you. I am going to leave here; I am going north to my own country. I do not want to see blood spilt about this agency. If you are going to send your soldiers after me, I wish that you would first let me get a little distance away from this agency. Then if you want to fight, I will fight you, and we can make the ground bloody at that place."

As indeed it was to be made bloody. The many Cheyennes who would survive the long sorrowful trek back to Montana did so in large part because of Little Wolf's skills at military planning. Camps were always located in places where the view was extensive and that were defensible against superior numbers. When there were battles – as there were all along the seven-month, fifteen-hundred-mile journey – Little Wolf fought harder than he had ever fought. "He did not seem like a human being," his friend Tangle Hair said of Little Wolf during the 1878 trek. "He seemed like an animal – like a bear. He seemed without fear."

After the exodus, and largely because of his initial negotiations once the last of the fleeing Cheyennes were caught, a reservation was eventually established for the Northern Cheyennes on a small part of their traditional homeland in southeastern Montana. That is where Little Wolf settled in 1879, intending to live out his last years surrounded by friends on the once open prairie. For a time it was so. He visited with old friends, hunted, and even worked with a white soldier on a book about Indian sign language.

Yet Little Wolf's life was never one of complacency, but of action – and one ultimately of anger and violence and of cultural codes passed down for generations.

That code was simple, and its rules few. It had been given to the generations after Sweet Medicine had received it at Noahvose, the Sacred Mountain, Bear Butte. Among its decrees was a central guiding light: a Cheyenne should never harm another Cheyenne. If someone killed a fellow tribesman, the consequences were harsh: the guilty was exiled, and the tribe's holy covenant, the sacred arrows, had to undergo a special renewal or bad times would come.

Witnesses say that on the night of December 12, 1880, Little Wolf was drunk and sullen when he walked into the trading post on Two Moon Creek. Starving Elk was there. Little Wolf had warned Starving Elk to stay away from his daughter, but rumors of Starving Elk's passion had been feeding the gossip circles for months. On this night Starving Elk was gambling for candy with Little Wolf's daughter. By simply showing anger and possessiveness over his daughter, Little Wolf was already breaking the code for a carrier of the Sweet Medicine bundle. Still, he raged onward, ordering the man to get away from his daughter. Others tried to restrain him.

"I will kill you," Little Wolf shouted. He left the building and returned moments later with a rifle, walked in, leveled it at Starving Elk, and pulled the trigger. Starving Elk died instantly. "I am going up on that hill by the bend in the creek," Little Wolf mumbled. "If anybody wants me, that is where I will be."

A local paper reported the event, getting the names wrong in the process:

> It is currently reported that Lone Wolf, a Cheyenne brave, . . . while under the influence of "firewater" shot and killed "Poor Elk." At the realization of what he had done "Lone Wolf" packed his traps and tepee and with his squaws, clandestinely skipped.

In reality, Little Wolf turned himself in to the army. Because of his fame as a leader and negotiator, and because they did not view intratribal squabbles as significant, the army did not prosecute him. But Little Wolf had broken the old code. His crime had been particularly dark because of his position in the tribe. Some said that no amount of purification would rid the tribe of the troubles. Since he had violated the central commandment, nearly all of his fellow Cheyennes shunned him. No one but the whites would speak to him. He was banished by his own people and went to live with his family in a remote place on the reservation on Muddy Creek. Even today, although his name is spoken, his great deeds for the Cheyenne people are not widely known.

Little Wolf spent his last twenty years in a dignified self-exile. He lived on the edge of the reservation on Muddy Creek. He did odd jobs and visited his white neighbors. He continued to carry the chief's bundle for a while, but eventually that too he passed on to others. Because no one knew how to purify the bundle, a new one was created, and the one tainted by a murderer's touch, the one that had been passed down from Sweet Medicine himself, was buried.

In the end Little Wolf even gave up his beloved horses. He went around the reservation on foot, now a blind old man dressed in pants, not even dignified by a breechclout. When he died, some of his glory was remembered; his body was taken to a high hill and stood erect, and stones were piled about it. It was said that he might continue to look out at the Cheyenne homelands of Montana.

Like many other Cheyennes who have struggled against this devil in the past century, Little Wolf's demon was alcohol. "Little Wolf did not kill Starving Elk," the victim's brother said years later. "It was the white man's whiskey that did it."

4. Kit Fox Drums and the Wild Dogs of Fonda

Stone dark and raining miserably, everything about this day is sinister. At 3 P.M. the sky is low and black. It has been raining since I started seven hours ago from a wet camp at the edge of a deserted lake.

It is my third day of hiking in this rain and I am standing at the gateway to a small, sad, abandoned cemetery on a nameless dirt road in northern Oklahoma. The steel-gray, snaky rain falls on the tombstones and slithers down into the tall, unmowed grass. I hesitate, then turn and walk through the gateway and into the cemetery. Most of it is overgrown, and wet tombstones poke through the tall spring prairie grass, but to one side it is neatly mowed at the resting places of the more recently departed.

Indian names: Nightwalker, Little Coyote, Medicine Woman, Old Bear, but no flowers or tobacco offerings, and nothing but the hiss of rain and the high lonely wind in the black sky.

I turn to leave, then turn again back toward a recent burial: a young man, "our beloved son," died last year, aged seventeen. I turn away, pulled by an unseen hand, an invisible other who has been in control of this day from its start.

North of the road, black trees mark the banks of the North Canadian River, the route the Northern Cheyennes took through here on their escape. A good twenty square miles along the river is a state wildlife area, and because of that, there are no other roads than the one I am on – and there hasn't been a car on this road all afternoon. The ruts of a few random pickup trucks are deeply set in the muck and mud. Still, I imagine I hear a car and jerk around back toward the cemetery. There is nothing except for the arrow flight of a great blue heron as she splits the sky of rain.

I am nervous and ill at ease in this vacant, ashen land. There is no rational reason for my vague fear, but all the same, I check my pocket for the slender can of pepper spray a friend had given me.

"For ranch dogs," she explained, "and . . . whatever else."

Not long ago "whatever else" would have included a wide range of predators once native to the Great Plains. Grizzly bears stalked the grasslands as far south as Oklahoma and Texas. The big bears roamed the riverbanks and hills of the prairie following the food supply through the seasons: fish spawning in the rivers, mice, rabbits, berries, and – although rare – buffalo. The journals of Lewis and Clark are full of stories of grizzlies they encountered daily on their trek west, but by the time of the Civil War the grizzlies had been hunted to extinction on the open prairies and had taken refuge in the high peaks of the Rockies and Sierras.

Just below the grizzlies in the hierarchy of plains predators were the wolves. While they seldom attacked humans, they were the buffalo's greatest enemy. Lying in wait in packs as the herd passed, they would silently stalk the bison and then attack like machines. An early witness to such an attack described the wolves' method:

> They seem to act in concert and as if by understanding. First they post themselves at proper distances in a line in the direction the victim is supposed to take; then two or three charge in the middle of the herd, cut out an animal and drive it to where their companions are waiting. The victim then runs between the two ranks of wolves. As it goes, fresh bands join in the chase, until at last, exhausted by fatigue, it stops and becomes their prey.
>
> I have several times come across such gangs of these animals surrounding and torturing an old or wounded bull . . . the animal had made desperate resistance until his eyes were entirely eaten out of his head; the gristle of his nose mostly gone; his tongue was half demolished and the skin and flesh of his legs torn almost literally into strings.

I shudder in the cold rain, still fingering the pepper spray. I see a mule deer a hundred yards from the road, its jerking, tall ears the only motion. It turns its head and then bounds away toward the sanctuary of the river refuge. Then I too hear the truck and turn to face it.

A battered blue Ford pickup is grinding its way over the muddy road from behind me. I step aside and wait. I wave as it passes, but neither the sullen driver, a man with no hat and gray eyebrows that meet over his nose, nor the thin, sickly woman next to him returns the gesture. I watch them plow ahead for another mile, then turn at a ranch road. The Ford disappears behind a hill and moments later reappears further away, headed toward a collection of buildings in the distance. The faint sound of the truck silences as it reaches the distant ranch house.

I walk on in the hushed rain.

The sky is still black and low and billowing. Blacker specks circle on the dark clouds. Vultures.

Except for the ranch where the truck has turned, I do not pass a building for another hour. The map says I should be coming to a tiny town called Fonda, but there is nothing save empty hills as far as I can see.

After a long stretch of short rolling hills, the roadway flattens on a wide creek valley, and in the trees near the creek there is a single house. No one appears as I pass, then two big dogs bound out from beneath the porch, startling me with their deep barking.

I have already discovered that my first line of defense against ranch dogs usually works: a stern "No!" spoken as if I am their master. Although they continue to bark, these two immediately stop running toward me. My second defense is milder, and often serves to send dogs running: I shame them. "Go on," I say out loud. "Who are you kidding? You two couldn't scare a mouse." Their heads drop at my tone and, although they bark a bit yet, they turn and trot back toward the house. The sudden appearance of the dogs has got me to thinking about my pepper spray again. I work around the tightly cinched backpack belt and dig the can out of my pocket. The thing is to be held six to twelve inches from the perpetrator – not much good for grizzlies anyway – and given a blast of one or two seconds. The slender can holds ten shots, no defense against a pack of wolves.

Although the ranch dogs are still barking, I can tell from the sound that they are not following me. At the time I do not think it is odd, but as I pass the trees near the creek, a howling erupts from deep in the woods. Behind me the ranch dogs erupt again with their own wailing. It is a dog probably caught in someone's steel trap, I decide, and keep moving out of the trees and into the open country again.

As I walk on I am distracted by pain. It has been a long day and I am weary, and yet miles from where I had hoped to camp. The pack has not gotten any easier to carry in the days since leaving Geary, and by this late in the day my legs have begun to shake. Abruptly, I realize that although I am a good mile past the house, the two ranch dogs have not stopped their barking. I slowly swing the huge backpack around in order to look.

Not more than fifty yards away a dozen wild dogs are silently following me. They have spaced themselves evenly in a line from one side of the road to the other. I am essentially surrounded. Instantly the pepper spray is in my hand. They have stopped and are staring at me.

I find myself yelling at them, unintelligible screams and hoots. I wave my arms and stomp my feet.

The line of them does not move. They stand frozen in a semicircle around me. I know I must not run, for they would easily catch me, but I am at a loss for what to do. I shout again, and they begin to prance and look about them. There is still no sound, but at some invisible signal the entire line moves, snaking through the light rain and into the field on my right. I turn, trying to keep the entire group in my view. I decide to wait until they have moved on in front of me, so that I might keep them in sight as I walk, but the lead dog has stopped and the rest soon stop as well, waiting.

I turn slowly and resume my walking, and as I do, the pack begins to move. They are now a hundred yards away in a long line parallel to the road. I shout again, but aside from a few mongrels who glance in my direction, they are not affected.

Except for a German shepherd and a couple of black Labs who run along at the end of the line biting at each other's heels, I have never seen such dogs as these. They are short, muscular brutes with steady, black eyes and a lean, loose gait. More like hyenas than dogs.

They continue to parallel my movement.

In a quarter mile the road will turn north, forcing me to walk straight toward them. I do not know what I should do but decide that I must keep moving and try to keep them in my sight. Just before the turn, however, the lead dog swings north around a low mound and the line of wild dogs follows him out of sight behind the hill.

I reach the turn and take it, my aches and pains long forgotten in the tingling, feverish aliveness of fear. I walk for a mile, turning constantly to study the horizon around me, but the dogs do not reappear. Instead I come upon four or five dark shapes in the twilight road. Vultures are feeding on something, and they wait until I am close enough to see the wrinkled, naked red skin of their heads before they stumble a few steps and take wing. In the road is the hollowed-out carcass of a large fish. Its eyes are gone, and part of its tail is missing. The vultures have disemboweled it, and parts of the fish litter the gravel.

At that instant a car appears on the road, coming toward me. It passes me, a window full of faces staring out at my figure in the drizzling dusk. The car slams to a halt, spraying gravel across the fish carcass, does a U-turn in the road, and returns to me.

"Are you the guy walking to South Dakota?" The driver has stopped just behind me and has rolled down his window.

"That's right," I say. In the back seat three faces stare up at me. I walk to the car. A slender girl of about nine thrusts a skinny kitten out the rear window toward me. "How did you know about me?" I ask.

The driver grins. "Oh, we know about you," he says. "Things get around down here. Why are you doing this hike, anyway?" He takes a sip from a Red Dog beer bottle he has been holding in his lap. A woman sits in the shadows on the seat next to him. The slender girl from the back seat is chattering at me, asking countless questions. Her kitten is now in my arms, its tiny claws piercing my fingers.

I begin to explain.

"You're following Little Wolf?" he interrupts. "Honey, listen to this man, listen!" He turns to look at me. "My wife," he starts, "my wife, she's a direct descendant of Little Wolf!"

"She is?"

The man sticks his hand out the window. "I'm Ronnie Harris," he says. "Where are you walking to tonight?"

"Oh, just to Seiling," I say, although it is still a hard two hours of walking to the town.

Ronnie hops out of the car. "Come on, I'll give you a ride."

"No, thanks," I begin to say. Since I started the hike at least a dozen people have stopped to ask if I would like a lift, and I give them all a standard answer. I tell them I may not make it all the way to South Dakota, but I want to try to walk as far as I can.

Ronnie will have none of it. "Kids," he says, talking to the three children in the rear seat and to me at the same time, "move that junk out of the way so this guy can get in there. These are my children."

I try another, feeble protest. "Really, there's no place for my pack . . ."

"Your pack . . ." He stops as if he hasn't noticed the gigantic thing on my back, but it barely slows him. "We'll put it in the trunk."

In an instant Ronnie reaches into the open front window, snaps off the ignition, and takes the keys to the trunk. It is filled level with empty aluminum cans. They are stuffed around the jack and spare tire and boxes and blankets and inside two large black plastic bags.

"No. You've got all these cans," I say.

"No problem," he says. "We'll just get rid of them. They clutter everything up anyway." He grabs plastic bags, one in each hand, and tosses them into the ditch. I had long ago forgotten what it was like to toss a gum wrapper from a window, and the action stuns me for a moment. What's more, by the looks of things Ronnie's family could use the twenty or thirty dollars they represent.

I squeeze into the back seat, which is crowded with jackets and boxes, cats and kids. I fold my feet in and wedge them on top of a twelve-pack of Red Dog.

"Kids, introduce yourselves," Ronnie says as we start off. "This guy's walking to South Dakota!"

L. R. is Ronnie's son. He is five and sits fidgeting on the far side, looking out into the gray evening light. L. R. has been taking tae kwon do lessons and is a green belt, Ronnie explains. "But my oldest there, Renecia, she's the one we are real proud of. She's a princess. An Indian princess."

Renecia smiles at the words. She is about fourteen, a stout, strong child with a wide face, bright eyes, and a big smile.

"My," I say. "A real princess."

"She's a junior princess, and she's going to be very important in the powwow down at Woodward," he explains. "This is my wife, Norene."

"Hello," I say. Next to me, the girl with the kitten has not spoken. "What's your name?" I ask her.

"Rebecca," she says.

"She's real smart. She's our student." Ronnie cuts her off and turns in his seat to look at his oldest daughter and speaks to her instead. "Renecia, tell him where we're going tonight."

Renecia laughs, and her smile brightens the darkening day. "No, you tell him."

"My daughter has a great honor. She's a member of the Kit Fox Society," he says. "They're having a powwow tonight, and she has to preside. She's only fourteen, but they treat her with respect."

Historically, the military societies of the Cheyenne culture consisted of most but not all of the men of the tribe. Their function was both social and political. A boy about Renecia's age could elect to join a society or not, but if he joined it was often the same one to which his father belonged. The boy's family went to the first dance of the society and had a great giveaway of gifts for the occasion. A few young women were selected to belong to the societies as well. It was a great honor for a girl to be selected, for it meant that she would attend the meetings and join in at the dances, often sitting and singing with the singers.

The Kit Fox men had a set of rituals and dances unique to the societies. Their dances were private and of great importance to the group. Often they painted themselves black, from the neck to the waist, including their arms down to the elbows. Food was also important, and no dance was held without it.

Ronnie is talking, explaining. "My wife was a member of the Kit Foxes, but then she got pregnant without being married." He laughs and pulls at his wife's shoulder. "She met me and couldn't resist. Anyway, they allowed her to name the person who would replace her."

"And she picked me," Renecia says.

"But you weren't born yet?" I ask.

"My wife told them whatever child was born would be her replacement, so Renecia here was born right into the Kit Foxes. She's learned a great many things from them. She goes to peyote gatherings, sweats, and all the private meetings, where they've been teaching her."

"And you're related to Little Wolf?" I ask Norene.

She nods but does not turn from the front seat to look at me. "He was my great-great-grandfather."

"Some of his people returned to Oklahoma," Ronnie explains. "She was born down here but met me in Montana. Lame Deer. I'm from there. She was a pretty wild girl. You liked to party some, huh?" He grins at her. "But she met me and that was that!"

Outside, the night sky is nearly night-dark. We are traveling toward a horizon dancing with distant lightning.

"Where are you staying tonight?"

"I'm not sure. I'd like to camp somewhere near Seiling."

"You shouldn't camp tonight. There's going to be bad storms."

I could use a shower, and after several nights in a sleeping bag, a motel sounds perfect. Fifteen minutes later Ronnie is unloading my pack from the trunk. We have pulled into a plain motel at the edge of the small town of Seiling.

"It would be my honor for you to come to the Kit Fox dance tonight," Ronnie says. "My daughter's honor." Despite the lateness of the hour and my exhaustion, I readily accept. Ronnie will pick me up from here in an hour.

The lightning is much closer, and now the distant low rumble of thunder can be heard.

"We used to live right over there," Ronnie says, pointing to a trailer park just across the road. He shudders visibly. "This is a horrible place for tornadoes," he says.

Thirty seconds later I am making small talk with the motel clerk. "This spot must be a horrible place for tornadoes," I say, repeating Ronnie's words.

She is a once slender woman of about fifty years. Age and time have caught up with the tight jeans, platinum blond hair, and red lipstick. "Oh, no," she says. "We're between two rivers, and the Indians say this is a sacred place."

I smile. "The Indians say so?"

"Yes, they say this place is protected from all tornadoes. You'll be safe here tonight." As she speaks the lights flicker and the rain starts again.

When Ronnie's late-model American car pulls in the lot a little while later, I am bone tired but showered and ready for him. The night is cool, and yet the wind rips summerlike storms across the sky. Waves ripple across the puddles in the parking lot of the motel.

I go around to the rear car door, expecting to see the children, but only the boy, L. R., is there, next to a thin man in neat clothes. Another man sits in front, next to Ronnie.

"Yeah, yeah, just get in there," Ronnie says. He is even more animated than earlier. "These are my brother-in-laws," he says, swinging a Red Dog toward each of them. "My wife's two brothers. This is Adolf up here, and that's James."

James nods at me, then turns to the drawing he has been making for L. R. In elaborate letters, on a tablet, he is spelling out the words "Martial Arts" for his nephew in the streetlight dark of the car.

The other brother-in-law, Adolf, turns in his seat and holds out a big, flat hand, and we shake. He wears a well-used green army jacket and sports a walrus mustache. Compared to the solemn and clipped James, Adolf seems quite social. "Ronnie says you're walking north. That's a long way to go. I don't know how those people did it way back then."

We drive down the main street of town. There is traffic on the street, but except for the collection of cars in front of the two or three bars, most of it is cruising the main drag, just like us.

"The women are going to the dance together, and that gives us a chance to drive around," Ronnie says. "There's no hurry. We have dances all the time, and for us these things can be boring."

Ronnie honks the car horn and waves at someone. "I finally had to teach him a lesson," he says to Adolf, indicating a giant of a man who is walking into one of the bars. "I warned him, and he just pushed me a little too far."

"What did you do?" Adolf asks.

"I was coming out of the grocery store and he was coming in," Ronnie explains. The hand with the beer waves in the air, while the other punches the darkness toward Adolph. He hasn't touched the steering wheel in a block. "He said something to me, and I set down my groceries and grabbed a ketchup bottle from the bag. I stood up and hit him with it as hard as I could. One hit, that was it."

James, who has remained silently drawing, snickers. Adolf laughs.

"That was all it took. It knocked him out cold. It worked. He has had nothing but respect for me ever since then."

I swallow hard.

"We've had trouble with that family for a long time," he says to me. "But we aren't afraid of them. We've all fought him. Adolf here has, and you too, right, James?" Ronnie stretches to look at James in the rearview.

"Yeah," James says, "I've fought him."

"We all have fought him. You earn your respect around here, and nobody can say we aren't respected."

The tires squeal a bit as Ronnie makes a U-turn at the end of the three-block main street of Seiling and into a package liquor store. James hops out and in a moment returns carrying two small paper bags. He hands Adolf one of the bags, then removes the bottle from his own and takes a swig. He is apologetic. "I asked them for a hundred proof," he says, "but they only had eighty."

Adolf is neatly folding back the paper of his bag so that the neck of the bottle is exposed. "This'll do just as well, I suspect," Adolf says, but he puts the bottle in the pocket of his army jacket without opening it.

"My brother-in-laws like their hard liquor," Ronnie says, cruising the main street again. "I just drink beer, is all."

Ronnie drinks, James drinks, and as we head out of town on a dirt road it begins to rain hard. Wind and water blast through Ronnie's open window. No one seems to notice.

We drive into the storm, driving and driving into the blackness. Ronnie's talking turns darker and darker. James, L. R., and I sit in the shadowy back seat. Silent lightning silhouettes James's thin figure staring out the window like a prisoner. L. R. sits between us listening to his father; James's drawing is on his lap, unfinished.

We drive for a long while, and just as I decide Ronnie has no intention of going to the dance and that we will simply continue to joyride through this dark night, we turn down a road marked with a dead-end sign. I take a deep breath. Ronnie pulls off the road and into a field.

"Oh, yeah, they're here already," he says. In the middle of the field a handful of cars are parked around a low aluminum building. Ronnie slows as we bounce over the ruts in the field. He reaches near his feet and lifts up a twelve-pack box of empty Red Dog beer cans. This he jettisons out the window, just as we turn and park beside a dark blue Chevy sedan. There is a bulky, dark shape in the front seat. It moves.

"That's their sister," Ronnie says, pointing to the figure. "She's not right in the head, but people look after her. She'll just sit there all night and listen to the singing from inside."

James pockets his bottle. Adolf lights a cigarette. The men get out of the car, and L. R. follows. I open my door, but Ronnie turns to me. "Wait in the car until we check out the situation," he says.

I close my door. No problem, boss man.

The rain has stopped, but the lightning and thunder continue in the distance. I am wet from the open window and cold, and tired beyond my imagination. L. R. and three other boys are racing around between parked cars. Adolf is at the edge of the lot, smoking. I do not see James, and all the women must be inside, because I see none of them.

Ronnie is talking to a man. The man is wearing a bright Hawaiian shirt and a pure white ball cap. Double braids hang halfway down his back. The man looks in my direction.

Ronnie steps over to the car and leans his head into the open window.

"That guy is Jay Dean Bull Coming," he says. "You should talk to him. He's the chief of the Kit Foxes. He'd be good for you to talk to. He knows a lot of stories. As long as you don't believe most of them, you'll be all right."

"So, what's happening here?" I ask.

"He said it was okay for you to attend the dance." Ronnie steps away from the car.

"Should I just go in?" I ask.

He stops. Turns. "Oh, yeah. There'll be food in a little while. Help yourself." In the dim light from the open door, I can see Ronnie's face. He smiles. "Go on. I'm going to hang around outside for a bit. When you go to these dances every week or so, they get boring."

The sister's figure moves as I get out of the car. There is a small thread of smoke coming from the Chevy's window. I walk across the dark lot toward the square frame of light that is the door to the aluminum building. All around me are shadows. Shadows of men, of cars, and in the distance far beyond the fields of prairie grass, the shadows of a massive cloud framed in lightning.

I step inside, and in the warm light on the concrete floor a small child of about two toddles uncertainly across the room. A woman speaks to her in Cheyenne and the girl laughs. The woman is about twenty-four. Her hair is a black silk ribbon against her shoulders. She turns to me and smiles. "Come on in," she says. "Have you had food? There'll be food in a moment." She motions to a table where women are arranging large, aluminum-covered pots and plates.

"Thanks," I say. It is a large room, about the size of a tennis court. Except for the edges, where small groups of people are gathered about chairs and benches, the room is empty. It is mostly a covered, well-lit slab of concrete.

Jay Dean Bull Coming is at the far end of the room. He has not removed his pure white ball cap, and it is hard to miss the Hawaiian shirt. He sees me and walks the length of the room to greet me.

"Sit," he says, motioning to the bench behind us. He is a young man of about thirty-five, with smooth skin. He does not smile, and yet his face is friendly. I begin to explain my hike, but he cuts me off. "Ronnie told me what you're doing," he says, and then without introduction, he begins to talk about the bombing in Oklahoma City. "That was a sad thing that happened – they call it a tragedy. But what happened to us, what happened to the Cheyenne people, they never once called that a tragedy. It's the same thing. What happened to us nearly wiped out an entire race. What happened to the Cheyenne people no one ever cried over, but it's the same as that bomb in Oklahoma City. The same thing." Abruptly, he stands. I rise. "Have some food. You're welcome to stay as long as you wish," he says and then walks away.

I turn and see Ronnie's wife, Norene, kneeling in front of her daughter Renecia, making last-minute adjustments to the girl's dress. The mother is calmly working around the daughter's impatient fidgeting.

Renecia is beaming, her smile as wide as the moon. She parades in front of me so I can see how beautiful her dress is.

It hangs like a spectacular black cape on her. White, round shells line its edges, and a breastplate of long ivory porcupine quills graces the front. The contrast of the black dress and the white trim of shells, spines, and bones is stunning.

She wears a wide gold banner that seems out of place for a moment. "Seiling Pow Wow Princess," it reads.

"At the larger gatherings she wears that banner so people will know where we're from," her mother explains. "She represents all of our people."

"Did you make this wonderful dress?" I ask.

Norene smiles and looks away. It is her daughter who answers. "She made it, and she works on it all the time!" Renecia says. A single eagle feather is held upright behind her head by a colorful beaded band. In her right hand she holds a fan made from the entire wing of a red-tailed hawk. The hawk's wing is attached to a wide beaded handle of beauty.

"Come here, now, come here," Norene says, and Renecia stands impatiently while her mother is before her on the floor, fixing a loose shell on the hem.

More kids and adults are coming in. A line has formed at the food tables. "Go get something to eat," Norene says through lips pressed around three safety pins.

When I return with my food, six or seven family groups have gathered in lawn chairs and on benches and folding seats around the edges of the room. People are eating and chatting. Children are racing around, playing tag and shouting. Norene introduces me to her mother and to cousins and children who have materialized around the radiant Renecia.

I turn my attention to the plate of steaming food: big, thick meaty strips of beef, cooked plain and unadorned. Potatoes. A stew. Cooked carrots. Jell-O and cookies. Fruit punch or piping hot coffee served smoking and thick in tall Styrofoam cups.

In the center of the room women are setting five or six chairs in a circle for the drummers. There is no hurry. There is laughter and smiles. The electricity dims twice as the drummers drift out one by one from family groups to join in the center of the room.

At the eastern end of the building Jay Dean Bull Coming taps at a microphone. Through the open door near him I can see lightning in the east. There are no windows.

"There's plenty more food," Jay Dean Bull Coming says and then cracks a few jokes. People everywhere laugh. "If the drummers are ready there, we'll begin with the flag song."

One by one, almost indistinguishable at first from the other sounds in the echoing building, a drummer starts to tap on the single bass drum, placed on its side on low crates. The other men pull their seats closer, adjust beaded straps about their drumsticks, and start. The drumming dominates all sounds; then the lead drummer leans back his head and begins the song.

His syncopated tremolo drifts out across the air in waves above us all. Now the others join him, and their singing fills the room. Before the song falls off with a long sliding note, a procession of loosely formed lines of dancers has formed about the drummers. Renecia is near the front of the procession. I look at Norene, but she is oblivious to me, eyes glued on her daughter. The Kit Fox dance has begun.

A young girl circles the room selling raffle tickets. I fish out a dollar bill and drop it in the pillow case she is using to collect the funds. "No ticket," I say, when she insists on trying to give me one. "I couldn't carry that prize shawl even if I did win it."

Between songs there is much chatting and gossiping. The dances are held frequently, but these friends and relatives still have much to catch up on. There are over fifty people in the room, and everyone knows everyone.

I have found an old friend. The woman I had met on the first day of my journey is here. Roberta Black, who had made my success sound easy by telling me she had prayed for me, smiles and waves. It hasn't been easy, but I am a good fifty to sixty miles further than when we last met. We chat for a bit, and as we are talking a woman near us turns and says, "They say there was a tornado touched down."

"Where?" Roberta asks.

"Two miles away. Between here and Seiling."

Ah, I think. Yes. Tornadoes.

Several hours later the lightning is still flashing. I have been sitting with Roberta Black's family, but at the west end of the building Ronnie has finally reappeared at the Harris family area. He is guzzling a large cup of hot coffee Norene has set before him. Adolf is there, too. He stands in the shadows watching the dancers. I do not see the thin, sullen James.

Ronnie motions to me, and I excuse myself from the Blacks and walk to him. I pull up a chair next to the one he has taken. He is red-faced, and he speaks in a nonstop flow of words. "You enjoying yourself?" he asks. "I've been drinking some: beer only. We have these dances often, so it's a good time for many men to talk." He takes a swig of the coffee. "My daughter has everyone's respect. Adolf there, you saw that vodka he bought? He hasn't had a drop of it. It's out of respect for my daughter. Everyone honors her. You enjoying yourself?" he asks again. "Renecia asks me all the time why I talk like a white man, you know: talk, talk, talk nonstop and not say anything. I tell her I'm proud to be Cheyenne, but I have nothing against whites." He laughs. "Although maybe I do talk a lot. Isn't my daughter lovely?"

"Your daughter is quite beautiful," I say. "Norene did a marvelous job on that dress."

"She spends more time with that dress than . . ." he starts. "The people pay a lot of attention to her."

I tell him that the attention his daughter gets is really nothing more than people paying respect to him. "After all," I say, "you were the one who raised her."

He sits silently a brief moment, considering. "You may be right there," he says, and the thought leads him to talk about his future. He wants to return to the reservation in Lame Deer, Montana, where he was raised, and teach at the high school. "I'd like to show them what I did with my life, and go back and teach there." For now, however, he will remain in Oklahoma and attend the Kit Fox dances and powwows to watch his eldest daughter, his pride and joy.

Renecia is running from her mother to the dancers to the far end of the room, where she sits for a while with the Kit Fox men.

But her sister, Rebecca, has caught my attention, and as I watch her, she runs up to where we are seated and giggles.

She throws a blanket over my shoulders and then backs away laughing and pointing at me. "You have to dance," she says.

"I do?"

"Yes! Go!"

Ronnie is smiling and nodding. "It's a shawl dance. If a woman puts a shawl around a man, it means he has to dance like a woman."

I stand up, reluctantly. There is no one dancing, although the song has begun. I turn to protest, but Rebecca shoves me to the center. On the aching feet of a white man I struggle around the circle to great cheers and laughter. Thankfully, soon other men join me; even Ronnie comes out, wrapped in his wife's colorful blanket.

When the song is finally ended, I slump back into my seat. Ronnie joins me and studies me for a moment. "You look like you could use some sleep," he says. "You let me know when you want a ride back to town."

The day has been so long, I think it has never had a beginning. "I should go now," I say.

Ronnie is headed for more coffee. "Okay," he says. "We'll get out of here right away." "Right away" in Indian time is yet another hour or two, and so I sit back and watch some more.

The shawl dance is followed by a hat dance, wherein men may place their hats on the heads of the woman of their choice and the woman, in turn, must dance like men. Without hesitation I capture Rebecca, and she twirls in her satin shawl and heads for the dance floor. When the hat dance ends she runs back to me excitedly. "They're going to do a blanket dance in your honor," she says. "They put a blanket down and people dance around and," she pauses, her eyes wide and glowing, "and they give you money!"

"The people have heard about your trip and want to help," Ronnie says.

I start to protest and then realize it would be rude of me to do so. Ronnie escorts me to the center of the room, and I am handed the little microphone and told to explain what I am doing. I talk a moment or two, then Ronnie gives me a blanket and instructs me to put it in the center of the room. The singers' high wail floats on top of the steady beating of the drum.

The dance begins, and the entire Harris family – Ronnie and Norene, the kids and Adolph, everyone except James – leads lines of high-stepping dancers, which radiate out like twigs spinning in a whirlpool of Kit Fox drums.

When the dance is over I am given the money from the blanket. I am deeply touched. Any number of the people here tonight could use this money more than I can, but as I make my way back to my seat there is nothing except pride and wide smiles on the faces of the people.

The evening is winding down, and I am so tired that mostly what I see is a blur. Then there is a buzz around me and I look to see an ancient woman being helped in through the door.

Norene introduces me. "She doesn't speak much English," Norene explains. "She's like the grandmother of us all."

The woman is seated on the long bench and is talking quietly as other women come up to her. She smiles at me and nods, then resumes her soft talking. The dark skin of her face is etched with deep wrinkles and folds of skin, but they do not diminish the aged dignity that shines through her eyes. She leans on a cane, even while seated. She watches the dancers and nods to the increasing number of women and men that are gravitating to her. All evening the feeling of family kinship has been strong, but with the arrival of this ancient woman it suddenly becomes clear to me that for the modern Cheyennes, clan and family and respect for the long heritage of bloodlines is of monumental importance.

Despite this insight and the presence of the wonderful woman who inspired it, despite the honor of the blanket dance, despite drums and the singing and the storms and the uniqueness of the night, I am falling asleep even while seated bolt upright. In my daze, I hear bits and pieces of conversations, some in Cheyenne, some in English. My ear fixes on something familiar. Some women are talking about Ronnie's silent, thin brother-in-law, James. I have not seen him since he stepped out of the car. One of the women says he has just been released from prison. Someone else says he has been there for the last fifteen or twenty years. Before I can hear more, Ronnie is at my side.

"You ready to go?" he asks.

I stand. After another fifteen minutes of handshakes and conversations Ronnie and I step out into the impossibly late night.

The shadows of men still line the parking area. A thin line of smoke still rises from the window where the bulky, dark outline of the woman sits in the car. To the west lightning still flares like fire.

Ronnie has had too much beer for my comfort, but he drives slowly and cautiously down the deserted dirt road toward town.

"Who told you that?" he demands when I ask him what James had done to be put in prison for fifteen years.

"I just overheard a conversation."

"Who told you that? Who?"

"I don't know who it was."

"Don't believe him," he says. "Some people around here get jealous of others who have a nice home and a good job. They'll say anything. No, he was never in prison for fifteen years." His laugh is short, like a cough. "Oh, yeah, maybe as long as six months, but not for fifteen years. I wouldn't believe whoever told you that."

Rain starts, then immediately pounds the roof of the car. We are heading west, straight into a gigantic storm. Lightning cracks over our heads, stabs at the woods silhouetted in black a half mile off the road, stabs again. The radio announces that a tornado has been sighted just southeast of Seiling, headed east, straight toward this road. We drive onward into the heart of the dark terrible night, but Ronnie does not notice the storm.

"My brother-in-laws are good fighters, but I'm not afraid of them," he says. "I'm smaller, but I beat James up. I had to; there was no choice. Now they respect me."

"You had a fistfight with your brother-in-law?" I ask.

Wind buffets the car, but Ronnie holds it straight. The rain is coming in diagonally through his still-open window.

"My wife's people are descendants of Little Wolf. Little Wolf was strong and brave, but I'm strong too. James doesn't frighten me," he says. "One night we were driving somewhere and James just hauled off and hit me in the back of the head. Just hauled off and hit me. I stopped the car and pulled him out and beat the shit out of him right then and there." Ronnie's words spit out like the rain and wind. "He just hit me in the back of my head. I nearly blacked out, but I knew I had to beat him or I'd never get respect." He is shouting to be heard above the roar of the storm. I am gripping the edge of the dashboard, trying to see the road during the brief instant the wipers clear the blanket of rain away. Lightning is almost constant. We are at the heart of the storm.

"We were driving somewhere and he just hauled off and hit me in the back of the head. Just hauled off and hit me," Ronnie repeats. In the wild darkness of the storm, something like callous iron is pressed hard against the bone behind my ear. Ronnie's cold fist pushes against my head. "Right there, he just hit me as hard as he could. Right there."

The fist lingers, a bony block of an anvil covered with thin skin. It is the first time and only time Ronnie has touched me. The anvil withdraws as a single blast of thunder shakes the car and the sky is filled with light.

PART TWO

Morning Star

The Cheyennes don't want to go back to the Reservation and be starved to death by Indian contractors and every mother's son of 'em should be murdered for such ingratitude.

Unsigned editorial in the *Omaha Herald*, October 1878

5. The Barren Wastes

If we ever knew it once, we have forgotten about solitude. It is hard to find, but true solitude does remain. For one thing, it's out here in the barren wastes of Major County.

I am passing north through the county and face thirty miles of emptiness. Except for a small burg just north of Seiling, there is nothing for two days of hiking until I reach Waynoka.

Nothing.

We have so forgotten solitude that when the grace of God allows us to come face to face with it we react with fear instead of gratitude. A good friend, who as firefighter, teacher, naturalist, and canoe guide has made his career in the most remote parts of the continent, defines wilderness as a place where there is something dangerous enough to kill you. Except for rattlesnakes, tornadoes, and lack of water, the greatest danger in this wilderness is my own self-doubt.

Intellectually I understood the nature of the wilderness I have to pass through, but now it is before me as real as these treeless, seemingly barren plains.

In museums they sell a poster called "The United States at Night." It is a composite of photographs from space on cloudless nights. There are no words to identify locations, but the outline of the country is obvious in the wide blotches of the lights from megalopolises. Pools of lighted cities blanket the nation. With care you can pick out small cities of twenty-five thousand inhabitants or so. In time you are drawn to those few areas where there are no lights at all. Alaska remains largely dark, but the West itself is stringed with pearls of lights – Billings, Cheyenne, Denver, Albuquerque, Phoenix – so that the large pockets of darkness representing the least populated areas of the country are surprisingly few.

My hike takes me across the largest of those dark places.

The soil here is a worn red – a color the mixture of rust and

Little Wolf and Dull Knife, 1873. Courtesy of Nebraska State Historical Society.

blood. It sticks to whatever few objects rise up from the land. Solitary trees bleed alive, while cars and trucks rust to dust.

Dull Knife and Little Wolf climbed this same divide toward the valley of the Cimarron. I cross the North Canadian on a bridge outside of Seiling. Two cattle egrets rise up white against a cloudless sky. Imperceptibly, the landscape rises toward the divide. By midafternoon I am still in the Canadian River watershed. In the direction I've come, the wide expanse of the Canadian River valley is framed by low hills in the foreground. A few cattle dot the red hills. There is a light breeze in the empty sunlit air.

I have not yet crossed into the Cimarron Valley when this flat land falls away before my feet and slopes rapidly into a cool canyon of pine and juniper. I set up my traveling seat and cook a lunch on the stove. I take off my boots. I am supremely relaxed and buoyant. The sparse woods here are inhabited by jays and chickadees, and their familiar calls soothe me. The trickle of the headwaters of Griever Creek and the warm spring sun lull me into a peaceful nap. I awake rested and strong. In *Thoughts in Solitude*, Thomas Merton writes, "the phrase self conquest can come to sound odious because very often it can mean not the conquest of ourselves but a conquest *by* ourselves. . . . Self conquest is really self-surrender. Yet before we can surrender ourselves we must become ourselves. For no one can give up what he does not possess."

I climb up out of the canyon to the lip of a vast expanse of seemingly featureless horizon. A nothingness. The Cimarron Valley is a dinner plate sixty miles across. I can see my next several days of travel. To the northwest, where I will be going, is a splotch of white, Little Sahara State Park, yet a day and a half away. Beyond it, however, is an even greater expanse, spreading out level into the distance all the way into Kansas.

I have not passed a house since long before noon, and at sunset I walk a quarter mile beyond an abandoned ranch house to set up camp in a small indentation on the east side of a hill.

I am camped in the bar ditch of a former ranch road. A few trees shade a blanket of wildflowers and green grass from the golden sunlight of day's end. Strangely, I am not worried about how low my water supply has gotten. I will need more by ten tomorrow morning, with yet ten hours of hot, dry hiking until I reach the next known water supply. I remember having seen a ranch house in the distance, a couple of miles west of here, and could hike there, or I can survive on the abundant rainwater that for the past week has choked most creeks with water.

The recent rains have made the prairie grass about me thick and lush with brilliant orange flowers. I sit in the grass next to my tent thinking of nothing and watching the sunset. I do have a healthy respect for rattlesnakes, however, and so once every few minutes I take one of my boots and tap the ground around my seat as a warning just in case one might be wandering near. A mourning dove *cook-coos, coos, coos,* from a nearby cottonwood tree. My body is deliciously exhausted and alive. The bird, the tree, the snake, the sunset, the soft breeze flipping the flap on my tent, they are all here now, absolutely and timelessly here now. A coyote, a pack of them, sing at the instant of dusk. I am in solitude and thank God for the gift of it.

The wildest beasts are those that have stalked me all of my life. Although I usually deny their existence and at best can but briefly turn away from their threat, in the isolation of this prairie dusk I face for one clear instant the twin menace of pride and ignorance. Neither I nor the beasts blink, and in that is a small victory. Wilderness is a place where we are allowed the opportunity to face the true dangers within ourselves: it is the solitude we each of us face in death.

"We must return from the desert," Merton wrote, "with our capacity for feeling expanded and deepened, strengthened against the appeals of falsity, warned against temptation, great, noble and pure."

I sit silently until the dark is nearly full and the light of stars is all I need to climb into the tent and fall into a blissful and deep sleep.

In the morning I use half of the remaining water for coffee, brewed on the tiny stove from tealike coffee bags, eat a breakfast of hot oatmeal and dried fruit, and am on my way.

The curve of the valley is so imperceptibly bowled that my view to Kansas is essentially the same as yesterday when I climbed out of Griever Creek canyon. I watch as my walking takes me further and further from the distant, occupied ranch house. I am convinced I will find water ahead of me, and indeed, three hours later and down to a couple of mouthfuls, I happen upon a small house at the intersection of two roads.

It is not a ranch house but a small framed house with a tiny porch and a half dozen black oil tanks in the rear. They are as tall as the house. I knock on the door. Pause, knock again. I can hear a television set playing inside.

The man who opens the door looks at me through the screen as I speak. "I was running low on water and was wondering if I might fill my water bottles from your hose?"

"Oh, sure," he says without hesitation. "Help yourself." He opens the screen and steps outside. He is a weathered man of about sixty. His skin sags a bit, but underneath it his muscles are taut and young.

"Oh, hell, don't use that hose water. Follow me, we'll get you some good water."

He leads me around the outside of the house to the oil tanks in the rear. They are arranged in a circle, with a fence around them. A utility pole sports a yard light, glaring brightly in the noonday sun. We pass through a gateway of some sort, and it is evident that large trucks frequent these tanks. We step across a short wooden bridge. Under the bridge is a square culvert full of thick, oozing oil.

I shudder. If we are passing through this polluted ground to get to the "good water," I wonder what the hose water might have been like.

The man pauses at a small shack. He is asking me about my walk. He opens the door and invites me inside. It is a small office of some sort. There is a TV playing in the corner of the single room, but the room is empty.

"Here, help yourself," he says.

Lining the far wall of the room are at least a dozen five-gallon glass jars of purified water. From a spigot where one of the bottles has been placed, I fill my water bottles. "You sure you don't mind if I fill them all?"

"Help yourself. I have plenty of clear water. In fact," he pauses and walks over to a refrigerator, "here, have a pop or two."

The refrigerator has nothing but shelf after shelf of cold cans of cola and orange soda. The frost steams up into the hot sunlight. "Go on, take another," he says. I take another orange.

Outside again the man shakes my hand and tells me to enjoy myself. I thank him once again and walk away tilting the second can to my lips to extract the last drops from the cold aluminum. The cool, clear water sloshes comfortably in the bottles in my pack.

The couple dozen words I have said to the man mark the first time I have spoken aloud in over forty-eight hours. The act has freed my tongue, and as I move across the prairie toward the Cimarron River I begin to chatter and sing and comment on the world around me. "It's all right to talk to yourself," I say aloud, "as long as you don't answer yourself."

"No problem," I answer.

The silence has not bothered me until it was broken by the stop for water. Where before it simply was, now I am self-consciously aware of the quiet. I play with it, testing the size of my own voice against its enormity. Not only does it always win, but it also ceases to serve my solitude, since now I am too aware of the quiet and try to listen for it. Finally, I simply pause to listen for sounds, which arrive like the single fluted note of a western meadowlark. In listening for sound I become aware of time passing, too aware of the unbroken pause between note and stillness. For a while I painfully insist on marking that period of unspoiled silence by breaking it with my own voice. But the day is long and the magnificent prairie wilderness of Major County far stronger than my patience. So it is that with grace and with gratitude I once again fall into the silence and solitude of open space.

6. Morning Star

The Heritage Acres Nursing Home is a low-slung modern building at the edge of the town of Hardin, Montana. It is one of two nursing homes in the town of six thousand a few dozen miles from the Crow and Northern Cheyenne reservations and a half an hour from Little Bighorn National Monument. It's not difficult to find the nursing home, since nearly everyone in Hardin knows it best as the county-run nursing home; that to distinguish it from the private and, to some, better convalescent center.

Because there is no nursing home on the Northern Cheyenne reservation, Heritage Acres is home to many elderly or infirm Northern Cheyennes. Inside its wide and inviting doors the clean, orderly facility buzzes with cheerful aides and nurses who hurry about in bright hallways decorated here and there with Indian-influenced art.

Room 210 at Heritage Acres was the last home of Ted Risingsun, great grandson of Dull Knife and Pawnee Woman, grandson of Broken Foot Woman, child of John Risingsun. Born in 1926, Ted Risingsun grew up on the reservation listening to the stories of his grandparents and elders – Dull Knife's children. Ted heard the stories of the long flight from Indian Territory from the ones who made the journey, and he learned of the battles from those who fought at Turkey Springs, at Punished Woman, and at Fort Robinson. Ted heard the stories and the stories before them, and Ted knew more about Dull Knife than probably any other living person. After he attended the BIA's Tongue River Boarding School in Busby, Montana, he graduated from high school and did some college work in Kansas and South Dakota. A modern dog soldier, Ted enlisted in the service as soon as he was of age and served his country in war and in peace. He became the most decorated Indian in the Korean War and was a frequent member of the Northern Cheyenne tribal council. After fighting the demons of democracy, Ted struggled for years until, through his own strength and courage, he overcame the impish trickster-enemy alcohol.

On a bright July morning a year before my trek, room 210 was nearly empty. There was no television, no books, no loose clothing scattered about. There was no radio, nor grandchildren's drawings, nor postcards, nor pencils and paper. Next to the bed was a nightstand with a large red plastic pitcher of water. On the bare wall, framed and centered near the window, was a portrait of Dull Knife.

Ted Risingsun sat propped up, the hospital-style bed cranked to support his torso, and a stack of pillows behind his back to finish the job. His black hair against his deep, golden skin was like a seam of coal on the side of a sagebrush-covered hill. "While I've been in here, all I hear is how dark my hair is," Ted said. "They say: 'You've got black, black hair.' I say it's because I'm a young man, that's why."

He wore thick, dark-rimmed spectacles, and although he was nearly toothless, his eyes were clear and bright. His cotton trousers were neatly tucked under his thighs, each one twisted twice at the place, just below each knee, where six weeks earlier they had amputated both of his legs. Ted had the sugar sickness, diabetes.

A portable table was spread out in front of him, and as he talked he rested his elbows on it or used it to softly bang a fist in order to underline a point.

"If you went on the reservation and asked a fifteen-year-old Cheyenne what they knew about Dull Knife, they wouldn't know a thing," Ted said. "There is no interest in our history. Other things have come along which have taken them away from their history. Other things such as drugs and alcohol."

His hand softly slapped at the table. "There's no real leadership on the reservation today. People today are more interested in being popular; they aren't interested in leadership." He paused a moment, peeling back the skin of a banana, then continued. "When he finally got to the reservation, Dull Knife said, 'We cannot live the way we are. We're going to have to change the way we're living.' He asked for schools to be built in our country so the children could go to them and learn the new way of life." Ted's voice, which at first had been soft and tired, grew stronger as he spoke. "The men would shoot their guns in the air, yell at him for wanting education, call him a white man's wife, call him other names, but that didn't stop him. He said the same thing over and over and over again. Whether he was unpopular for saying this didn't change it. Being unpopular didn't change the truth of his words. It took the Cheyenne a hundred years for that message to penetrate. Now the people say, 'We want a high school.' What for? Why do they want a high school? Why do they want a junior college? Why do they want these things if they didn't like education so well? Dull Knife kept saying the same thing over and over again. He kept repeating the truth." He stopped, the sudden outburst still echoing in the room. "That's real leadership."

Across the room, partially divided by a half-drawn curtain, Ted's white roommate Ed listened intently. He sat in an ornate rocking chair near his bed. He had a box of tissues on his bedstand, near a framed color photograph of a young couple and three children. A stack of newspapers was on the floor, two clean shirts were folded on the edge of his bed, an award of some kind hung on the wall, and a crucifix looked down from above his bed. "Ted's just as bored as I am in here," Ed said in the silence.

Ted looked at him and slowly fed the banana into his mouth. He munched on it a moment, then spoke again. "I retired from the military in 1993 and after a lifetime of service I get something like eight thousand dollars a year," he said. "So I can lay here the rest of my days and get eight thousand dollars a year and not do a thing for myself." He paused. "Ehh," he said, "I wouldn't want to spend the rest of my life here at Hair-it-age Acres, I'll tell you that much." He held up the peel of the banana. "This is what I would be eating the rest of my life."

"Bored," Ed repeated.

"They give me anything I want here," Ted said. "I don't have to do a thing here, they do it all for me. Hair-it-age Acres is just like the reservation: we don't have to do a thing for ourselves."

Ted Risingsun turned his head slowly toward the portrait of Dull Knife on the wall, motioned with the palm of his hand, and then spoke as if addressing his comments to the picture. "We could have our own nursing home right on the reservation. That's my dream. There's no reason people have to come all the way to Hardin just to see their loved ones; there's no reason why people have to leave the reservation and come here when they're old. It's not the Cheyenne way. It can be done," he said. "There's no telling what people can do when they want to do it. People are too used to having everything served to them, like here at Hair-it-age Acres."

"People don't want to hear that," Ed said. "They don't want to hear that they're lazy."

"People don't want to hear things, but if it's the truth, then it must be said." Ted pointed to the portrait of his great-grandfather. He paused a long moment. His mouth's half-slanted frown was identical to the way Dull Knife's stern lips were held. "Dull Knife said things that weren't popular, but when they needed a leader to take them north, who did they turn to?"

Ted ran his hands across the portable table in front of him as if smoothing an invisible cloth. "Someone may have given Dull Knife advice which he did not heed. There are those who claim that had he taken this advice so many would not have been killed at Fort Robinson. Some people, even today, don't think well of Dull Knife. Those feelings may be related to that – to stories passed down about how he didn't heed advice that may have prevented the tragedy where so many were killed at Fort Robinson." The hands tightened to fists, and the fists rested on the cold steel of the table "They don't understand that it's because of that man we are alive today. There were many killed, it's true, but Dull Knife is the reason we're still here today: Dull Knife is the reason we're strong."

Without legs, Ted Risingsun could not walk across tiny room 210 at Heritage Acres, much less the thousand miles from Oklahoma, but he was right about the vitality of his people. The reason the Northern Cheyennes are strong is not simply because of Dull Knife, but because all true leaders – men and women like Dull Knife and like Ted Risingsun – know that strength is much more than the fortitude of the body.

One month before I began my hike, Ted Risingsun passed on.

Morning Star, that was his real name, Wohe Hiv, a Cheyenne name. "Dull Knife was a kidding name," Ted Risingsun told me. "His brother had always teased him about the sharpness of his hunting knife, and before long the nickname was how he came to be remembered." Although he was a member of the Dog Soldier

Society, he was most trusted for his wisdom in counsel rather than his abilities as a fighter.

Morning Star was born in the 1820s and died in Montana in 1883, five years after the long trek from Indian Territory, five years after he was among the few who survived the bloody massacre at Fort Robinson that brought to an end his part in the long odyssey.

The first written record of Dull Knife was made in 1856 after soldiers claimed that four horses had been stolen by the Cheyennes. When Little Wolf refused to give up the horse he had found and the soldiers retaliated by capturing a Cheyenne man, Dull Knife was the one who negotiated with the commander at Fort Laramie for the release of the captive. That was his first contact with the *veho*.

Dull Knife reappears in the written record of western history ten years later when the legendary lust for gold brought whites into the traditional homeland of the Cheyennes. Even though in 1851 a treaty had been signed promising the Powder River country between the Black Hills and the Rockies to the Sioux Indians, when gold was discovered in Montana, miners immediately violated the treaty and invaded the territory on a freshly built road known as the Bozeman Trail. Red Cloud's Sioux were the main opponents to the use of the Bozeman Trail, and the Cheyennes were allied with them.

On December 21, 1866, Captain William J. Fetterman, disobeying explicit orders not to go into an area outside of Fort Phil Kearny, met a combined force of Red Cloud's Sioux, Arapahos, and Cheyennes, including Dull Knife. According to an eyewitness, Dull Knife and some of his warriors initially lured Fetterman and his troops even further from the post. After chasing Dull Knife's small band, Fetterman suddenly found himself surrounded by fifteen hundred warriors. In the vicious battle that followed, probably less than fifty Indians were slain, and all of Fetterman's command – seventy-nine soldiers and two civilians – were killed.

Two years later President Ulysses S. Grant appointed General William T. Sherman to head a council to hammer out a new version of settlements with the Indians of the Great Plains. On May 10, 1868, at Fort Laramie, near the present-day border of Nebraska and Wyoming, Dull Knife and others signed the treaty

Sherman negotiated. This treaty gave them the choice of settling in the south with the southern band of the tribe, or in the north near either the Crows or the Brulés and other Sioux.

One year later Dull Knife, Little Wolf, and other Cheyennes went to Washington DC to meet with the commissioner of Indian affairs. When the commissioner told them they had signed a treaty agreeing to go south, Dull Knife protested, saying they had never agreed to give up the Cheyenne homeland in Nebraska and Montana. The commissioner simply said that Dull Knife's "pretense of misunderstanding" would not get him far and that he would have to go south to Indian Territory.

The next day the Cheyennes were taken to the White House to meet President Grant. According to the *Evening Star* they "formed a circle in the main lower hall, looking as stolid as tobacco signs." Again Dull Knife protested, this time directly to the president. He said that he refused to go south. Grant responded by saying that the interpreter at the treaty signing must have been at fault, for he was certain that Sherman would never had done anything to harm them. Neither side changed its interpretation of the treaty.

A man who met Dull Knife during his trip to Washington wrote in his diary:

> Dull Knife was tall and lithe in form, he had the face of a states-man or a church dignitary of the grave and ascetic type. His manner of speech was earnest and dignified, and his whole bearing was that of a leader with the cares of state.

The Washington photographer who took the pictures of the visiting Indian leaders posed Dull Knife seated next to his friend Little Wolf. In the photograph the two men stare, unsmiling, into the lens.

Dull Knife is clearly the older man; his eyes squint in the light of the photographer's studio, his lips held in a tight, thin line, framed by deep wrinkles creasing his face. He holds his pipe, resting it on his right knee, his long, delicate fingers poised on his blankets. His black, thick hair puffs up off his forehead in a nearly modern way, then entwines in thick braids behind his head.

Ted Risingsun said that when Dull Knife and the others went to Washington, they had a cook assigned to them. In Cheyenne tradition, they always would leave a little food on their plates out of respect. This went on for days until finally, out of exasperation, the cook couldn't stand it any longer and spoke to the Cheyennes. The cook said that he would make them anything they wanted if they just would eat it all. That night the cook prepared what they had requested, and when he checked the table after they had finished, he discovered the Cheyennes had eaten everything on the table: all of the salt, all of the pepper, and even the flowers on the centerpiece.

Although Dull Knife, Little Wolf, and the other Cheyennes left Washington without an agreement reaffirming that they had been promised a northern homeland, the meeting probably did give the Northern Cheyennes a few years of grace in the north before the killing started again. For four years after the Washington visit, Dull Knife and other Northern Cheyennes were able to live as they had for centuries, hunting the high prairie grasslands of their traditional home, camping together in ten large bands through the winter months, and moving off into hunting camps when the ice broke on the great Missouri and Yellowstone Rivers.

The end to the old way was sudden. Once the final wars began, it would take only a little over two years for the way of life of the open plains to end and the confining life of a reservation to begin. Dull Knife was not present at the event that signaled the beginning of the end. He and his followers were not on the Little Bighorn that June afternoon in 1876 when Custer and his soldiers from the Seventh Cavalry were wiped out, but his son Medicine Club was there and was killed that day.

That fall Dull Knife and the village moved into the Bighorn Mountains to camp for the coming winter. They settled in on one of the prime winter camping places in the west. The wide valley up on the Red Fork of the Powder River is enclosed by a long, high mountain to the north and an arc of red ridges to the south. The creek cuts through red rock canyons and white stone bluffs and then opens to a wide, flat meadow for a mile before it closes in again and climbs into the Bighorns. A mile below the flat campground are warm springs that remain ice-free all winter, attracting a steady supply of game. Protected by the high, surrounding mountains, the icy winds and frozen blasts of drifting snow don't pound here as they do elsewhere. For centuries native peoples had treasured this camping place, even fighting battles for the right to use it.

By November over two hundred Northern Cheyenne tepees were set up across the meadow, where in the early hours of November 26, 1876, Ranald S. Mackenzie's troops – who were combing the area looking for revenge on Custer's defeat – discovered them. The Cheyennes had not fled the coming of the massive encampment of troops. The army claimed it was because they had taken the Cheyennes by surprise, but it is unlikely that the Cheyennes would not know about the movements of such a large invading force. Ted Risingsun said Dull Knife and Little Wolf and other leaders had known the troops were nearby and had wanted to leave, but that a powerful medicine man of one of the soldier societies said he had seen in a vision a great victory for the Cheyennes. He said his vision told him they could not be defeated. Ted claimed that when Dull Knife and others tried to leave anyway, the medicine man had warriors cut the cinches on their saddles and travois in order to keep them in place. They had returned to camp and built breastworks up the valley in preparation for the attack.

Mackenzie's Indian scouts lined the southern ridge top while his force of nearly 1,300 men, along with several hundred Pawnee and Bannock auxiliaries, began the attack, supported by 168 wagons, 8 ambulances, 219 drivers, and 400 pack mules.

It was said that a second of Dull Knife's sons was the first person killed. He had spotted the soldiers and was running through the sleeping village trying to warn others when he was shot down by a dozen bullets. A soldier later recognized the body as that of Dull Knife's son Young Bird. "His face to the sky, peaceful, a noble young man in a blanket of fine cloth, one half red, the other blue, doubled and suspended from his waist. Around him was a belt holding his gun, an army rifle pointed diagonally across his body."

At the first instant of the attack Cheyenne warriors ran naked from their lodges into the point-blank range of the thousand troops. A number of defiant Cheyennes ran directly at the soldiers' heavy fire. Ted said the medicine man who had insisted the village not retreat was among the first killed. One unidentified young man scrambled out to retrieve the body of a fallen friend, surviving what a witness described as hundreds of shots fired directly at him.

Although the Cheyennes were outnumbered at least two to one, the fighting continued all day. Mackenzie set up his field headquarters on a flat ridge that extended out into the valley from the tall mountain ridge on the north. Behind him a similar hill served as the army's field hospital. That night, with the battle still raging, the Cheyennes had to abandon the village in order to seek a better defensive position. Believing they had the Indians trapped, soldiers chased the last of the warriors up the canyon. A quarter mile later they ran into a wall of Cheyenne bullets, which came up from a nearly invisible ravine at their feet. The soldiers fell back, but the Cheyennes were forced to leave behind the objects on which their survival depended. Not only did they abandon a thousand robes, a season's worth of dried meat, and all their lodges – their stores for a healthy winter – but they also lost many sacred items. Family keepsakes and medicine pouches, sacred pipes, and painted hides had been left behind because of the sudden attack. As soon as the Cheyennes departed, Mackenzie ordered everything burned and smashed and destroyed. That night it snowed two feet, and the deep blanket of white covered the smoldering ashes of centuries of Cheyenne culture.

In the spring of 1877, starving, sick, and decimated, 550 survivors of the attack on Dull Knife's village surrendered at Camp Robinson, Nebraska. By late spring, the number of Northern Cheyennes who had surrendered at the camp was close to 1,000.

It was decided the these 1,000 Cheyennes would be taken south to Indian Territory, where the United States had been trying to consolidate Indians for a decade. When told what was intended for them, the Northern Cheyennes protested. They had been getting government rations at Camp Robinson since 1868; besides, here in the north was their home. If they were to be forced onto a reservation, they should surely be given one where they had always lived. While leaders such as Little Wolf, Dull Knife, and Wild Hog said they wanted to stay north, a leader named Standing Elk apparently agreed to go south. Later, people said the reason was that Standing Elk had relatives among the Southern Cheyennes in Indian Territory and missed them; others say Standing Elk had been tricked into agreeing. In any event, most members of the tribe wished to stay north, but the officer in charge wired Washington that the majority of Northern Cheyennes being held wanted to go to Indian Territory "if they are to be moved at all."

Despite being well aware of the Northern Cheyenne resistance and protest, Lieutenant General Philip Sheridan, commander of the Department of the Missouri, then forwarded a recommendation to Washington that the Northern Cheyennes be sent to Indian Territory. Sheridan's recommendation made no mention of the overwhelming reluctance of most of the Indians to leave their home country.

So it was that on May 28, 1877, 937 Northern Cheyennes, under military escort, left the pine ridge beauty of the Red Cloud Agency at Camp Robinson, Nebraska, for the Cheyenne-Arapaho Agency near Fort Reno.

After seventy-two days of travel, the large group reached Indian Territory. Immediately after arrival the Cheyennes protested the poor conditions they found waiting them. For the next year the Northern Cheyennes faced disease, insufficient food, and poor shelter, and they were placed in competition with their Southern Cheyenne cousins for what scanty provisions existed. These poor conditions grew intolerable through official neglect and ineptitude. Pleas for additional provisions and for medical attention went unfilled throughout the winter months and into the summer of 1878. After an epidemic struck two-thirds of them ill, Dull Knife and the other leaders, "homesick and heartsick in every way," began to plot for their escape north.

They fled on September 9, 1878, and after a month of running battles reached the familiar hunting area of southern Nebraska. Once into Nebraska the Northern Cheyennes split into two groups. Some of them, under the leadership of Little Wolf, hid through the winter in a secluded canyon. In March, a hundred miles from the Powder River in Montana, they would surrender. These would survive.

Others, under the leadership of Dull Knife, would not be so lucky. Approximately 122 Northern Cheyennes would follow Dull Knife as he headed toward what he thought was still Red Cloud's

Agency and Camp Robinson. There he hoped to find sympathetic help from his friend Red Cloud and his people.

Unbeknownst to Dull Knife, however, the government had moved the Red Cloud Agency further north into South Dakota during the time that the Northern Cheyennes had been held captive in Indian Territory. Instead of finding Red Cloud and protection with the Sioux, Dull Knife's band of fleeing Northern Cheyennes were captured in late October and taken prisoner to the newly fortified and renamed Fort Robinson.

Initially they were treated well, but then orders came from Washington that even though one of the coldest, snowiest winters had slammed down on the Sand Hills, the prisoners were to be returned to Indian Territory immediately.

The Cheyennes were imprisoned in a barracks and told they would have to return to Indian Territory. They refused to go.

The commander at Fort Robinson issued orders to withhold food, water, and fuel from all prisoners, including the children, until the Indians agreed.

On the night of January 9, 1879, after a being held in a sealed room without food or fuel, the Cheyennes pieced together the rifles and pistols they had taken apart and concealed as women's jewelry before their capture. Dull Knife spoke to the people. "Let us never give up to these people, to be taken back south to the country we have run away from. We have given them everything we have and now they are starving us to death. We may as well die here as to be taken south and die there."

Just as the 10 P.M. bell sounded from the large clock in the fort's central building, the Cheyennes tore through the boarded windows of their prison and poured out into the thirty-below-zero night. In the first few minutes twenty-one were killed; by morning an additional nine others were dead. Twenty-two of these were women and children.

During the next week the rest were pursued into the badlands above the fort. Day after day the soldiers attacked and tracked the few remaining Cheyennes until, on January 22, after a bloody standoff in a pit above a remote Nebraska creek where twenty-five of a group of thirty-two Indians were killed, the last of these were captured.

Of the more than one hundred who attempted to escape, all but about seven were killed or captured. Among the seven who escaped was Morning Star – Dull Knife himself.

The death count for the week was seventy-seven Cheyennes and about a half dozen soldiers. What was called the Fort Robinson Massacre, but soon came to be known as the Cheyenne Outbreak, was over.

Ma i you'n, the mysterious power that controlled the affairs of humankind, is silent now. The bones of Dull Knife have returned to dust in the soil of his home country. The descendants of many of the Cheyennes and of the pioneers and soldiers who died are scattered now far away from the reality of those times, far away from the memory of the stars and heat lighting, the storms and the full moon of the long prairie march into time.

In 1913 an old Northern Cheyenne by the name of Porcupine Bull recalled a song from those times:

HI tA
In I' O mon i,
nA niss' On i.

All will
Be gone,
My children.

He was an old, old man, but his voice rang out as if he could hear the echoes of those times as clearly as the speech of the wolves:

HI tA
In I' O mon i,
nA niss' On i.

All will
Be gone,
My children.

7. Andy

The late-model American car slowly crests the hill in front of me just as I reach the bottom of a little draw. Even though there is no traffic on this empty dirt road, it pulls well off into the bar ditch and stops. In a moment the door opens and a figure emerges slipping into a jeans jacket. He moves to meet me.

He is a tall, slender man, whose walk is an easy, solid, and erect gait. He wears a felt black cowboy-style hat. He is an Indian.

Although we have never met, there is no doubt about who the other might be.

"Andrew," I say. His eyes briefly reach mine and we smile.

"Alan," he says. On this remote and emptiest of back roads, Andrew Sooktis has found me.

A year ago when I visited the Northern Cheyenne reservation in Montana I had met Andrew's sister. She said it was a good thing for someone to walk the route and thought some Cheyennes would probably like to join me. I returned home for a year of preparing and planning, but it wasn't until a week before I left for Oklahoma that she called on the phone to say who might join me.

"My brother Andy is one of the ones who wants to walk with you" she had said. "He'll meet you in Oklahoma."

I had spent a year studying maps, plotting the Cheyennes' route across large, unpopulated spaces. It would be impossible for a pack of bloodhounds to find me, much less a complete stranger randomly searching the remote plains of Oklahoma.

"Meet me? Where?"

She had laughed her deep, soft laugh. "Oh, don't worry," she said. "He'll find you."

As I tell him the story, Andrew's laugh is rich and soft like his sister's. He passes off the compliment about his tracking abilities.

"Oh," he says, "that sounds like her."

I unhitch my pack and let it slide to the ground. We stand in the grass and breeze at the side of the road and talk. He would have caught up with me earlier, Andrew says, but he's been busy doing genealogical research. He and his sister are direct descendants of Dull Knife, and Andrew is the leading authority on the complex Dull Knife family tree. He is anxious to show me his latest research, and I am anxious to see it. He reaches into the cluttered back seat of the car and pulls out a briefcase full of papers. From this he unfolds a wide sheet of paper. It is a family tree. I recognize Ted Risingsun's name.

"Dull Knife had three wives. His first wife died fairly early," he says pointing his long, bony finger at the lines before us. "He married Pawnee Wife next. She was my great-great-grandmother." His finger slides across the chart and stops at her name.

The words lift themselves off the page, and I follow them up to his face and out across the prairie earth. From the slope of the small hill where we stand, a rough-legged hawk rises above the carpet-green ground on a thin thermal updraft.

"One of his wives died on this journey north," he says. "My grandfather told me she was kicked by a horse when the army discovered one of their camps and they had to move quickly. She was packing a horse and it kicked her in the head. She died a few days later."

It shouldn't surprise me that the history I had barely glimpsed from my reading was for Andrew a rich web of family stories, but in his respectful and familiar tone I suddenly see the human connection to the past I had blindly missed in my study of the words on history's pages.

"Maybe we can find the place where it happened," I say.

He pauses a long moment and our conversation develops the slow and relaxed pace it will carry the rest of the voyage. "Maybe so," he says, smiling. He wears a wisp of a mustache on his thin upper lip. He smiles frequently and then his narrow face returns to some calm place.

He folds up the chart, places it back in the briefcase, and tosses the case on the front seat. His dark hair spreads out across his back. It reaches midway to his waist. "I still need to talk to other descendants in this part of the area. It'll take me another day or so; then I'll walk with you."

"Fine," I say. We lean over the hood of the car and study the map from my map packet and agree at a time and place to meet, then he climbs back into the car.

Almost imperceptibly, he lights a cigarette. Andrew smokes as I replace the backpack. I snap the belt and cinch it tight, then lean on his open window, supporting the weight of the backpack by resting my hands on the frame. We chat a moment or two longer and then part. "See you later," I say, "Good-bye."

Instead of "good-bye," Andrew only says, "Okay," then turns the big car around in the grass of the bar ditch and pulls back onto the road. I wave as he drives away.

Andrew Sooktis was born on the high, empty rangeland of southeastern Montana. There are few fences to break the expanse of grass and hill; the coulees run down to the creeks, and the creeks roll down to the winding Rosebud or ease into the broad valley of the Tongue River. On the higher hills are pines and junipers, and the golden cliffs of ragged rock jump from open miles of thick golden grass.

Andrew and his wife live on the reservation in a ranch-style house amid a small cluster of homes occupied by his parents and other members of his family. He is a well-respected employee of Lame Deer's major store, where his skills at everything from carpentry to computers keep him busy. Although his life on the reservation is that of a modern man, Andrew grew up on the back of a pony crossing and recrossing that gigantic, open place, following the horse of his grandfather, Dan Dawn Seminole.

His grandfather was a direct link to the old ways of the Cheyennes and one of the last to shun modern ways. The grandson of Dull Knife and Pawnee Woman, Dan Dawn Seminole was raised by his uncle, Buffalo Hump. When Buffalo Hump's daughters said, "We don't have a brother; can we have Dan Dawn Seminole for a brother?" Seminole's mother gave her son to her brother.

Because Andrew's grandfather knew skills most others had forgotten, men sought him out for work that required a special sensitivity to the land. Andrew's grandfather tracked cattle rustlers to earn the little money he required. Even in the 1950s men still rustled other men's cattle, but few were able to study the bent blades of grass or read the scratches on bedrock well enough to track rustlers for days across southeastern Montana's coulees, foothills, and rivers.

As a young boy Andrew rode with his grandfather for weeks at a time. Zigzagging across the land for days without seeing a soul, his grandfather worked for the ranchers who hired him, tracking the thieves and collecting evidence that could be used to prosecute the rustlers. As they traveled, the old man taught Andrew about the old ways of the Cheyennes. His grandfather knew the location of every cabin in every remote creek bottom, as well as the isolated hillsides where the wooden shelters and pole corrals marked the lodges of other, nearly forgotten ones.

They would ride out in the blistering dry August and camp miles from home. They would ride out in the freezing cold December with just a blanket and jacket and spend a week in the wilderness. On one such ride, with their faces numb in the bitter cold, his grandfather pulled out a bottle just as they stopped to camp for the night and said, "Take a bit of this so at least your insides will be warm." Andrew took a single sip of the alcohol. No matter how much he asked, Seminole refused to give him another one the rest of the night. "Too many men have been ruined by whiskey," he explained.

Once his grandfather wanted to catch some weasels for a braid he was making for his daughter, but they were far from town and didn't have anything to catch them with. Seminole told Andrew, "I'll show you something you'll remember a long time." They had some food in cans, and the old man opened two of them partway and took some hamburger and rubbed it along the rims. These he placed near some weasel holes he found. In the morning he had his two weasels, their tongues tightly wedged between the lid and the edge of the canned-food traps.

One time his grandfather told Andrew to saddle up because he had a special place to show him. Before light they rode to the northern edge of the reservation and crossed onto the land of a white rancher who, Andrew knew, didn't like trespassers. They came to place he had never seen before where the rocks were twisted into strange and unearthly shapes. He noticed how medicine bundles and other offerings were placed carefully about.

"This is the place where Sitting Bull had a great vision," his grandfather explained. The great Sioux holy man Sitting Bull had been camped at this place in the spring of 1876 when he had a vision of soldiers falling into his camp. Less than a month later Custer and many soldiers from the Seventh Cavalry would meet their end on the Little Bighorn. Many said that Sitting Bull's vision had foretold that victory.

Andrew gained a new respect for the rancher because he now understood that the reason the man so disliked trespassers was in an effort to protect this holy place. The thought only made him more uneasy, however. "What if the rancher finds us?" Andrew asked, but his grandfather only laughed. "He doesn't ever get up until eight-thirty," he said. His grandfather's powers of observation were so acute that he knew not only the habits of the wild creatures of the land but those of its human inhabitants as well.

By day the two of them would track vague hoofprints across the grass and sage and rocks and sand, and at night, after his grandfather had carefully logged the day's findings in his journal, they would sit before the campfire. The old man told Andrew story after countless story about his own grandfather, Dull Knife.

By the time Andrew was a teenager he had stopped riding with his grandfather, though he still sought his advice. One time Andrew had some extra money. He bought a car and some clothes but still had some money left over, so he drove out into the countryside to his grandfather's cabin to ask him what he should do with the rest of the money. He thought it would be a quick trip, that he'd be told how to invest it and then be out of there. Instead, Andrew spent the day with his grandfather, fixing a fence, shoeing horses, and resetting some fence posts for the corral. During the entire day his grandfather didn't say a word about how to invest the money. The evening came on and the two of them went for a long ride into the hills. It got late enough that Andrew had to spend the night. In the morning, as he was preparing to leave, his grandfather said, "Buy some horses." Andrew took the rest of his money and bought some horses. For months to come his grandfather would come into town to teach him everything he knew about horses.

Andrew's grandfather lived outside the town of Lame Deer in a log cabin he had built himself. He would often leave his horse at home and walk the distance into town because he said the walk kept him healthy and feeling young. When he was very old, people were afraid he would get hurt walking all that distance and made him move into town. According to Andrew, the move into town was what finally killed Dan Dawn Seminole. "For all of his life Dan Dawn Seminole had little use for money," Andrew said. "For years his only expenses had been eight dollars a month – the cost of enough electricity for a bulb to read by. Everything else, his water, his food, and even his clothing, he provided by himself. Now, the electricity for his town apartment alone cost over thirty dollars, and there was rent, and grocery bills and . . ."

Andrew was in New Hampshire attending a Quaker high school in the mid-1970s when he got the news that his grandfather was near death and was asking for him. Andrew raced back to Montana and for the next eight days sat at the old man's side, sleeping at nights on the floor of the hospital room. On the morning of the eighth day, Dan Dawn Seminole passed away in Andrew's arms. The next day, grief-stricken and drunk from whiskey bought at Jim Town just off the reservation, two of the old man's daughters were killed on the dangerous curve coming back from the bar.

For years Andrew was worried that he had forgotten Dan Dawn Seminole's many stories, but his mother told him not to worry, that even if he couldn't remember the words, he would remember the stories when he needed to.

Sure enough, Andrew Sooktis has begun to remember his grandfather's stories.

The next time I see him, Andrew is sitting in the shade of a big cottonwood tree just across the Cimarron River, where we have agreed to meet. At first I see only that his car is pulled way off into the bar ditch, and until he rises and waves to me, I don't realize there is someone near it.

Thousands of swallows rise up around me as I cross the bridge over the swollen Cimarron. Their chittering, jerky flight is a choreographed dance of feathers. The land breaks from its pancake flatness into bright red cliffs along the river's shore. The hills crumble their blood into the high crimson water.

"I've been watching two or three turkeys over there," Andrew says as I walk up. He points to a distant clump of trees along the river's edge, but I do not see a thing. Apropos of nothing he says, "There are some people here I'd just as soon avoid."

"What people?" I ask.

"I stopped in a store to buy some pop and there were a couple of these Freeman people," he begins.

"I don't understand."

"Those hate group people. There are a lot of them around here, I guess," he says, calmly. "These two men said a few things to me when I was in the store. We have these hate groups in Montana, too. I'd just as soon walk around their town."

A pickup truck clatters across the bridge, scattering the swallows. It slows and two men stare down at us.

Andy is not looking at them. "So, are we going to walk?"

I watch the truck slowly move down the road. "You sure you want to do this?" But he is already tying a plastic bottle full of water onto a piece of string. This he swings over his head so that it rests across his chest. Next he slides out of his cowboy boots and slips on a pair of sneakers. He adjusts his hat and checks for his pack of cigarettes. We agree to a complicated shuttle of walking and moving the car so we can cover the distance on foot while keeping the car along.

He tosses me the keys. "I'll see you the other side of Waynoka, then," he says.

Two hours later we are together again and stopped for the night. I have used the time well, located the name of the man who owns the land where the battle of Turkey Springs was fought. Andrew has seen two deer but no more turkeys or white separatists. There are hawks flapping gentle wings away over a neighboring hill.

"Tomorrow the others should find us, I hope," Andrew says.

"The others?"

"Sam Spotted Elk and Barbara One Bear Spang," he says. "They've come down from Montana to walk some with us. Barbara is Sam's aunt. They're driving around looking for us with another aunt and Sam's mother."

"They're all going to walk?" I ask.

"Only Sam, and maybe Barbara," he says. "I halfway expected them before this. If they don't find us soon, we may be in Nebraska before they catch up."

Darkness comes in a long, slow graying of the sky. My legs are killing me from the long stretch of hot asphalt I've covered today, but Andrew seems unaffected. He is talking about pipes.

"I've been trying to get Dull Knife's pipe back to the reservation. It's now at Pipestone National Monument Museum in South Dakota," he says. He explains the complicated procedure for establishing heritage and ownership and the assurances of safekeeping one must provide in order to regain possession of such an artifact. "But I think I'll get it back. I want to bring it back to the reservation and find a good safe place to keep it. Dull Knife took that pipe on this journey north."

"Perhaps they camped right here," I add and wave my hand across the empty bowl of twilight sky.

Andrew smiles. "You know, in 1976 I did a sundance. My brother was our painter, and as he was painting the man next to me, he told me to fill my pipe. As I was filling it he said to think about what I was going to pray for.

"Because I was the youngest I had to pray last. Well, I listened to what the others were praying for: keeping their jobs, or a new truck or house payments. Those things were all just for today, those things they were praying for wouldn't last, so I thought and thought what I might pray for."

The sunset is complete and the night has become suddenly dark and full. I wait, and in a moment, Andy's soft voice continues.

"I thought and thought, and when it came my turn to pray, I had the shortest prayer of them all. I just prayed for health, because that was the one thing I thought of that could last."

I am politely not looking at his eyes, but in the twilight, I can see his hands fingering a blade of grass.

"I didn't think much about it then, and I put my pipe away after that. It was in a drawer for years. My father recently told me that you had to use your pipe and not just let it sit there. Well, as I was leaving for this trip I was running late. I was all packed, but I thought I had forgotten something. I thought it was a photograph of my wife. I went back inside to the dresser where it was. I saw my sundance things and opened the drawer beneath them, and there was my pipe – so I took it with me. I think maybe this Turkey Springs might be a good place to use it."

Then we are asleep in the dark center of the night.

8. Grace

I am walking west, following the Cimarron upriver. I am in a small jumble of low hills in the breaks north of the river. It is early afternoon, but the light from the flat gray sky casts no shadow and tells me nothing. A mile away there are trees along the Cimarron, but here it is ranch land and open. The grass is stiff and sharp in the fields.

The tallest of the grass here is just knee high, but an hour ago I passed an incredible sight. On the cool side of a natural cut through these breaks, there arose a forest of grass. It towered above me, an emerald stand of jointed stems as thick as my finger and loftier than my head. An acre of tall grass prairies – an invader from the east – the patch had flourished in this mostly short-grass range.

Tall grass – big bluestem and Indian grass – once covered all of Iowa and large parts of the states that surround it. No trees grew in the tall-grass prairie because, in part, the massive jumble of dead grass, composted for a thousand years, created a thick mat above the rich soil that choked out the seedlings. The sod, once it was broken by the pioneer's long, mud-shined plow, uncovered the surface of a thousand-foot-thick layer of the richest soil on earth.

Most of the thousands of pioneers who came west from the densely wooded hillsides of New England, or Europe, or Ohio, falsely reasoned that since the endless open expanse of prairie was treeless, it must be infertile. As a result, the image of a fruitless "Great American Desert" was born, and for a generation the prairie remained nothing more than an enormous wilderness, not unlike the wilderness of a gigantic sea. To set themselves adrift in such a featureless wasteland was for some pioneers "like putting into Lake Michigan in a canoe." In her book *Grasses: An Identification Guide,* Lauren Brown quotes an early traveler after he crossed a part of the tall-grass prairie in 1824:

I do not know of anything that struck me more forcibly than the sensation of solitude I experienced in crossing this, and some of the other large prairies. I was perfectly alone and could see nothing in any direction but sky and grass. . . . Not a living thing could I see or hear, except the occasional prairie fowl, or perhaps a large hawk or eagle wheeling about over my head.

I wandered at the edge of the tall-grass remnant for a full half hour before I moved back up out of the cut and into the short-grass rangeland of northwestern Oklahoma. Here on the short-grass prairie there isn't enough rain for tall grass species, and except for anomalies such as the intruder acre of tall grass I saw earlier, the red soil is dotted everywhere with short clumps of bunchgrass, buffalo grass, and blue grama grass.

A car with Montana plates pulls past and stops a few feet beyond me. A woman from the back seat turns to look at me as I approach. Her smile is as immediate and lasting as time, her face full of calm grace. Squeezed next to her in the back seat, and struggling to free himself from the small space, is a muscular young man.

The front door opens and another woman, the driver, gets out. "You must be Alan," she says. She wears long, beaded earrings and sunglasses. "We have Sam for you. He's anxious to get out of this car full of women, eh, Sam?" She reaches in to lift the bucket seat, and a stocky, muscular young man unfolds himself from the small car. "I think Sam has had about enough of us. Introduce yourself."

"I'm Samuel Spotted Elk Junior," he says and lightly shakes my hand. He wears a blue bandanna across his forehead, and on his white T-shirt is a picture of a mountain in flames. Below it are the words: "Montana Firefighters – 1994 Season." He glances briefly in my direction and then looks down the long road before us.

"You want to get walking, don't you, Sam?" the driver laughs.

"Hey, about four days ago," Sam mumbles.

She turns to me. "My name is Barbara One Bear," she says. "These are my sisters," she says. "Carol and Phoebe."

I lean into the car. In the front seat is another woman with short, curly hair. She stretches out her hand for me to shake. "Pleased to meet you," she says, "I'm Sam's aunt Carol." She turns to the woman in the back seat whose graceful smile had first caught my attention. "And this is Phoebe."

Phoebe's arm juts out at me, her palm facing down. When I take her hand, she shakes it vigorously. "Phoebe!" she says. She nods her head at me. "Phoebe!" she repeats.

From the front seat Carol says, "Phoebe, Barbara, and I are sisters. Phoebe is Sam's mother."

"All right, Phoebe," Sam is saying. "I'll see you later, then."

"I think you'd better get to walking with Sam or he's going to take off for South Dakota by himself," Barbara says.

Barbara gets back into the car, hands Sam a small plastic water bottle, and then drops the car into gear. "Where am I going to meet you again?" I show her on the map where I had hoped to reach by day's end. We agree to meet there in a few hours, and I back off so she can drive away.

Sam is still speaking to Phoebe, nodding and assuring her he will be all right. "Yeah, Phoebe," he says, "Go on now, Phoebe." He waves at her as the car pulls away. We watch it growing smaller and smaller on the long road ahead.

Sam starts walking briskly in short, slightly uneven steps. He carries his head low on his shoulders, a little bit like a man trying to ease some as yet unspecified pain.

Sam is young, perhaps twenty-three; his faint beard does nothing to harden the still youthful skin of his oval face. He wears a thin mustache, and his black hair is curly and long enough to cover the tops of his ears. I manage to catch a glimpse of his eyes, although he is looking everywhere but at me. They are close set and very bright; a glimmer on the brown pupils flickers with the polished sheen of life. When he smiles he shows the bottom, not the top row of his front teeth.

"Phoebe's your mother?" I ask for openers.

"Phoebe's my mother," he answers, "but I was raised most of the time by my grandmother, so I called her Mother and I call my mother by her name: Phoebe."

He tells me he works as a firefighter in the summertime, which is how he gets his money. He tells me he was always a good athlete in school but that he did not graduate from high school. He says he is strong and he tells me he intends to walk all the way north as a gift to his grandmother and Phoebe.

"Dull Knife was my great-great-grandfather," he says suddenly. "I'm a direct descendant of Dull Knife."

"And so you and Andrew Sooktis are – "

"Cousins," he finishes for me. "He's a cousin."

He seems a little nervous, talking quickly in short sentences that jump from subject to subject. During one such jump he tells me that he has been having the exact same strange dream for the past several nights. It is the old days. He is running across open country. Running and running. There are Cheyenne Indians following him. It is the same dream each night: part fear, part courage, running toward some unknown thing, behind him are all the other Cheyennes.

"What do you think it means?" he asks, excitedly. He is happy to be out of the car, having left Montana a week ago, visited Oklahoma relatives, then finally found me on the way back north. "Do you think it might be those people – Dull Knife and them others from back then – in my dream?"

"I don't know what to make of it," I say. "Have you told that dream to Andrew? He would be good at interpreting it."

He shakes his head. "No. Not Andy. I wish I knew what the dream meant."

"You should tell it to him," I say once more, then: "You going to be warm enough with just that T-shirt on?" He nods, but he carries nothing other than the small bottle of water Barbara had given him. I say, "It's been raining almost nonstop since I started more than a week ago."

"I'm strong. I can make it all the way. I have a strong body and a strong heart. I'm making this hike for my grandmother," he repeats.

"Well, if you do get cold, I have an extra sweatshirt in my pack," I say, and he nods slightly.

"You think we can make it all the way north?" he asks. A cool wind has risen but thankfully the rain has stayed away. "I want to walk all the way north."

"It's a long ways," I say. "But if it stays like this we're going to be pretty cold before we get there."

"I'm not cold," Sam says, marching fast enough for me to have to hurry. "I feel like I've got a blanket on!"

The six of us – Andy, Sam, Barbara, Phoebe, Carol, and I – are at a tiny country store that makes up the entire town of Camp Houston, Oklahoma. It is late in the afternoon and we are all tired and hungry. I have set up my stove on a patch of grass and am boiling water to make dinner. There is a picnic table at the side of the store, and the others sit at it and talk or take turns at the pay phone to make calls home.

Just to my side, lined with concrete and covered with a screen, is a square hole in the ground. At the bottom of the pit and curled on the concrete, two rattlesnakes lie motionless. The owner of the store comes out, turns on a hose, and waters the snakes. She does not speak to us.

Andy wanders over to my stove.

"I've got some freeze-dried chili I'm going to cook up," I say. Despite the Cheyenne tradition that expects men not to do much cooking, I'm going to cook up a week's worth of my chili to feed our hungry crew. I'm convinced it is the best-tasting food from my supply.

"Ah," Andy says. He walks over to the table and sits. In a little while Phoebe asks him something in Cheyenne. Andy answers, and I recognize the word "chili" among the Cheyenne words.

Barbara comes back from using the phone. The conversation is repeated in Cheyenne and Andy nods toward me and says "chili." I pretend to ignore him and lift the lid of the pot to see if the water has started to boil. Young Sam is at the table devouring an entire bag of cheap potato chips. Barbara turns and walks back into the store.

"What do you know about that Turkey Springs place?" Andy turns from the table to where I am seated.

The site of the first battle between the fleeing Cheyennes and the army is our destination for tomorrow. "I've got the name of the man who owns the property," I say. "As soon as we eat I'll give him a call to ask if we can go there. I think it's about eight miles north of here. We could get there before noon tomorrow."

"Yeah," Andy says in his characteristic way, softly cutting the *h* off in his throat. Though we have only been together for a short while, there is an ease and naturalness to the way our plans are made. Instead of having a leader – one who decides where we are going and what should be done – we have quickly come to a relaxed sense of community. Without planning or debate each of us contributes what we can to ensure that our voyage continues. Tonight my contribution is this chili. When there is a discussion of group plans, not many words are wasted. Everyone contributes their thoughts, and a consensus is quickly reached. A few minutes earlier, for example, Andy had talked to the store owners about setting up camp in an empty lot across from the store. After a brief conversation, we all had decided that although it looks less than inviting, the lot would have to do for tonight.

My fine little camping stove has heated the water into a rapid-bouncing rattle of boils. I have laid out my spoon, the single plate I have with me, and two plastic bags of the orange and brown powder that will soon be our meal.

"That's the chili there, huh?" Andy says, eyeing the small pouches.

"Yeah," I answer. "It doesn't look like much, but it's pretty good." I decide not to tell him that there's dried tofu in the mix. I open the bags of chili and set them back on the grass, at the ready. In a single fluid motion that would put a ballerina to shame, I lift the lid off the pot of boiling water and put it on the ground, dump in one of the bags of chili, and follow it immediately with the other. I tip my face into the steam of rich spices that rises up and then stir the concoction with the spoon, flip off the flame, and replace the lid. "Five minutes of sitting there and it'll be ready," I say and stand, "but I'm afraid I have only one plate and only one spoon."

"I got some coffee cups and some spoons for the chili." Barbara has returned and is passing these around the table and opening a box of crackers. This she hands to Sam, who removes a packet, rips it open, and grabs two fistfuls.

Although everyone is very hungry, I watch the time carefully. If you serve freeze-dried food too soon, it will be chunky and have the consistency of paste. Phoebe says something and Barbara translates with a laugh. "Phoebe says she's hungry."

"Me too," Sam says.

"I don't know how Sam there could still be hungry after all those chips and crackers," Andy says, smiling.

"I walked far today, *eh-nah*," he says. "How far did we walk?" he asks.

I have squatted back at the stove. "Ah, I don't know," I say, "maybe ten miles since you joined me." Everyone is watching me from the table, but the chili needs another full minute.

"Ten miles?" Sam says. "I didn't know I would get this hungry after just ten miles."

For a moment I can't figure out how to get the hot pot from the grass to the table, but I grab a pair of socks from my pack and use them as mittens. I set the pot down in front of my companions. "Dinner is served."

One by one everyone scoops the smoking, thick chili into tall Styrofoam cups with thin plastic spoons. They eat. Cans of soda pop are opened. Andy is the first one to take a handful of crackers and crush them into the chili. Then Phoebe laughs, speaks in Cheyenne, and she too takes several crackers and crushes them into the cup.

We fall silent. Nothing about the silence is unusual: six hungry people are concentrating on their meager meal. Even so, the quiet feels awkward to me. Just when I become convinced something is wrong, Phoebe speaks again, this time in English.

"Hot," she says, pointing at the pot.

"Uh-huh," Barbara says.

Phoebe begins to laugh. "Hot," she repeats, and then says something in Cheyenne. Suddenly everyone except me is laughing.

"Phoebe says this chili is pretty spicy, eh, Phoebe?"

"Hot," Phoebe repeats. They laugh again, Phoebe the loudest. After a second's pause, I realize that in my culinary bravado I had failed to consider the different cultural definitions of "good" food. Barbara goes to her car and rummages in the back seat. She returns to the table with a small container of canned meat, which she opens and passes around.

We continue to eat, but every few moments someone suddenly looks at Phoebe and begins to chuckle.

Phoebe is eating a piece of the canned meat, which she has put on a cracker. She waves this in the air. "Hot," she says.

I laugh too and decide I won't serve the chili again for a long while. I am thankful I did not tell them about the dried tofu.

A half hour later we are sitting at the big table in the dining room at Dewayne and Lillian Hodgson's ranch house. Lillian, a gracious woman with pretty silver hair, has just set big cups of steaming coffee in front of us.

"Now, you five are all Cheyenne Indians?" she asks my companions.

"Northern Cheyenne," Andy says. "The Cheyennes are all one tribe, but we have both a southern and a northern group."

The Turkey Springs battle site is on the Hodgsons' property. After the chili, I had called from the phone booth at the tiny store in Camp Houston to ask if we could explore the site, and Lillian Hodgson had answered.

"You're walking all that way?" she had asked. "For heaven's sake, why don't you come on up to the ranch."

"Right now?"

"Of course! We'd love to have you all here. It would be a treat to meet you all," she said.

In less than ten minutes we had turned down the long drive toward a low-slung ranch house. The house is built into the side of a hill as protection from tornadoes, but the wide front expanse has an open and inviting feel about it. As soon as we pulled up, Lillian was out. She whisked us immediately into her home.

Now Lillian moves about, asking questions, serving coffee, and listening, all the while trying not to trip over her three grandchildren, whose vacation week at the Hodgsons' ranch is climaxing with our unannounced visit.

They would deny it, but the two junior-high-age boys are shy. They roam around the edges of the room, watching carefully and talking of sports anytime someone draws attention to them.

The third grandchild, Hilda, on the other hand, is edging closer and closer to us while her grandparents ask questions.

"What do you all know about Turkey Springs?" Dewayne Hodgson is a solid, muscular man in his sixties and wears a recently ironed western shirt.

After a pause Andrew tells them that Little Wolf chose the place for the fight, and that their ancestor, Dull Knife, tried to talk with the soldiers before the fighting began.

"We've collected a lot of articles and such about the battle site," Dewayne says, rising. "Let me go get them."

"I have some photographs," Barbara announces.

"Can we see them?" Hilda blurts out. She no longer tries to hide her excitement. She is about ten.

"Wait until you tell the kids at school about how Cheyenne Indians visited your grandmother," Lillian says.

Barbara stands up. "I'll get the photographs from my car," she says.

"Can I come with you?" Hilda races to hold the door open for Barbara, and together they walk outside.

The grandsons still hide at the edges of the room, but the rest of us are clustered at the table. Dewayne has a folder of articles and information about Turkey Springs. "There's been a lot written about that place," he says, sliding the folder toward me. "We've kept it untouched; we just run a few cattle on it."

The talk continues, but I step away into the quiet kitchen area to flip through the folder of articles. The perfect host, Lillian has gotten up to make another pot of coffee.

"How long has the battle site belonged to you?" I ask.

"Oh, it's been in my family for a couple generations," she says while moving about her kitchen measuring coffee, washing cups, and popping a large package into the microwave. "It was deeded to Dewayne and me by my mother. We raised our children right here – well, in the old house. Both Dewayne and I grew up, oh, within twenty miles of each other." As she moves in a dozen different directions, she shares with me the story of her family and their home on this lonely open land.

"My grandfather, Heinrich Reutlinger, was born in Zurich the year Dull Knife and Little Wolf passed through here. He married Hilda Eckert – young Hilda out there was named after my grandmother – in 1903." The coffee maker is bubbling and the dishes fly through Lillian's soapy fingers as she stands at the sink and talks. The land itself is as much a force in her heritage as any ancestor, and she speaks about it with pride. Her grandparents purchased section 13, 28 north, 18 west – the site of Turkey Springs – at the turn of the twentieth century.

"It had been School Land Commission land at one time," she says. "It was eventually deeded to my mother, Alice Reutlinger Seivert, and from mother it came to me. My grandfather built the rock wall around the spring so it would be a better water source for his cattle. You'll see it tomorrow. You read there a moment. I'll be right back." She flies off with the fresh pot of coffee to refill everyone's cups.

In the hallway leading to the back door are a half dozen hat hooks. A cowboy hat hangs on every hook. Through the open back door I can see Hilda and Barbara standing at the car. Hilda's blond hair is tied back in a tight ponytail, and she stands directly in front of Barbara. Barbara is speaking to her and Hilda is hanging on every word.

Lillian returns and refills my cup with coffee. She sets the empty pot on the counter, then looks at me. "You've visited the reservation in Montana?" she asks. There is a polite hesitation in her voice. "I don't know very much about what their life is like today," she begins, "they say all the Indians in Oklahoma are all on welfare, but I don't know . . ."

"Money's not the only thing of value on the reservation," I say. I tell her about Andy's grandfather, and how eight dollars a month was all the money he needed, since he could provide all of life's necessities on his own. "But his times are mostly gone, and it's true a lot of people are poor."

For the first time Lillian pauses from her role as a perfect hostess and looks at me. "I don't know a thing about modern Native Americans," she admits. "Are there jobs?"

We talk then about how the isolation on most reservations has created intense economic problems for tribes. Even though the Northern Cheyenne Reservation, like many others, sits on a gold mine of natural resources, precious little of the profits from the sale of its coal and water have reached the residents. A few have gotten rich, but the corrupting seeds of power and greed have choked the life out of the buried wealth of the reservation.

"There's evil and selfishness everywhere," I say.

Lillian turns from me to return to her preparations, "Yes," she says softly, "And yet there are always good people like you folks who have blessed our home today."

Lillian has insisted we spend the night. She is fixing up beds for the women in another part of the house. The sun cracks through the clouds at the furthest edge of the world just before the long, early summer dusk begins.

Dewayne has gotten up and gone outside. Barbara has returned and has spread out photographs of her relatives on the table. "This is Maggie Seminole One Bear," she says. "She just recently passed away. She was the last of that generation."

"Who was she?" Hilda asks.

"She was our mother," Barbara says, sweeping her finger toward Carol and Phoebe. "And she was Dull Knife's granddaughter."

"Wow," Hilda says.

Outside in the light of sunset, I can see Dewayne seated on a tractor. He is mowing a field a quarter mile below the house. For a moment I think he must work because the constant rain has kept him from it until now, but one of the boys, Sage, tells me his grandfather is mowing the field to make a smooth place for me to set up my tent. Sage and his cousin race outside to the barn and in a moment they too are in the field, setting up a large canvas tent for Andrew and Sam to use.

A half hour later we are all in the field. The boys have built a large campfire, and Dewayne has lit a barbecue and set up lawn chairs around the fire. The Cheyenne women drive down to the field in a car, with a tape of traditional Indian singing playing on the car's system. They leave the door open so that the rhythm of the voices and drums fills the graying light.

I have set up my tent and helped the others arrange camp, but when I try to help him at the barbecue, Dewayne orders me to sit and enjoy myself. I unfold my camp chair and sit next to Carol near the fire. A slight woman with a flat, oval face and sorrowful, tired eyes, she is studying the shapes of flames. She is worried about her home situation, calling there constantly, she says. It is not an easy story to tell. When she was only fifteen years old, Carol had gotten pregnant. Her daughter was given up at birth. Although she knew a little about her first-born's life, she had no contact with her daughter for twenty years, and then suddenly she called asking Carol to adopt her first-born child – Carol's grand-child.

"I thought it was a good way to pay something back for having given my own daughter up," Carol says, those heavy eyes flickering back the light of the orange flames. She took the boy – the child of her daughter's relationship with a man from the city – into her house. He is now five years old and still living with Carol, staying with another of Carol's daughters until she returns.

"But I may have to go back to Montana very soon because my daughter decided she wants him back," she says. "She thinks he should be raised where there are other black kids, not other Cheyennes, but I said I wouldn't give him back. I'm afraid she might just come and take him away while I'm down here." She tells me of other trouble brewing at home as well, of abusive men and broken love.

Carol talks of her hard life and the difficulties of parenting. She says that even though she knows she would not have been a good mother at age fifteen, no one knows the anguish and doubt of giving up one's child. "Maybe things might have worked out for the better if I had kept my daughter. Who's to say what pain might have been avoided, what troubles might have never happened, if I had only kept her."

She pauses. "It doesn't matter what people say," Carol says. "A person always tries to do what they think is right and best. There's just no way of ever knowing for sure."

"You're raising your daughter's child," I remind her. "That counts for a lot."

In the light from the fire I see her smile. "Yes, he's a fine boy. He's half black, and one hundred percent Cheyenne as far as I'm concerned." Others have joined us around the fire, balancing paper plates and cups of soda pop or coffee in their hands. Soon Carol's sadness has been replaced by laughter. That laughter is full of dignity.

It is at that very moment that Lillian, who has spent the entire time preparing food and organizing our sudden party, appears before the fire. She speaks loudly and clearly so that everyone hears. "We'll all hold hands and say a grace," she says.

The fire lights our faces as we stand. I take Carol's hand in mine, and Lillian's grandson Zac takes my other. The circle gathers tightly before the warmth of the fire. There is a silent pause. The soft echo of the Indian singers from the car's tape deck only serves to expose the profound silence of the great, open night all around us.

Lillian's grace is the most beautiful I have ever heard. With her head bowed, she speaks humbly in a firm and quiet voice to ears beyond our own. On and on her blessing of praise and thanks radiates out into the vast circle of sky and earth. It is a benediction, a blessing of the bountiful gifts of food and friends and family and farm. While her grace is worship for the precious gift of the holy mystery that brought us here together, and rich in wisdom and dignity, balance and virtue, it is the charity of this humble and remarkable woman that brings us all to joyful tears.

9. Turkey Springs

Turkey Springs is at the bottom of a short, steep hill in a maze of low ridges and hills on the Oklahoma-Kansas border. To the south the valley of the Cimarron River is so flat and featureless that the view from even these low ridges is expansive. On a dustless day the red banks along the distant river shine like blood-red sunlight on the golden grasslands. Much farther to the south, beyond the river, the low divide that separates the Cimarron from the North Canadian is a pale yellow line in a grand distance of sky.

Trees and brambles line the small wet pool of Turkey Springs, and the stagnant water is choked with weeds and mud. Still, animals and humans have come here seeking a dependable source of water for centuries. The Cimarron River is a dry day's journey to the south. To the north, over the divide, waterless gullies wind miles before their sand spills into the banks of the silty Salt Fork. It may not be the sweetest water, but even after a hot and dry summer Turkey Springs – named for the wild turkeys that frequent the grass at its edges – can be counted on as a place of rest and nourishment.

Turkey Creek, born at the springs, cuts a complicated path of intersecting gullies and dry washes as it moves down out of the hills to the faraway Cimarron. Someone unfamiliar with this place could easily become disoriented, wandering back and forth over the ridges, or stumbling blindly through the gullies, seeking the proper way out.

In short, for warriors like Little Wolf and Dull Knife, Turkey Springs was a perfect place to stop the people and rest. On Friday, September 13, 1878, after moving 120 miles in the five days since the escape, the Northern Cheyennes halted at Turkey Springs. The women and children set up camp at the springs itself, while the warriors spread out over the hills. Under Little Wolf's direction some men went north, securing an escape route, while others tended to the horses and still others sought defensive positions behind the horse-size rocks between clumps of chokecherry bushes.

The women dug up the cached pemmican marked here and there on the ridges by rocks the size of two men. Slender rocks had been placed upright a season or two earlier to mark the places where food was buried for insurance against hard times. The women left some of the food undisturbed for others who might come later, but much of it they used, or packed in the parfleches for the journey ahead.

Except for the scouts who traveled apart from the main body in all directions, the Cheyennes most likely had been traveling together as a group since escaping captivity, climbing up shallow draws so that their silhouettes could not be seen against the sky, while a few scouts rode on the ridges to keep watch. As the main group camped at the springs, one such party of scouts came upon two cowboys a few miles to the north.

Like many men after the Civil War, Reuben Bristow and Fred Clark had come west seeking a life that was simpler and more open than that which they had known in the east.

Bristow was a young Kentuckian who had come west to work at his uncle's ranch. His uncle, Charles Colcord, had been a colonel in the Rebel army but now ran the Rancho Grande spread in southern Kansas.

Fred Clark was a tall, slender man with a fair complexion. Folks knew him as congenial and friendly, and – unlike many men in the west – he was well educated, having gone to school in Virginia before he moved west.

On that Friday afternoon the two men were on their way from Colcord's ranch to gather salt from the flats near the Cimarron River. They rode together in a wagon pulled by a team of mules across the high, dry frontier on the divide north of Turkey Springs. Like most men, they rode the ridgeline trail to keep clear of the rocky ravines and sandy washes of the lowlands.

Clark was probably the first one hit, since his body was found with a silent arrow through his heart. Bristow, seeing his companion's fate, whipped the mules in a wild desperate dash across the ridges. He was shot from behind by a rifle; the shots pierced his head and back.

The Cheyenne scouts took the mules but, after stripping them for their clothing, left the men's bodies unmolested in the wagon.

It was several days before Colcord and two other cowboys from the ranch found the bodies. They buried Bristow and Clark on the ridgeline and left a crudely carved stone to mark the burial. Rising a few feet above short grass on the lonely frontier divide, that stone still stands to mark the cowboys' cemetery.

With the two cowboys dead, the Cheyennes turned their attention to the troops they knew were closing in on them.

Captain Joseph Rendlebrock, with thirty years of service in the military, was a year from retirement. In those thirty years he had fought in the battles of the Civil War and on the dust-choked grounds of the Indian wars and had never turned away from the fear of death. He looked forward to climbing down from his saddle and taking the government pension that was due him.

Now, near the end of his career, he had been placed at Fort Reno patrolling the treaty Indians and guarding the meager herds of skinny cattle from the hungry and ill-fed Cheyennes and Arapahos.

In the early hours of September 10, 1878, Rendlebrock was awakened. His sole orders for a week had been to keep the Northern Cheyennes under close observation. Several hours earlier, while his command was sleeping soundly, the entire camp of Northern Cheyennes had slipped away unnoticed.

Eight hours after the Cheyennes made their escape, Rendlebrock, two Arapaho scouts, four officers, and eighty-one enlisted men from Companies G and H, Fourth Cavalry, started their pursuit from Fort Reno. Their orders were to overtake the Cheyennes and to return them to the agency. The first day they picked up a faint trail and followed it for over 30 miles, trailing it northwesterly toward Dodge City, 150 miles off. At 2:45 P.M. that day, September 10, Rendlebrock sent a messenger to Camp Supply:

> Have struck trail, will continue pursuit as long as the daylight holds, and do the same the next day. Send cavalry to join me. Last information through indians was that troops were close, and have good prospect of overhauling them. Indians well mounted with plenty of good stock, chase will prove a long one, hope to intercept indians at crossing of Arkansas, said to be high. Abandoning lodges means greater desperation than anticipated.

Word of the Cheyenne outbreak was telegraphed to the division commander, General Philip H. Sheridan, and soon the Departments of the Missouri, Platte, and Dakota were alerted to the Cheyenne escape. Detachments of troops all over the high plains began to be placed at strategic locations to intercept the fleeing Indians. The War Department gave orders that unless the Indians surrendered immediately and agreed to be dismounted and disarmed, all troops were under orders to attack without mercy.

At dawn on the second day out of Fort Reno, Rendlebrock's troops hurried on, traveled forty-five miles, and then camped. The third day out they made forty-two miles and camped near the Cimarron River. On Friday, the 13th, at 9 A.M. they had traveled thirteen miles from their camp when they spotted some Indians on a hillside, three miles ahead.

Rendlebrock set his soldiers at a trot and met the Indians at eight hundred yards. The Cheyennes were concentrated around a bit of timber the Arapaho scouts called Turkey Springs.

Rendlebrock later testified that the Cheyennes seemed to be waiting for the troops and made absolutely no effort to flee. The cavalry column rode to within four hundred yards, and as they did so the Cheyennes moved about, leading their horses here and there. There was much movement of the Cheyennes north and south through a ravine. The soldiers rode across a deep gully at the bottom of a high hill where Dull Knife and a few other Cheyenne leaders sat on their horses, not moving back and forth like the rest the Indians.

At 10 A.M. the army's Arapaho scout named Chalk, who the Cheyennes knew as Ghost Man, rode up the slope to parley with Dull Knife. Dull Knife held his pipe; the rest of the mounted Cheyennes on the hill were unarmed. Chalk translated Rendlebrock's orders that Dull Knife and the rest of the Cheyennes must return to the Darlington Agency. Although Chalk repeated the order several times, the parley was brief and the Cheyenne answer was short. Dull Knife said simply that he did not wish to fight but would do so before he would return to see his people starve at the Indian Territory reservation.

As Chalk turned his horse to ride back to the troops, a group of Cheyenne warriors moved down a side ravine to encircle the soldiers. Rendlebrock gave the order, and men from Company G opened fire. Instantly gunfire erupted everywhere across the hillsides and gullies. His soldiers' Springfield carbines were ill matched to the Cheyennes' superior Sharps carbines. A group of Cheyennes rushed out and met the troops. The troops were concentrated on the slope of the hill and in the gully immediately to the south. A few soldiers had scrambled up the south side of the gully to a small knoll, but the Cheyennes held the far side of the knoll, blocking a retreat. Rendlebrock held the center of the command, while Lieutenant Abram Wood held the right and Lieutenant Wilber Wilder the left. The Cheyennes dropped back and then moved about, concentrating their men on two or three hills and in ravines near the soldiers. The soldiers dug rifle pits for protection.

Although the fighting continued all day, the heavy gunfire did not last long because Little Wolf, who was leading the warriors, gave the command to preserve the limited supply of ammunition and make every shot a good one. Still, he led the warriors in three assaults on the troops during the long afternoon.

The sun climbed in the dry, prairie sky, and the day grew hot. The soldiers began to ration their remaining water. By nightfall the gunfire was sporadic, and Little Wolf called to his men to stop fighting and come into the camp at Turkey Springs. The Cheyennes kept guard on the troops so that at about eight o'clock that evening, when seven soldiers tried to reach fresh water under cover of darkness, they were driven back. Then the Cheyennes set fire to the prairie in hopes of bringing the soldiers out of their camp, but the wind changed and the fire did not drive the troops out or stampede their horses.

There was not much sleep the night of September 13, 1878, in these hills of buffalo grass and chokecherry. Three soldiers lay wounded at the fireless, dry battle camp, and the bodies of two others, Corporal Patrick Lynch and the Arapaho scout, Chalk, were stretched out at the edge of camp, covered with horse blankets. Six army horses had been killed too, and already their stench had made it hard to keep the remaining horses calm.

At the Cheyenne camp the women tended to the five or six wounded, including a six-year-old girl who had been hurt by a stray bullet during the most intense part of the fighting.

At dawn the fighting resumed, and an army reconnaissance revealed that the Indians were in ambush completely around the troops. Rendlebrock decided to retreat back to the safety of the Cimarron River and water. He ordered a detachment to charge the Cheyennes while the rest of the command retreated down the long twisting maze of a ravine. Cheyenne warriors fired down at the soldiers from the steep banks overhead as the soldiers fled southward. One soldier, George Sand, was killed during the retreat.

Once the troops reached the Cimarron they stopped briefly to rest. While there a soldier scribbled a crude map on a piece of parchment. A wavy, jerking line shows the path of the retreating troops through the twisting ravines, while at the top, sides, and bottom of the map the fear and horror are evident in the soldier's large, dark scrawl: INDIANS HERE ALL DAY! INDIANS CHARGED HERE . . . MORE INDIAN CHARGES . . . INDIANS HELD RAVINE . . . INDIANS HERE ALL DAY! And then a sweeping line to the south labeled: DIRECTION OF RETREAT.

A year later, the first charge in the court-martial of Captain Joseph Rendlebrock stated that "in command of expedition in pursuit of hostiles and after engagement with enemy in which his command was defeated and forced to retreat, did lead said in retreat in a careless and unsoldierly manner and, by his personal example, did destroy the morale of the soldiers under his command, creating confusion and disorder, to the jeopardy of the command and disgrace of the service, at or near Turkey Springs IT on 9 /14 / 78." He was found guilty of the charge.

All that next day, and probably through the night, the main body of Cheyennes remained at Turkey Springs, tending to the wounded and letting the warriors rest. Then the Cheyennes began to move again, this time using an old trick to confuse any who might follow: they split up into several smaller bands and moved north, each band leaving a trail along parallel draws that climbed up and over the long wide ridge of the divide.

PART THREE

Ghosts

Do you remember? We'd come jogging
To town with jingle in our jeans,
And in the wild night we'd be bogging
Up to our hats in last month's dreams.

BUCK RAMSEY, *And as I Rode Out on the Morning*

10. The Divide

"All my life nearly I have been hearing that the voice of a coyote will not echo," wrote the great chronicler of southwestern life and literature, J. Frank Dobie. The legend is that no one can duplicate the sound of the plains' greatest survivor and trickster, for unlike the call of other wild beasts, a coyote's yodel will not echo. Of course, Dobie pointed out, "The claim must have originated in prairie country, where there are no echoes."

Here, on the high ridge of the lonesome divide between Oklahoma and Kansas, there is nothing to ricochet the yelp of a coyote or a person. This great rise of prairie rift between the Canadian and Arkansas watersheds is home to coyotes and other survivors of the frontier, but not much else. There are no houses, no people, no cars – that's the easy part – and there are no distractions of the modern world. Nothing of the past to cling to, nothing in the future to fear, and nothing to ignore in the present.

This is open range, and the route I am following crosses large tracks of fenceless grasslands, green and thickening in the damp spring. On this frontier there are no sounds save the wind, and no barricades save those of my own making.

The border between two political units – the area the rest of the world calls a *frontier* – is a neglected land. With notable exceptions, neither country nor state nor people see much use in maintaining borderlands. Why spend money on roads, sewers, schools, or towns through which so few of the constituent people pass? It is the same on this border between Kansas and Oklahoma, and these fenceless hills of grass resemble nothing so much as the *frontier* – the way a person from the American West uses the word – an open, boundless sky and an exhilarating sensation of walking on the brink of some world-changing moment.

Each step of mine balances on that abrupt edge, regardless of the gentle slope of creek beds splitting on either side of me. I walk

Little Wolf, ca. 1879. Courtesy of National Archives.

on the divide between all that I have been and all that I could, or will never, become. Behind me is where I have been. I am north of Turkey Springs, leaving Oklahoma by myself while the others have returned to the ranch for lunch and conversation. I am headed cross-country into the second state of my trek and only now am beginning truly to understand how long and difficult might be the trail ahead; only now slowing down enough to understand that all of it could end in an instant.

It is the divide. The past recedes, the future yet a step beyond. What is the struggle for life if not simply the attempt to experience our existence unencumbered by time? At the center of great religions, at the heartbeat of great love affairs, is that same desire to be present in the otherness of a single moment. The greatest thought of all is no thinking at all. The greatest time in history is no time at all.

It is the divide. Beauty walks here, suspended between the precipices of death and birth. Hawks hang in the air, while yucca stabs the earth. The truest moments of my life, I suddenly realize, are the fleeting instants when time ceases and everything simply *is*. It is a matter of accepting every horror and joy, every moment of beauty or of pain, as a gift.

Beauty walks here on the divide, and a miracle of sorts has begun to present itself. I have been walking eight to ten hours a day for over a week, and the slow, endless movement has brought me to a holy place. As always my undisciplined mind is busy thinking of the past and planning for the future, but now, through the grace of it all, my focus has become quite narrow. Instead of reliving ancient history from my past or imagining distant scenes in a faraway hereafter, I have begun to think no further back than the day just past, and no further into the future than the day before me.

Like all objects of beauty, once I try to capture this realization, it flies. In the very act of recognizing my place as here and my time as now, I once again lose both mysteries to a wandering mind. Still, the miracle lingers and I am willing to settle for nothing more than a day's life on either side of now.

It is difficult to walk here, through herds of nearly wild cattle and the stares of gigantic bulls; across the open flat land still changeless for centuries; around yucca and prickly pear and dried rattlesnake skins; through waterless dry land where a simple sprained ankle might become life-threatening; over the dust trails of pioneers and Indians, now so irrevocably lost to time. It is a difficult passing. I have almost walked myself out of existence: traversing a narrow strip of land across a narrow strip of time. It is difficult and beautiful to walk the divide where the voice of the coyote has no echo, but I would not trade it for any other life.

11. By Cheyenne Campfires

Our campfire consists of my small backpacking stove, which hisses faintly before us. The six of us are around the stove, stretched out on the lawn behind the Mennonite Church in Protection, Kansas. My companions are speaking in Cheyenne, then English, then Cheyenne again. We are telling stories of the day.

Barbara One Bear laughs. Her gentle and genuine chuckle mingles with the sounds of the pot of stew quietly boiling on the stove. The Cheyenne language sounds like the murmur of wind through pines on a moonlit ridge. The few vowels are often voiceless and whispered, and words change pitch, like singing. In Barbara's kind and soft voice, the song is beautiful.

Barbara has found us this quiet spot in the tiny village in southern Kansas. She met the minister's daughter in a store, and soon the minister himself was opening the back door of the church so we might wash up.

"No one will bother you back here," he had said, waving his hand across the lot. On one side of a lawn tall, thick bushes bordered the grass, and on the other the low brick church itself blocked us from the quiet street. "I called the town sheriff, and he'll drive by throughout the night to make sure you are all right."

As Sam Spotted Elk Junior and I sought out a place to unroll our bed gear on the soft lawn, the others stood in the dusk talking to the minister. When the minister left we had gathered around the stove to prepare the meal. Someone produced a can of stew, and soon we were all seated on the grass talking and watching the stew bubble on the stove.

I lift the lid of the pot to pour in some water and a good portion of freeze-dried pea soup from the supplies in my pack. Just as I replace the lid, Phoebe speaks.

"*Wa — teh-fff*," she says. Deer.

"Oh, how could I forget," Barbara says. "We have some dried deer meat." She produces a large plastic bag and removes a half dozen long strips of the black, leathery, jerked deer meat. Barbara gives Phoebe and Carol some of the dark ropes of it, and as we talk the three women begin to pound at it with fist-size rocks they have gathered. "Most of us like to break the meat into long strings first," she explains for my benefit. "It makes it easier to chew."

Phoebe speaks again in Cheyenne, laughing. I recognize a single word, but it is enough: chili.

Barbara translates. "Phoebe wanted to make sure we added some deer meat if you are fixing us chili again." Everyone laughs.

The story of my chili-cooking expertise is told and then retold. Then other stories, unfolding from one to the other as effortlessly as pages in a book: The graciousness of the Hodgson family at Turkey Springs. Barbara's long day of walking. How Phoebe and Carol have shuttled the car forward. Sam's counting and recounting of the miles he thinks we have made. Andrew's story of the coyote and eight deer he has seen today, the tale of each animal's appearance given equal time in the dark, calm night.

Car lights flicker across the lawn and shine briefly on our group. A squad car pulls slowly past and the figure of the sheriff waves from the front seat.

"Probably looking for you," Barbara says amid laughter. It is an invitation for me to tell the story of my day again.

I had been walking east, toward Protection, on a long straight stretch of asphalt. Although U.S. Highway 160 /183 was nearly deserted, the one or two cars every ten minutes was more than I was used to. At midmorning a brown patrol car approached me and I stopped. The police car pulled to the side of the road twenty yards ahead and the door of the car opened. I waited.

The policeman stood up slowly from behind the opened door of his car. There was something not quite right about his overly muscular torso, which I could see through the window of the door between the two of us.

"Howdy," I said, walking toward him.

"Hello," he said. "We've got three or four reports about you on this road."

"Well, I'm pretty easy to see," I said and, without being asked, told him what I am doing.

"Any others with you?" he asked.

"Yeah, there's two or three retracing the route with me, and some women in a car. We're all walking alone. The others must be within ten miles or so of me." He waited. "They're Cheyenne Indians, if you run into them."

He nodded. "Oh, we've had reports of them too," he said. Although it was a gray day, he wore dark aviator sunglasses. The round, black glass completely hid his eyes, and in their reflection I saw flashes of the road and the abandoned windmill in the field beside us. "Can I get your name?" He reached back into the front seat and grabbed a clipboard from inside and then finally moved from behind the door to stand at the front of the car.

A man in his midthirties with a neat, trim haircut and a smart military mustache, he stood as if at ease in his precisely starched uniform. His name was Lynn Kelly and he was the deputy sheriff of Comanche County, Kansas.

We talked then of the weather and of the miles I had walked. Briefly, too, we talked of the recent bombings in Oklahoma City, and how a suspect had been caught not far from Comanche County.

With some prodding, I got a bit of Deputy Kelly's story. He had moved to sparsely populated Comanche County nine years ago from the town of his birth, Los Angeles. He lowered his head a notch. "I belonged to a gang there for a while," he said. His unsmiling expression had not changed since getting out of the police car. "I saw that side of the law, and thought maybe I'd try the other side."

He grew up in the sunny, whirling world of the nation's second city with gang brothers instead of friends. He seldom traveled alone but always as a part of a pack, scurrying through fields of concrete blossoming in spray paint bouquets of color. Then one day he just packed up his wife and children, pointed to an empty spot on the map, and left.

"It's nice here," Kelly said, snapping his pen onto the clipboard, "you end up having to go quite a ways to get your kids to and from baseball games and such, but it's mostly quiet." As he turned to throw the clipboard back into the car, I realized why his torso looked so unusual. Under the light blue uniform and above the thin white line of his T-shirt was a bulky black slab of material: a bulletproof vest. He turned back toward me. "It's mainly a quiet place," he repeated. Not a single car had passed us on the wide U.S. highway connecting what remained of yesteryear's wild Kansas cowtowns: Dodge, Hayes, Wichita. Just a few generations ago, men like Wyatt Earp and Bat Masterson patrolled gangs of cowpunchers and killers and marshaled citizens against a moving band of three hundred Northern Cheyenne Indians; now this man from California rides the lonely road, keeping the peace in this yet untamed country.

"I'll bet he keeps plenty busy even here," Barbara says, lifting the lid and spooning out the steaming stew. Between us we have almost enough plates for everyone. Sam reaches to fill the empty can that he is using for his bowl.

"I'll bet he hasn't ever had a white guy walking through with a bunch of Indians, *eh-nah?*" Sam says.

"I doubt he's ever had a bunch of Indians walking through *without* a white guy," I say. The others laugh.

The conversation lulls as the thick, hot meal is distributed and we eat. After a bit, Barbara speaks. "The people never had even as much as this to eat, do you think?" She means her ancestors of course. Dull Knife, Pawnee Woman, and the rest of the Northern Cheyennes passed by this very spot. There is a long natural moment of silence in the slow pace of the campfire way. "I kept thinking about those people all day long today," Barbara continues. "The women, especially, with all those children to feed and to keep moving." She shakes her head. She is a youthful woman whose strong body shows nothing of the sixty years it has lived. "I'm more tired than I've ever been from walking." This from a woman who is known all across the reservation as a long-distance jogger and walker. "All my life I've heard stories of those days, but you really never understand."

"People still talk about the trek north?" I ask.

Barbara nods. "The older ones, not so much the young ones."

"The young ones don't even know what you're talking about," Sam throws in. "People my age are ignorant about our history."

"Why?" I ask. "If the old people still talk about it, don't the younger ones listen?"

"The older ones speak Cheyenne. Many of them barely speak any English," she explains. "My generation, and Andy's generation, were all raised speaking Cheyenne as our first language, but then, I don't know, things suddenly changed. All of a sudden people starting thinking that if they wanted their children to be successful in school they had better only speak English at home, so there's an entire generation now – Sam's age – who were raised speaking English first. Cheyenne is a very difficult language to learn if you're not raised speaking it, so the young people today have lost the language."

There is a silence, filled with the sounds of crickets behind the darkened church. Then Sam speaks. "There's no one for the older people to tell the stories to. The younger ones aren't like me; they don't seem to care about history."

Barbara sighs softly. "Yes. What Sam says is true. I'm afraid so many stories are being lost. But not all young people have forgotten, so there is still hope."

Into the easy silence that follows, the voices of those who passed here so long ago whisper on the night breeze.

12. Henry Ford and Mr. Goodnight

A little after eight o'clock one spring morning, the bandit Jesse James noticed that the picture on his wall needed straightening. He propped the chair up against the wall and, with his back to the room, climbed onto the cushioned seat without removing his boots. At nearly point-blank range, Robert Ford withdrew his pistol and shot poor Jesse in the back, ending the outlaw's long career as a robber of trains and banks. It was April 3, 1882.

Henry A. Ford sits in the cab of his pickup truck staring out at the miles of open, roadless Kansas range. It is land his grandfather settled the year before Dull Knife and Little Wolf passed through, the land his father patrolled as cowboy and later as sheriff. "Oh, yeah, I'm related to Bob Ford, the man that done shot Jesse James." His voice is a western drawl; each word strolls out unrushed and relaxed, every syllable taking its own good time forming around his tongue and teeth. "My grandfather came from Missouri. My grandmother knew the James family quite well." Ford's hands are resting on the steering wheel. They are gigantic hands, thick and meaty and strong, thanks to his seventy-three years of tough living on the Kansas prairies. "I have to put a stone in my shoe to remind me how old I am. My poor memory was caused by too much drinkin' or fightin' or lovin' when I was younger, but now I can't remember which it was that done it." He lifts one of the big hands and points to a darker green splotch in the emerald fields near the truck. "Buffalo wallow," he says. "You can still find them all over the place."

Ford leans forward; his round, weathered face looms over the steering wheel. "Damn. Now, he swore this gate would be unlocked. I talked to the owner just this morning." Ford has brought us and his friend, Don Goodnight, twenty miles out from town and across three miles of open country to the site of the largest of several battle sites, thirty-five miles south of Dodge City. Bouncing and jolting the eight of us like so much cattle feed, he has driven over open fields, plowed across muddy swales, and slammed over grass-covered boulders to find the place where the Cheyenne Indians fought the cowboys in Clark County, only to come across this locked gate.

"You can see those white bluffs over yonder," he says, pointing to low chalk hills two miles in the distance. "Well, it was right about there in that canyon down toward Spring Creek where they fought."

Despite the folklore, there were very few battles in the old West between cowboys and Indians. Most of the fighting with Indians was between different tribes or involved the U.S. Army. For whites, bloodshed was mostly due to gangs of disgruntled Rebel soldiers like Jesse James or, especially in Kansas, wild groups of cattle drivers and the barely more civilized lawmen hired to control them. There were few times when the two lifestyles came into direct conflict, but in 1878, as the escaping Northern Cheyennes moved north through "the new southwest," as southern Kansas was known, local cowboys panicked at reports of marauding Indians and formed posses to ride out in search of the Cheyennes.

The cowboys were jittery enough, since only three years earlier there had been widespread rumors of raiding Indians' storming isolated homesteads and massacring dozens of pioneers. The rumors were false, started by ranchers trying to scare away the plowmen pioneers, but the stories had spread so quickly and convincingly that groups of settlers banded together to build stone breastworks and fortifications around high points of land.

This time around it was more than hearsay, for on Tuesday, September 17, 1878, cowboys from Driscoll's ranch rode into Dodge City, stampeding up Front Street and shouting out how the Cheyennes were swarming over the cattle land forty miles to the south. Fed by news reports of the Cheyenne escape from Indian Territory, and nurtured by the story from the Driscoll ranch, the town of Dodge started to panic. As word spread, more and more people from surrounding ranches flooded the town, seeking safety.

After the battle at Turkey Springs the Cheyennes divided into several smaller bands and moved northwest up the various creek beds that parallel one another in this dry country. As they moved through the once open land, speckled now with ranches, they had at first tried to purchase horses in order to replenish their beleaguered stock. Local ranchers, already aware of the escape from Indian Territory, responded with raised weapons. No one will ever know for certain exactly how many people were killed during this part of their trek, but it seems likely that between September 17 and 22 the Cheyennes were responsible for perhaps three or four deaths (including the death of a black cook for the Chapman and Tuttle spread, twenty miles south of Dodge), had stolen about twenty horses, and killed perhaps a hundred sheep and cattle. By Thursday evening nearly every rancher and pioneer within thirty miles of Dodge had come into the city seeking protection. Even the *New York Times* reported "panic and all kinds of fighting" just outside Dodge City. The paper said that a house was burning two miles to the south of town where a farmer had seen the Indians coming and fled. The *Nebraska State Journal* reported that dozens of men and women had been killed in raids. The *Russell (KS) Reformer* reported that a Swedish farmer was so flustered by the Indians that "hearing of the impending danger, [he] bundled his wife and two children into the old prairie schooner, mounted one of the ponies and struck off across country, leaving his family in the barnyard; he had forgotten to hook up the traces."

On Saturday morning, fortified with ammunition and supported by 107 cavalry and 40 infantrymen under the command of Captain Joseph Rendlebrock, about 50 cowboys and ranch owners headed out of Dodge City. Before the day was over they had made contact with one group of Cheyennes, but according to Rendlebrock's court-martial records, "when one company of his command was fighting the enemy and the firing distinctly heard by him, [Rendlebrock] failed to support said company or make any disposition whatever to fight the enemy with the rest of his command." As a result, the cowboys and soldiers were forced to retreat as night fell.

The next morning they found a trail in this white-rimmed canyon that runs into Spring Creek. They circled around to the west, trying to surround the group of Cheyennes. A cowboy who was there said the Cheyennes "had dug holes around the top of the canyon large enough to hold two to six men in each hole, and we advanced to within 300 to 400 yards of them and fired around them all day. Everybody was anxious to charge into them and endeavor to capture them, except the ranking captain."

Although Rendlebrock was in command of three companies of cavalry and one infantry, he used only a portion of his command to skirmish with the hostiles while he remained with the rest of his command nearby.

The cowboy claimed that later that evening the leading men in his bunch tried to persuade Rendlebrock to put guards around the Indians and hold them in their position in order to send for reinforcements and heavier artillery. Instead Rendlebrock, who was "under the curse of Custer," according to the cowboy, withdrew all of his forces a mile away, where they went into camp for the night.

At Rendlebrock's court-martial he was found guilty of neglecting to send a messenger to the commanding officer at Fort Dodge to notify him of the engagement and of the position of Indians and their probable direction of travel. Even more serious was the charge that he actually "withheld information necessary for intelligence and the co-operation of other troops in the attempt to capture or destroy these Indians." When he returned to camp, "under the pretense of procuring supplies," the Cheyennes made their escape, "thus allowing Indians to gain a march of 36 hours on his command." The cowboy who testified at the court-martial said, "The next morning the Indians were gone again, having taken a northerly direction and crossed the Arkansas River up where the Deer Trail was located at the time." The Cheyennes had their wounded with them and about two hundred head of horses.

Disgusted with the army, the ranchers fired off telegrams to the governor. Soon the newspapers picked up the story, and three days later the secretary of war issued orders to General George Crook, commander of the Department of the Platte, telling him to "spare no means to kill or capture these Indians for if they are successful in reaching the north, it will endanger the whole northwest and affect for a while the whole Indian reservation system."

Within a week charges were brought against Rendlebrock for his conduct in Kansas and at the Turkey Springs battle. Captain Rendlebrock, who had served the U.S. Army for nearly thirty years and was only months from retirement, was found guilty of neglecting his duties. He eventually settled in Kansas City. Years later his pension was restored by a pardon from President Rutherford Hayes.

My traveling companions have spread out across the landscape overlooking the distant battlefield, sharing the same view that Rendlebrock had of the fortress of white cliffs where Dull Knife and Little Wolf had been entrenched. Andy and Sam have climbed over the locked fence and are about a mile distant, on the very edge of the canyon. The women are not as far away, stooping over to inspect plants and rocks as they walk.

Henry Ford leans against the hood of his truck. "My father worked out this way riding for the Goodnight-Craven's crew," he says. Earlier in the day he had given me a copy of the book his father wrote during the 1930s. Henry Ford's father led an adventuresome life, eventually becoming the sheriff of Clark County. His father's third grade education didn't stop him from writing his story down, picking out the words a single letter at a time on the old typewriter that sat on the rolltop desk in the Clark County sheriff's office. Henry and the other children, when they got within hearing distance, would spell words for him. "The Kid," as his father was known during the 1890s when he began to ride for the area's cattle companies, not only knew every square inch of land for a hundred miles in any direction but also knew more about horses than anyone else who lived in that expanse. In 1898 the Kid rode all the way into Nebraska to obtain horses, earning his keep by bringing along a short, mean bronco and betting on its ability to throw any cowboy along the way who thought he could ride it. The Kid had just about every kind of job a man could have in the west in those days: breaking horses, ranch hand, longshoreman, merchant marine, bartender, and logger. He enlisted in the army during the Spanish-American War and survived a month of seasickness for a tour of duty in the Philippines. He rode horses and roped steers in dozens of traveling shows that were riding the coattails of Buffalo Bill's popularity. But his greatest adventure might have been escaping from jail after being falsely accused of horse stealing. The Kid hid out in these same canyons and camped on the high mesas; he rode the rails and worked wherever he could, finally turning himself in after more than a year on the lam.

He served a year in prison for his jailbreak and came out a changed man, determined to stay on the right side of the law.

"He went to work for your grandfather about then," Henry Ford calls out to Don Goodnight. Mr. Goodnight stops snapping photographs and comes back to where we are standing.

"That would have been about right," Mr. Goodnight says. "Henry's father was foreman of my grandfather's spread on the old Ben Johnson ranch, north of Englewood." In sharp contrast to Henry Ford's blue jeans and ball cap, Mr. Goodnight wears a brown, western-style corduroy jacket, pearl-button dress shirt, and a gray felt western hat with a small, tightly rolled rim. After sixty-seven years his inquisitive blue eyes and friendly smile seem a natural part of his face. With the ease and love of men who have spent a lifetime coming to know one place in the world, both men lean on the truck and talk of the history of the land. "My grandfather Frank hired Henry's father," Mr. Goodnight says.

His grandfather, Frank Goodnight, was the cousin of Charles Goodnight, the first white man to settle this part of the United States. Colonel Charles Goodnight served in the Confederate Army and, when that dream failed, blazed a trail west where, in 1876, he established the first ranch in the Texas panhandle. The J. A. Ranch was jointly owned by Goodnight and John Adair, an Irish nobleman and financier. The J. A. Ranch at one time totaled more than one million acres.

"I grew up on the ranch at Englewood," Mr. Goodnight says, pointing off to the south across fifty miles of yellow valley land.

"Right there?" I say, joking.

"Well, yes, most of the land you see there. My maternal grandfather, Charlie McKinney, came here in 1884 and had control of thirty thousand acres. Frank Goodnight had that much or more."

"Your son has nearly that now, don't he?" Henry Ford cuts in.

"Yes," Mr. Goodnight says, "nearly so."

"I guess you could say we come from a long line of cow men," Henry Ford says.

Charles Goodnight invented the chuck wagon, a portable kitchen and pantry that traveled with a camp cook so that cowboys didn't have to worry about fixing a hearty meal after a long day in the saddle. Although Goodnight was a visionary man – in addition to the chuck wagon, he experimented with cross-breeding buffalo and cattle to produce cattalos – ranches like his were chiefly great reservoirs for cattle. For over twenty years following the Civil War, millions of cattle were sent up the trails from his and similar ranches to railheads in the new towns of Nebraska and Kansas. It was during these years that Dodge City found its fame as the toughest cowtown in the West. Dodge was a busy place, but soon, in search of fresh grass and new markets, the cattlemen made other trails northward. Goodnight himself figured he could find a market for his cattle to the west in the gold fields beyond New Mexico's Pecos River, and so he and partner named Oliver Loving set out up the Pecos one spring with a herd of fat steers. To their great surprise they were able to sell the entire herd at Fort Sumner. They hurried back to the ranch for another herd. Soon the busy Goodnight-Loving Trail extended up to the northern border of New Mexico, to Colorado and Wyoming.

"There's trails all over this land," Mr. Goodnight says. "Why, you can still see the Tuttle Cattle Trail right there." He points to a ridge where a strip of lower, greener grass winds north and south across the face of the earth to the horizon.

"You headed up to Wichita today, Don?" Henry Ford asks.

"Yes. Going to pick up a couple of fellers and fly them to Kansas City." Mr. Goodnight checks the clear blue sky as he answers. "I've been flying since I got out of the service in 1948," he explains. He has made a living all of his adult life as a flight instructor, teaching ranchers and business executives and others how to fly the small planes that have replaced the horses and chuck wagons of his grandfather's day. He flies J3 Cubs these days, and loves the way his home land looks from the air.

He gazes out across the open, treeless land, past where my Cheyenne companions are walking, spread out like distant tumbleweeds; beyond the white rimrock of the canyon where the ancestors of these cowboys and Indians battled so long ago; far across the vast green and yellow buffalo rangeland turned cattle empire and empty. "I've been all over the world," he says after a pause, "and this is a pretty good ol' place to live."

13. The Speech of the Wolves

It was late at night when Dull Knife's people set up camp north of the Many Geese River. It was a familiar place; the people had used the place for centuries of buffalo hunts. Here they stopped to rest. Some people fell to the ground without unpacking.

Pawnee Woman, a wife of the leader Dull Knife, knew better. She knew her horse needed a rest too. She unpacked her horse and then gathered her children near her to make them a little something to eat from the wild turnips she had found nearby.

Then, an alarm.

Someone shouted. The soldiers were near. The woman rushed for a horse. As she grabbed the rope the horse rose up. Hooves flickered in the night air an instant, then snapped at her head. Someone lifted her body and threw it on a travois. The camp had to run again, and there was no time to tend to her wounds. In a few days of rough traveling she was dead.

No one spoke much about it. Those who had passed away were many, and many more would follow, but her death must have been particularly sorrowful, for she was a strong and powerful woman, wife of Dull Knife and mother to fine children, and, it was said, among the few who still understood the speech of wolves.

In times past those who understood the speech of the wolves had many times saved the people from great danger. One time during a hungry season, for example, wolves had come to the village and howled. All of the Cheyennes who were there tell it in the same way. The wolves had howled, and one who understood their speech said, "The wolves tell me that we should go straight to the two mountains right beyond these mountains before us, and after we have passed them we shall find buffalo." A day later and beyond the two mountains they found such a great number of buffalo that the village was saved.

Now one of the last who understood the speech of the wolves was gone. It was said that on the night before she died some wolves had come near and howled from the steep hills. After that many came to her. She had told them what the wolves had said. They had said: "Look out, for the way in which you are going and the place toward which you are heading are bad."

"They say girls liked his wavy hair," Andy says as we talk about Dull Knife at our camp just west of Dodge City. Sam and the women have gone into town and left the two of us seated on the grass, studying the sky and talking. The night is clear and cool and peaceful. "They thought he was pretty. His family was known as the beautiful people." Andy laughs and motions at the layers of dust on our skin. "I don't know if they would still call this Dull Knife descendant beautiful or not."

"Your mother is descended from Dull Knife," I say, "but tell me about your father."

"Both my mother and my father were married once before, and so I have a lot of stepbrothers and sisters," he begins. "My father drove the ambulance on the reservation for many years. He knows just about everybody, and I think he's seen just about everything you can see of people in trouble. He's delivered babies, seen the old ones pass on, and everybody knows who he is because he had driven that ambulance everywhere for so many years."

Andy pauses. The silence is filled with early night sounds: an owl, handfuls of crickets, whisper wind.

"My father had some health problems this spring," he continues. "He's had poor circulation all of his life, and here lately it got so bad that he couldn't really walk much. The doctors told him the only thing they could do was to amputate his leg."

I shudder, remembering how soon after Ted Risingsun lost both of his legs that the end had come.

"My father resisted it for a long time," Andy says. "I think maybe it had something to do with the fact he had seen so much of pain and suffering for so long. Anyway, he resisted it, and the family didn't know how they were going to get him to do it. Then one day he found his courage and announced he would have it done right away."

"How has he managed with it?"

"He was pretty strong about it. Now he's learning to get around with his cane and he's as strong as ever."

We talk for a while more about his father, then about how Dull Knife must have been a strong father, despite so many hardships and a tradition so different from our modern one. For one thing, Dull Knife's first wife killed herself. Goes to Get a Drink, as she was sometimes called, hanged herself after Dull Knife took the captive Pawnee Woman as his second wife. In Cheyenne tradition a grievance that caused a suicide could result in chastisement for the offender, but even her grandmother said that what Goes to Get a Drink had done was a foolish thing. As a good Cheyenne man would do, Dull Knife soon married his first wife's sister, Slow Woman, and it was with both Slow Woman and Pawnee Woman that he fled north from Indian Territory.

We talk more about the nature of fatherhood: how it requires such an odd combination of guidance, nurturing, and instruction, as well as an ability to see beyond the present moment. Andy has no children of his own but stepchildren and a swarm of nieces and nephews.

There is another pause.

"It takes a lifetime to learn how to be a good father," Andy says.

I agree and fall silent a moment, thinking of how sweet were the voices of my children as they chattered at me on the phone an hour ago. "Some men seem to learn faster, or are just naturally better at it," I say. "Perhaps those are the ones, like Dull Knife, who realize that good fatherhood means more than just taking care of your own children."

Andy thinks about this for a moment before he answers. "If fatherhood doesn't go beyond your own offspring then you're just selfishly protecting what you think belongs only to you. Dull Knife understood the danger in that kind of fatherhood. In a way, he was a father for all of the children, even down to children of this day."

There is another silence. The night is full now, stars in a cloudless black.

"What about yours?" Andy says. "What about your father?"

I pause before answering. "He's been dead for twenty-five years," I begin, then start again. "I still can learn from my father even though he has been dead now all of these years."

Andy waits. And in a moment I begin my story.

14. The Ghost in My Father's Tackle Box

Not long ago my younger son had two friends over to play. The three of them were huddled together on the living room floor, designing a complex game involving sticks, paper, rubber bands, and marbles. Feeling pretty good about myself, and trying as always to be the perfect father, I crouched down to them.

"Hi, guys," I said. "Whatcha doing?"

The two friends smiled at me politely, but my son's eyes caught me off guard. They were far more serious than I believed was possible. He spoke to me in an even, calm voice, but with such authority that I was taken aback.

"Go away, Dad," he said, and stared at me. "Please go away, Dad."

I paused just an instant and then said a quiet "okay" and left the room.

I did what he said, bemused by the serious tone of his voice and a little saddened because I recognized his voice as my own. For a moment I thought of my own father and then I saw that ghost again. The ghost in my father's tackle box.

It was just after that monumental year of change, 1968, that my father had a heart attack and died. He had been at work. After a coffee break he had stopped by the restroom. The next person in had to throw his entire weight against the door, for my father's crumpled body was blocking the entrance.

I was nineteen and just coming out of the long blinding fog of adolescence. During that year I had only a handful of conversations with my father that did not involve some kind of confrontation. Either I was seeing too many girls or not studying enough. Either I was staying out too late or my hair was too long. And after I purchased a used army jacket from Goodwill and wore it to march in an antiwar protest, I began to argue with the indignant pride of political righteousness.

Our arguments usually took the form of an exchange of angry

words, followed by my father's outlining a series of restrictions and my silent vow to break those restrictions in every way possible.

Our fights were marked by the way he set his jaw in a tight, muscled box, the way he would tip his head and look at me under a furrowed brow, and his terse, strained voice. I don't remember the words, but I now realize what he was always saying. "You are no longer a child, and I must let you go. It hurts me to let you go. It hurts me."

For that last year our relationship followed the same pattern: a period of polite conversations, followed by one intense disagreement.

Such was the pattern, that is, except for our game of golf.

On the golf course we seemed to set aside our roles and treat one another as equals, or if not equals, at least as wary friends.

"What are you thinking about doing?" he asked me one bright Saturday morning when we had the course to ourselves.

"I think I'll chip it out to that flat area there and see if I can get a shot at the green," I said.

"No," he paused, "I mean, what are you thinking about doing when you leave home?"

The tall grass and weeds of the canyon sheltered insects, and their singing filled the air.

He was asking me a question like that during his game of golf, during our game of golf, and his voice carried no threat, only curiosity.

And so I answered truthfully.

"I want to move to New Mexico," I started, pretending to flip through my bag for the correct club. "I'm going to move to New Mexico, get some kind of job to support me so I can write the rest of the time."

"Yes," he said.

My future had been a topic of conversation before, but it had always been in the form of an argument about the value of a good education or about my responsibilities to serve in Vietnam. I had never before told him of my dream of a writer's life in Santa Fe.

My father waited and I shot, a sputtering hit that was saved only by the grace of a good roll. He stepped to his ball and swung. It fell within a few feet of where mine had landed.

"I always forget how hard it is to get a clear shot from down here," he said.

As we walked he spoke again.

"You might think about finding some career you'd be happy in," he said. I was about to tell him my career meant nothing, as long as I could write, but some faraway sadness in his voice made me stop short.

"You've got some things you're happy doing," he said. He turned his attention to his clubs. "Pitching wedge for me here."

He pulled the club from the bag and bent over his ball. It was a short chip up out of the last of the canyon and onto the green.

His club slid in a semicircle, a pendulum against the sky. It stopped at the apex and hung there suspended in time. The metal flashed, and the ball floated to a landing inches from the cup.

"How about forestry?"

I stopped. "Forestry."

"Sure," he said. "You like the outdoors, you know a lot about it. A career in something like forestry would keep you doing things you like to do, like hiking and being in the wilderness." He paused. "Something where you'll be happy."

"Well, maybe," I heard myself saying. I had never thought of it before, and was about to tell him I didn't think it was for me, but something in his voice made me stop short.

"I always wanted to play baseball," he said, apropos of nothing but the singing of the insects.

"You did?" This was news to me.

He nodded. "Wanted to play professionally, and took it pretty seriously."

We were walking up the far end of the canyon toward the green. The green on this magical hole sat on the edge of the canyon where it rose back up to meet the prairie. It was beautiful, poised between the dark, wild canyon and the endless horizon. An emerald oasis that waited peacefully.

"So, why didn't you?"

He laughed his rare, deep-chested laugh. "I was good," he said, "but not good enough. I played on a few league teams in northern Iowa before the war, but then . . ." The laugh faded and he shrugged. "Then the war came . . . the war came and that was that.

"Forestry, or something like that," he said, pulling a club from his bag. "It's something to think about." Across the long sloping green hill his eyes met mine and for a long moment we embraced with them.

It was the beginning of a new relationship between us. Had he lived a little while longer – until I had grown out of the self-centeredness of youth – I would have come to appreciate his life the way he had begun to appreciate mine. I would have been able to tell him so, as he had told me just then.

His death cut short any hope of me being able to tell him, but twenty years after his death, while sitting in the cold basement of my boyhood home, I could still learn to value his life. A startling series of apparitions rose suddenly in front of me, and before those ghosts had vanished into vapor, I would learn a final lesson from him.

When my mother finally decided to let us sell her house, the big, two-story house my brothers and I had all been raised in, each of her sons did what we could to sort through the crumbs of forty-five years of living. That was how I found myself in the basement with my father's ancient tackle box sitting before me.

Although we'd gotten a line or two wet over the years, fishing was such an infrequent activity in our family that I had always assumed my father never liked it much. I had never seen my father touch this tackle box. In the twenty years since his death it had been moved from one corner to another in the big, dank basement, collecting such a thick sheen of dust and spider webs that when I ran my finger across the top, a gray sheet of the stuff rolled under the tip of my finger like a piece of felt.

Even with the dust, cobwebs, and age, the box was still beautiful. The brass corners and wooden pegs that held it together were cool under my thumb. A zigzag pattern of thin dark slats worked their way up the side of the box, and a thick wooden handle arched over the top. Looking at it then, I could not understand why my father had decided to paint it black.

A small hook held the box closed. I slid it out and folded back the lid. The top shelf held an orderly collection of lures and hooks. Patient wooden fish, with a row of hooks instead of dorsal fins, gleamed with bright colors as fresh as spring. Near them was a tightly wound spool of dark fishing line. It had a label with a drawing of a fish bursting through the water and, in the distance, the faint outline of a man on the shore.

In the corner of that large shelf my eye caught on a shred of paper. I pulled it free from a box of small lead weights.

It was a fishing license. Lettering edged the faded red paper. "The State of Iowa Game Department grants" – and here a fat, jolly imitation of my father's controlled left-handed scrawl had written "Arthur Boye" in big letters – "a resident of Osceola County a license to fish the waters of the state for the year 1941."

In 1941 my father would have been twenty-one years old. As I sat there in the dark basement the bright colors of the lures swam before me. I imagined that glorious summer long ago in Iowa. The cornfields green and golden in the powerful sunlight, the streams thick with bass, my father's youth held on the tip of a bamboo pole.

By the year's end he would enlist in the army. In another year he would be fighting in North Africa, touring Europe, watching his friends die.

My father never talked about his World War II experiences.

Never. When pressed, my mother hinted vaguely at secret work he had done, at mysterious responsibilities he had had for the army.

Now I sat with the relic of his last youthful summer before me on the floor. Soon after the war he would be married and raising us. He would never return to live in Iowa, or to fish the streams of his endless youth. The tackle box was his alone, opened in the warm and golden moments of long-passed summers, on the sunlit shores of lakes and the banks of solitary streams.

The tackle box opened like an accordion, one level at a time, and I lifted out the deep top shelf and exposed the space below it.

There were no more lures, or weights or even spools of fishing line. There was nothing, really, except a small brown book of some sort. I was disappointed. Finding the last fishing license my father had as a boy had sent my imagination racing.

Aimlessly I picked up the book and flipped through the pages, still imagining my father's last perfect summer.

The book was a scrapbook of some kind, but the photographs were nearly as small as postage stamps. I squinted at them.

One seemed to be a picture of some kind of foundry. Despite the smallness of the photograph, the yawning opening of a kiln of some sort gaped at me. On the opposite page I recognized my father in a photograph. He was in uniform, unsmiling, standing at a gate of some kind.

An hour later I placed the scrapbook on my mother's lap as she sat in her wheelchair in the nursing home.

"Can you tell me about this?" I asked. I expected her to be as puzzled as I was about the strange book, but she recognized it at once.

"Oh," she said, "Art's photographs."

"You know about these?" I asked.

"Your father took these during the war," she said. "When he was on assignment."

She slowly lifted the cover and began.

My father had grown up speaking German. Since he spoke it so well, my mother explained, the army began to assign him to special units. Some of his work during the war took him into German territory.

"After the fall of Berlin," my mother said, her hands resting on the open scrapbook, "he was one of the first to be sent into Germany."

She paused, her voice straining for control.

"He was among the first inside Germany," she repeated. "The first to see . . . the first to know about the horrors."

"This," she said, pointing to the photograph of the kiln, "is one of the ovens. He was the first one to see them." She tried to explain, "no one really knew yet."

"A concentration camp?" I asked stupidly.

My mother nodded. "He had been with the group that freed the remaining prisoners. Your Dad found the ovens. He was one of the first to see the piles of bones, to see the ashes, to hear the survivors' stories, to . . ."

Her hand waved in the air over the pages of tiny photographs. It was as if my father had tried to limit all of the horror of the death camp by containing it in these tiny brown images.

"Where did you find this?"

She nodded when I told her, as if it made perfect sense to her that he would put the scrapbook in his fishing tackle box, as if that black box of his youth could contain the phantom of humanity gone mad.

All of us are haunted by ghosts, and to try and keep still the fear of their haunting is an endless task. Perhaps our lives are nothing more than a series of exorcisms, a series of delicate dances with the specters of the past.

"Go away, Dad," my son had said, and I'm sure I must have used the same words on my own father time and time again.

And now it is my turn to dance with the spirits of glorious youth and the painful passing of time. My own ghosts lie hidden deep within some emerald box of a summer's dream, and they drift, echoing across the long golden green of fading fairways:

Go away Dad. Now come back.

Go away Dad. Come back.

Go away.

Come back.

Come back.

PART FOUR

The Rattlesnake Way

There stands Minos, grotesquely, and he snarls,
examining the guilty at the entrance;
he judges and dispatches, tail in coils.

DANTE, *The Inferno*, canto 5

15. Chaos and Order

We have lost Samuel Spotted Elk Junior. He was supposed to be somewhere on a stretch of U.S. Highway 50 east of Garden City, Kansas, but it is an hour past the time we were to meet him west of Pierceville. I am riding in Andy's car, and this is our third fifteen-mile sweep of the busy highway. At first we had joked about Sam's tendency to lose his way, but now both of us are silently considering possibilities. The last time through Pierceville we stopped at the grain elevator and I ran inside to ask if anyone there had seen him walk past.

"What is he? An *Indian?*" a man had said. "No, didn't see any *thing* like *that.*" Another man in overalls who stood nearby laughed. I got back in the car feeling even more uneasy.

"They see him?" Andy asked.

"No," was all I said.

Andy swung the car around and we headed back toward Garden City.

"Maybe we shouldn't have trusted him to find his way," Andy says.

"How can someone get lost on this highway?" I say. "You simply keep walking on the pavement." It would be difficult to get lost, but I knew the highway had other dangers. All day we have been walking west from Dodge on the busiest road of the journey. The only shelter from the massive grain trucks, semitrailers, and roaring stream of traffic was a narrow shoulder with the dubious safety net of a stinking drainage ditch beyond it. All day I have been nervously eyeing approaching cars, stealing glances over my shoulder. It is most dangerous when cars approaching from the rear pass each other. The driver in the passing lane hasn't seen any oncoming cars, but he hasn't seen me, either. I don't expect cars from the rear to be on my side of the road, and three or four times during this nerve-racking day I had to dive for the edge of the asphalt

Dull Knife. Courtesy of National Archives.

just seconds before the whoosh of a screaming car sliced my shadow in two.

Andy has slowed down at the outskirts of Garden City. There's no way Sam could have made it this far into town, but I study the strip of malls, filling stations, and fast food dispensers anyway.

"Now where are they going?" Andy says.

"Who?"

He turns his head around to look at a passing car.

"Barbara and them," he says. "I thought we told them to wait for us at the campground, but there they go." He mutters softly, which is as upset as he gets. "I must have been speaking Spanish when we were talking," he says. Barbara's car turns into the parking lot of a mall.

We drive to Garden City's tidy downtown district to report Sam's disappearance to the police. The utilitarian, squat government office building that houses the police station is just a few blocks away from the newspaper office.

"Maybe we shouldn't have done the newspaper interview," I say. Andy does not respond. After I had walked into town a couple of hours earlier I called the newspaper office to arrange an interview. I had convinced Andy to go there with me. Once there everything seemed wrong. The reporter, a polite and proper woman in her sixties, had spent much of the interview talking with me instead of Andy. She had stumbled over the spelling of his name. The answers I gave her seemed shallow and silly.

"You go report him," Andy says, nodding at the police station. "You're better at that kind of talking."

The policewoman takes the information and enters it into a computer. She is professional, and the neutral lack of concern on her face does nothing to calm my worries. She lists Sam as "reported as missing" and explains that a notice will go out across the area for all police to keep an eye out for him. If we still haven't located him by morning, they will issue an all-points bulletin for a missing person.

We drive back out of town, past the mall, past the commercial campground where we had planned to camp for the evening, and out beyond the airport.

The shadows are long; massive thunderheads are on the western horizon. No Sam. A long shuddering semi, loaded and racing, passes us in a roar of diesel smoke. We watch the road, but it isn't clear what we are looking for. I talk about the day in order to break the tension.

I had managed to get off of the busy U.S. highway for a few miles moving cross-country on a route that paralleled the Arkansas River. A mile or so of open sky and air had almost eased the anxiety that had been building all day. Electric thin bolts of fluorescent green darted into the weeds: lizards. Big hawks, with wings in the reverse pattern of a vulture's black on white, circled overhead and dropped straight down on their prey. They were buteos, rough-legged hawks that feed entirely on rodents. Below the hawks were woodpeckers everywhere along the Arkansas. Their graceful flights – a swooping flap-flap-flap and glide – came constantly from the trees along the river.

Except for those few trees, the earth was either open rangeland or cut into huge fields of alfalfa or wheat or oats. Although sand hills occasionally rippled up on either side of the river, the land was flat. On some hills and in places where streams had cut away, the soil was the red I had seen for days, but even that was giving way to a somber gray sandy mixture that provided the route for the flat Arkansas.

That route has long been used by travelers. Just a century after Columbus, Coronado and his conquistadors came up and down the Arkansas, claiming ownership of the strange land for distant Spain. Some say that to this day pieces of metal from their crested helmets still appear behind air-conditioned tractor cabs peeling back the earth.

Slicing the hillsides along the Arkansas in green parallel lines, traces of the Santa Fe Trail are still quite obvious. The initial use of this route as a trade trail to Mexico was in 1821, when a financially strapped farmer from Missouri by the name of William Becknell decided to head west on a horse-trading expedition. He crossed the Missouri on a ferry, then headed southwest until he reached the Arkansas River somewhere near present-day Great Bend, Kansas. He went up that river for eight days until, along this very way, he set off across the *jornada* – a journey of sixty waterless miles to the Cimarron. Thinking there might be a profit to be made, the

U.S. government soon passed into a law a bill to mark and promote Becknell's Santa Fe Trail. Suddenly hundreds of traders, trappers, soldiers, investors, and pioneers wore their wagon ruts over the farmer's original route. According to Gregory Franzwa, who has spent a lifetime tracking and writing about this and the other great western trails, the ruts often split into several sets of parallel traces. "Northeast of Elkhart, Kansas, for example," Franzwa writes in his *Maps of the Santa Fe Trail*, "there is a sharp four-track pattern in the land, characteristic of the trail in Indian country, where wagons went four abreast to reduce the time needed to form a defense in the event of attack."

Dull Knife and Little Wolf and the others came this way because they knew from centuries of tribal experience where best to cross the river. Even today it is easy to see the ford where they forded the river just west of a rest area on the highway near Ingalls. Becknell had found it an easy place to cross as well, and the places where the pioneers led their wagons down swales to the river are still visible today as little dirt roads and paths where cattle and men in pickup trucks and on horseback yet cross the shallows.

"I must have been speaking Spanish," Andy repeats as we turn around again in front of the Pierceville grain elevator. "When people agree to something, they should stick to it. Now there's no telling where the women have gone shopping, and Sam is lost."

On the drive back into Garden City we talk about the problem with the day. "This busy highway sure hasn't helped things," I say. "I don't care where Dull Knife and Little Wolf's route went, tomorrow we aren't walking on this road."

"Yeah," Andy says, cutting the last letter off in his throat. "It seems like when things go wrong, everything starts to unravel. Dull Knife and them, they were a well-organized group. They followed patterns of behavior everyone understood. Everyone could operate just fine when everything went as it should, but if something came along to upset that system, then the entire operation started to fall apart."

I wait a moment, then he goes on.

"Just like us. When Sam disappeared all of our good organization and collective decisions went out of whack. After the Turkey Springs fight and after this other battle up north we're going visit,

Dull Knife and Little Wolf lost control of the young men for a while. Things with them went haywire for a while."

"And when there was chaos like that was when people were in the most danger," I say. Andy nods. "You could draw a comparison to the history of the entire West. The sudden arrival of all these whites in the middle of Indian land upset a system of order that had been in place for a thousand years."

"That kind of thing, that kind of chaos could explain why there were so many violent men in them days," Andy says. We are almost back to the airport, and the thunderheads tower above the nearby city. "Maybe that's why there was so much bloodshed. Today, too. Too many people lose control when the system gets all messed up. There were very few people back then who could see through all that. Dull Knife saw through it, though."

"Maybe even Buffalo Bill," I add. "No matter how artificial his Wild West Show seemed, at least he tried to preserve a view of what things were like before they got all messed up."

I'm not certain Andy agrees with me, but the give-and-take of our conversations has evolved into a deep and trusting friendship that allows us the freedom to explore any idea. And so he simply nods again. "Yeah," he says. Then he points. "At least the women have found their way back to the campground."

Barbara's car is parked in front of the commercial campground office. She is standing at a phone booth, the receiver pressed to her ear. We pull in and park beside her car. As I am getting out of the car, I see Phoebe and Carol seated in Barbara's back seat. In the front seat, calmly eating an apple, is Sam.

Barbara hangs up the phone. Andy goes to her instead of Sam and talks. I try talking to Sam, but he seems a bit sullen and only mumbles a response to my questions. I walk over to Barbara and Andy.

"He was just sitting at a filling station about a mile closer to town from here," she says. "We saw him there when we came out of the shopping center. He was just sitting there drinking a can of pop like nothing was the matter."

"How did he get there?" Andy says. "He couldn't have walked that far."

Barbara explains that Sam's foot had started hurting and so he decided not to walk any further. He didn't want to wait to be picked up as we had discussed, so he hitchhiked all the way into Garden City.

Sam has climbed out of the car and hobbles over to us. He is clearly favoring his right leg.

"Sam," Andy says. "How did you expect for us to find you?"

Sam shrugs. "My leg got to hurtin' and I didn't think I could walk much on it."

"How is it now?" I ask.

He shrugs again. "Okay," he says. "I'm pretty strong."

"Sam," Barbara says, "Andy and Alan have been driving all over for the past three hours looking for you. We even reported you to the police." Sam has held his face in a slight, impassive frown, but I catch a glimpse of a faint smile, which vanishes instantly.

"If we are going to make it all the way north," Andy says, "then no one can operate on their own agenda. When people just follow their own agendas then everybody suffers."

Barbara says, "You should have waited for us to find you."

"You found me, didn't you?" Sam's voice rises a slight bit, but already Andy and Barbara have moved away.

"Should we set up camp, then?" Andy says, turning to me.

Behind the tall wooden slats of a fence, trailers and campers are squeezed together in tight rows between narrow gravel paths. Broken picnic tables, not enough for everyone, are scattered near a few of the behemoths. We set up our little camp in a small space designated for tents only, but it appears the most common use for the area is as a dog exercise yard.

Out of sheer exhaustion and in the interest of frayed nerves, we order a pizza instead of trying to cook for ourselves, and in twenty minutes a pale youth driving a beat-up Ford hands the greasy boxes to us and then turns as if to run.

Over our meal, and under the gathering thunderstorm, Barbara talks at length of her adopted brother, whom her father adopted in an instant at a powwow long ago. "Our father has had four wives," she says. Carol nods. "His first wife was our mother, a Cheyenne woman. After they were separated she never wanted him to visit his two sons. Then he had a Sioux woman, an Arapaho, and now he's married to a Samoan." Phoebe interrupts by saying something in Cheyenne. Barbara translates, "She said, 'A fly sucked my blood. I killed it.'" For a moment we all turn to Phoebe, who sits near Sam, watching her son devour his pizza. Barbara says, "Phoebe once had a degree to teach bilingual students," she says. "Then she had her first breakdown. She's had three or four now, and she's mostly been like this."

Phoebe looks up. "I know Sam Senior and Sam Junior's birthdays," she says in English and out of the silence of heat lightning and distant thunder.

Later, I doctor two ugly blisters on Barbara's feet and give Carol a couple of aspirins for a headache. Carol is worried enough about things back home that the women have decided to return to Montana in two days after we visit the site of the battle at Punished Woman Creek.

A few drops of rain hit the tent at dusk, and the conversation has slowed. Sam stands and limps away to the restroom. Andy watches him. "I don't know if he can walk tomorrow," he says.

"Sam," Barbara says. "He always wants to keep moving, no matter what."

Andy is still watching the dark shape of Sam's figure moving away from our campsite. "My grandfather had a saying," he says, "He said, 'Be in the country and walk in order to become a patient man.' But Sam just wants to keep moving."

16. Punished Woman

We are gathered around the newspaper on the motel table as if vultures over a dead calf.

Andy turns away. He is the first to speak. "It can go one of two ways when a person has a lot of experience at something," he says, referring to the older reporter who wrote the story, "either they put that experience to use, or they just want to get through it all as fast as they can."

For a moment I experience a slight thrill at seeing my name in print, but then I search the story for the names of my companions. It is a long search: Andy and Sam's names are buried deep in the article, and it gets worse. In the last paragraph it says we are also traveling "with some Indian women."

Barbara and Carol turn away from the table. "What do you expect," Barbara says softly. "It's no different than it ever has been."

I read it again. The article about our journey is on the front page. It is full of errors and misquotes. It reads as if a Great White Man is leading a handful of trembling redskins north.

"I'm sorry," I say. I realize, much too late, that my enthusiasm with the reporter probably contributed to the perception I was somehow leading the group. The mood in the room is dark and uncomfortable.

"Hey," Sam says. "My name is in here." He has finally located it, low on the page. No one answers him, and no one mentions the article again. Sam turns away from the paper and sits on the bed. He grimaces. He removes his sneaker and sock. His ankle is red and swollen.

"That doesn't look good," I say, trying to change the focus. He had painfully hobbled into the motel room after a day spent mostly riding in Barbara's car. "It hurts," he says.

Andy looks at him for a moment, then turns away.

In an hour I have called my physician back in Vermont and described Sam's symptoms. "Tendinitis," he says. "He could do some damage if he continues walking on it. The only way it'll get really better is to keep off of it for a few days."

"I can keep walking," Sam says when I tell him the news. "I'm strong."

"If you want to keep walking, you're going to have to give it a rest," I say. I study one of my countless maps. "Tomorrow we're going to this place called Punished Woman. There was a big battle there, but it means walking over open land."

"I've got a strong body," Sam says. "My grandmother always told me to have a strong body, a strong mind, and," he slams his fist against his chest, "a strong heart." His face is red and flushed. "I'm going to walk all the way north."

I turn to Andy. I want to believe that he will speak to Sam as an elder. Andy is stretched out on one of the two beds in the motel room, quietly smoking. The women have gone to their own room. The television is on, but no one pays it any attention.

"I'm walking north for my grandmother," Sam says.

Andy swings his legs over the edge of the bed and sits up. "That's your agenda," he says to Sam, "but there's a greater thing here than just your agenda. Barbara and them are going back to Montana tomorrow after we visit this battle place. There won't be any other way for us to get you back home after they leave." Sam's face glows, but he does not answer. Andy goes on. "Do you know what happened at this Punished Woman battle? The people had the soldiers in a trap. They were waiting for the soldiers to come just a little bit closer and then they would have won. But this young man – he was about your age – had his own agenda. He didn't want to wait. He didn't want to follow the group decision. He thought he could do things himself, and so he shot at a soldier too early. Because of that many people were killed. The times got very hard for the people after that battle, and it was because of that young man following his own desires. The fact that he wanted to go with his own agenda jeopardized the entire tribe."

"You think I'm not strong enough to make it?" Sam says.

"It's not that," I say. "You've just got to stay off that leg for a while."

Andy says, "The actions of that one young man threatened the entire tribe. He had a responsibility to the group, but he decided to do only what he thought was best."

"I'm going to walk all the way. I can make it."

"Well, you've made a decision for yourself," Andy says, "but I'm talking about something else. I'm talking about learning something. About wisdom."

Sam stands up. "I'm a young man. I can walk further than you two. Faster too. You think I can't make it?"

"You already have your agenda, like I said." Andy stands, puts on his jacket, and goes to the door. He turns to me. "We ready to meet that history guy?" He opens the door and walks out without waiting for me.

I stand. I turn to Sam, who has gone to the TV and is rapidly flipping the channels. "Is it pretty swollen?" I ask. He nods. "The doctor told me it might swell up. You have to keep off your ankle." Sam does not answer me, but concentrates on a cowboy movie he has found on the television.

Albert Maddux orders a bacon, lettuce, and tomato sandwich from the waitress at the Chaparral Restaurant. "And I'll have some mashed potatoes and a baked potato on the side," he says. The waitress doesn't flinch but writes down the request for a double dose of potatoes and walks away.

Maddux is a short but stocky man with a rubbery face and a friendly, western-style smile. He sits at the table still wearing his cowboy hat. A retired county extension agent, Maddux has spent years studying local history. He is the foremost local authority on the Punished Woman battle and has been instrumental in preserving the battle site. He has been talking nonstop since we introduced ourselves. "This is the greatest thing in the world to have you here," he says to Andrew. He is like a small child on Christmas morning, waving maps and notebooks in the air. He points to a huge pile of photographs and old newspaper clippings he has placed in front of us.

"Discipline was a problem with the army," he says. "You see, Congress froze the military budget the previous year, and the soldiers out this way may have wondered if the same would happen to them. That might explain something like Rendlebrock's court-martial."

"You think he didn't have control of his soldiers?" I ask.

"Rendlebrock?" he says to my question. "Now, there's a story. Hard to say. Here's a man who fought in the Civil War, who has been in charge of soldiers most of his adult life, and then, at the end of his career, is found guilty of, well, of cowardice." Maddux takes an instant to grab a quick breath before he continues. "I suspect he may have thought he would have it easy out here. I figure he didn't want to die in a battle so close to retirement. Maybe he just grew scared. He was found guilty on all counts in his court-martial, but President Hayes eventually pardoned him because of his many years of service, so he got his pension after all. He moved to Kansas City and died there at sixty-six years of age."

The waitress sets our meals in front of us, but Maddux ignores his, talking to us of the details of Punished Woman.

General John Pope, who had been in charge of the Division of the Missouri and ultimately in charge of Fort Reno when the Cheyennes escaped, said that among the Cheyennes, women and boys could fight as well or better than men. He claimed the Cheyennes left Indian Territory because the government did not keep its promise. Whenever Indians are placed where there is poor hunting or no hunting at all, Pope argued, the government should keep its promise by at least supplying adequate food. Pope was somewhat sympathetic to the Natives' cause and often said that the Indians suffered privation and hardship more patiently than many whites would. "In my twenty-five years on the plains, every outbreak by the Indians has been because of bad faith by the government," he said.

At first Pope refused to believe the Cheyennes had made it as far as Kansas, but when he was finally convinced – if for no other reason than the outrageous reports of Rendlebrock's behavior – he detailed Colonel William Lewis and about 250 men to the area.

Pope believed that Colonel Lewis was an efficient and capable officer. Lewis himself thought Rendlebrock's campaign was badly managed, and as soon as he arrived in southern Kansas he took immediate charge of the troops.

Lewis's scouts found the trail where the Cheyennes had crossed the Arkansas – where I had seen the rough-tailed hawk diving for rodents just a few days earlier. The soldiers camped that night at the crossing and the next day started out on the Indians' trail. Though the scouts said the Cheyennes were moving quickly, the broad trail of horses and people was easy to follow. Lewis kept his soldiers marching all day, and they made a dry camp after moving forty miles.

The next morning, Friday, September 27, was a clear, cool, and sunny day. The soldiers followed the trail ten miles to a creek, crossed it, and found signs of an Indian camp with live coals in the ashes. The fresh trail led straight into the Smoky Hills. The scouts moved out ahead of the long line of cavalry, infantry, and wagons and up the west side of Famished, or Punished Woman, Creek.

There were no flankers, and the scouts were nearly to the head of the narrow canyon when a man named Brown turned back to show the soldiers how to get around the big canyons. He rode the two or three hundred yards back to where Lewis and the soldiers were lowering the wagons down a bad place on a hillside. Brown stopped to warn Lewis that the Indians were probably close, then went on to meet the wagon train. Just as he was getting the lead wagon swung up and around the canyon, he heard a shot from up ahead.

The Indians opened fire at 350 yards.

Lewis ordered the men near him up onto the steep ridge fifty yards to his left. The entire cavalry dismounted and followed his command, firing at the mounted Cheyennes, who rode down upon them from the ridge. Every fourth soldier held horses while the others climbed over the rough terrain of hills and hollows, driving the Cheyennes back. Then most of the command fell back under cover. Companies were organized, and those men holding the horses were sent to the ravines in the rear for cover.

The Cheyennes gathered in the shelter of the large rocks at the head of the narrow canyon that was supposed to have served as a trap for the soldiers.

The army wagons were brought up to the flat prairie above the canyon and corralled in a large circle on the ridge top. Using a large, flat rock to level it, Lewis set up a table to serve as his field headquarters and then, in full sight of the Cheyenne position about four hundred yards off, rode out on his big bay horse, urging men to take positions to the front. As the afternoon wore on, the troops maneuvered around the top of the narrow canyon, surrounding the Cheyennes on three sides. They were able to fire directly down not only on the Cheyenne warriors but also on the women and children who were pressed behind rocks and squeezed into the small caves of the canyon.

The troops were closing in, and the shots were coming much faster. Lewis remained on his horse, riding to a point of rocks 150 yards above the battle canyon, his long saber flashing in the late sunlight. The scout, Brown, yelled at Lewis to dismount because he was drawing the Indians' fire. Lewis shouted back that he could do no good on foot because walking was too difficult. Besides, Lewis believed the command gained confidence from his actions.

In the confusion of the first Indian fire, men had become separated from their companies. From the point of rocks Lewis next ordered Brown to the rear to pick up the stragglers. On his way Brown met another scout, who showed him a little creek bed full of Indian horses with not a single Cheyenne around. The men fired into the herd, scattering the horses far across the open plains.

Brown was occupied at this when a cavalry man came along and told him Lewis had been shot and was bleeding to death. Brown quickly rode to the field headquarters and saw soldiers carrying the wounded Lewis. A bullet had hit the inside of the colonel's right leg about six inches below the groin and had come out through the large muscles behind, cutting his main artery in two. A strap had been cut from his saddle, tied above the wound, and twisted tight with the barrel of a pistol. He had been shot just as he had dismounted in full view of the Cheyennes on the brow of the hill. He had been carried three hundred yards, during which time he had fainted twice. The soldiers who were carrying him on a stretcher shot and wounded two Cheyennes.

The surgeon and a few other men left the battle site for Fort Wallace with an ambulance carrying Lewis and two other injured men. Lewis's pain was very bad during the night. When they stopped to rest at the Smoky Hill River crossing, the colonel was delirious and wanted to get up. Thirty minutes later his ambulance stopped. Colonel Lewis was dead.

Captain Clarence Mauck was the senior officer on the field of battle and assumed command of the troops after Lewis fell. As darkness approached he called a cease-fire, pulled the troops together, and placed a strong guard around the camp, leaving some of the approaches to the canyon open. By morning the Indians were gone. The soldiers found one dead Cheyenne and then Mauck headed north, following the Cheyennes once again.

Brown and some others stayed behind to round up the Indian horses they had scattered. They found about sixty of them, well over two-thirds of the Cheyenne stock. Many of the horses were loaded with traveling packs, ready to flee. Brown cut one pack open and found it full of trinkets and a pair of buckskin gloves. He took the gloves and left the pack. At 9 A.M. in a small natural cove the horses were all shot down and killed.

The bacon sandwich is cold, but both the mashed and the baked potato have somehow disappeared between our new friend's many words.

"Had Lewis lived two hours longer, the Indians would have been captured," Maddux says. "He was the only officer who seemed vigorous enough in pursuit and ability to take advantage when it was offered to him."

I have been trying to listen to him, read through some of the piles of documents on the table, take notes, and gulp a meal in order to stave off my heavy hunger, all at the same time. I take a breath long enough to look up at Andy.

Some paper on the table has caught his eye. He studies it a moment and then passes it to me. It is a photocopy from the front page of the *Dodge City Times,* October 5, 1878.

A Dead Squaw

On the Indian trail five miles west of Cimarron and two miles north of the river lying within a few hundred yards of the trail on Saturday last was found the dead body of an aged squaw. The body was discovered by a Cimarron party, it being wrapped up in two blankets and covered with buffalo robes and placed on two poles or two sticks. Such was an Indian burial by a roving band striking terror where ever they go.

"What do you have there?" Maddux pauses to see what I am reading.

"Andrew's great-great-grandmother was killed on the way north," I say. "She was kicked by a horse while trying to break camp after some soldiers came upon them. We're trying to figure out where that might have happened."

"It wasn't her," Andy says.

"No?" I am disappointed. Some of the details match what we know of her death: near a river crossing, just off a main travel route.

"My aunts say she didn't die until several days after she was kicked," Andy says. "And that says it was an aged woman. She wasn't all that old."

"Hot dog," Maddux smiles. "I'm sure glad you people came along. I can't wait to show you the battle site in the morning."

The morning. If the way Andy looks is any indication, I must be dead dog tired. We say a quick goodnight and walk out of the Chaparral Restaurant. The night is hazy; a few of the brightest stars filter through thin clouds. Just before we open the door of the room I mutter, "I don't know what's going to happen with Sam." Andy does not answer me. Inside the television is blaring. Sam is fast asleep on the bed.

Andy and I are following Al Maddux's car north out of Scott City. We can see him chattering nonstop at Sam, who sits next to him.

Andy chuckles. "There's Mr. Maddux talking and talking about 'eighteen hundred and something,' and there's Sam thinking of that pretty girl who gave him a ride into Garden City," he says.

I laugh, but as we packed up to leave the motel early this morning, neither Andy nor Sam had spoken. Barbara, Carol, and Phoebe have remained at the motel to finish packing for their long drive home, while we are headed off for a tour of Punished Woman.

The early morning sun filters weakly through a hazy gauze of clouds. The landscape is as flat as we've seen it. Long low waves of hills spread out to the horizon like the ripples on a pond after a trout has just brushed the surface. The spring rain has been good to this dry land, where most tiny creeks disappear into shallow, nameless parched basins.

Maddux turns off the highway onto a side road, marked with a sign for a summer church camp. We cross a cattle guard and enter a sheltered area, different from the flat land around. Trees line a grassy field, and the dirt road begins to wind and twist a bit up into a range of hills.

Maddux stops his big American car next to some small barns at the edge of several cottonwood and box elder trees. Andy laughs again. "Yeah, he's talking eighteen hundreds and Sam a hundred miles away, thinking of that pretty girl." It is our established pattern: to repeat and laugh again at jokes and stories of the voyage.

The buildings of the summer camp are deserted, and we follow Maddux through the cottonwoods and out into a flat, plowed area, boxed on either side by a rocky cliff. This is where the troops entered the canyon, he tells us, and points down the long valley, to its boxed-in furthest edge, a half mile away. "Down there in a side canyon is where the Cheyenne were waiting."

We climb up out of the canyon to the ridge above the narrow valley. Andy walks with Maddux, listening as he explains where each company of troops was positioned and how they moved in on the trapped Cheyennes. Sam drifts out over the hills to the west, walking by himself.

Except for the cottonwoods, there are no trees, nor anything taller than my boot tops. All the same, the earth is green and growing. Everywhere the prairie is blooming. Single stars of bright yellow flowers flicker every few feet. Fainter, tiny blots of color rise up in the greening grasses. Pinwheels of flowers dot the land, and in the ravines the chokecherry bushes are spotted in white blooms.

The short grass itself is in bloom. Soft and golden in the diffused sun, it shakes with each light breeze. The grass is thickest on the top of the ridge, but even in the rocky vees that break back down to Punished Woman Creek, bunchgrass shoots up in small patches from the rocky soil.

The Cheyenne historian and author Margot Liberty told me that there is some evidence that Punished Woman is so named because it once served as the location of a brutal attack on a woman, probably given as a punishment for an infraction of tribal law. Trail cowboys knew these tormented cliffs and canyons as a cattle rustler's haunt. But their blood, and the smoke and screams of the

Battle of Punished Woman Fork have done nothing to stop the flow of flowers: asterlike fleabane; thin, solitary stalks of showy goldenrod; butterfly wings of blue flax; and out of the yucca's arsenal of dagger leaves, sabers of flower stems stab skyward.

The yucca's upward thrust is so dramatic that it would be easy to miss the spiny, crawling brittle prickly pear as it hugs the stony dirt were it not for its telltale flowers. The short, plump stem segments break easily away and give it its name. The camouflaged segments are so covered with thorns that except for sitting on one, or checking the ground to lay out a sleeping bag, the plant is hard to find except in spring, when its pale yellow flowers are glowing.

Maddux turns and from a distance calls out, "You're standing where the soldiers corralled their wagons." Sam and I are crossing a particularly level area. I pause over circle of flat stones laid out like symbols among the grass. Maddux is gesturing wildly. "Those stones are where Lewis had his field table," he shouts.

"Kind of a spooky place, *eh-nah?*" Sam says.

We walk single file, spread out in a line back toward the lip of the canyon. Andy and Maddux are in the lead, and Sam is far behind, his gait a limping and stuttering shuffle.

Soon Maddux and Andy are at a sharp pinnacle of land that juts out into the Punished Woman's narrow, flat valley. I walk out to them, and we tower fifty feet above the canyon's floor on a steep slope of large rocks. "Dull Knife and Little Wolf probably stood here and watched the troops coming," Maddux says. The view from this height of land is immense. We can see at least forty miles back over the flatlands toward Garden City and Dodge.

"They must have been waiting for something," Andy says.

"Well, this makes a pretty good place to have trapped the army," Maddux says. "If it had worked right."

From this point of rocks, watchers could have reported the soldiers' every move for hours in advance. They would have seen the scattered scouts spread out before the long lines of cavalry and foot soldiers. For hours they would have watched the clouds of dust rise above the long train of wagons.

"The Indians left a trail right up the floor of the canyon," Maddux says, swinging his arm back toward where we had left the cars an hour ago. "It led straight up the canyon here, around this point of rocks where we are, and straight up that narrow side canyon there." The rocks and caves of the side canyon made good protection, and with the added defense of freshly dug breastworks, this was the best defensive location in fifty miles. They had found buffalo here, and the women had quickly set about to cut and dry the meat while the men waited and prepared for the battle.

The plan was to lure the soldiers well into the small side canyon, wait until they all were bunched up in the narrowest place, and then fire down upon them.

"But someone didn't want to wait," Andy says.

Maddux nods. "Yes, sir, the scouts got as far as right below us here when someone shot at them from right about where we're standing."

"Maybe the young man who fired on them did it on purpose, as if to say, 'I can kill you all easily, but I won't,'" Andy says.

Just as he speaks, Sam arrives at the top of the mound. He says, "Is this where that kid shot at the soldiers?"

"Yes, sir," Maddux says again. "By the time the wagons had climbed up to the ridge top and been corralled, it was a pretty hot and heavy battle, with gunfire constantly."

The soldiers spread out and shot as they moved in skirmish lines toward the Cheyenne stronghold. The Cheyennes had limited ammunition, and Little Wolf told his men to hold their fire until he gave the order to shoot. He sat smoking a pipe as the bullets from the soldiers came in so thick that the dirt from shattered rocks covered him in dust. He called out to his men and encouraged them to be brave in the face of what now appeared to be certain annihilation.

When the soldiers were so close that they could be seen on the tall hills all around the Cheyennes, Little Wolf gave the order to fire and to let every shot count for a man. Three soldiers fell. One of them was riding a tall horse. It was Lewis. Although the battle continued until dark, the soldiers fell back after that. During the night the Cheyennes fled the canyon on foot. Three hundred men, women, and children were moving north on foot because now the horses had been lost.

Although he has been a wonderful guide, Maddux has walked far enough. After he turns around to head back to his car, Andy and I scramble down from the steep point into the canyon. Sam drifts away from us back across the open ridge top.

The side canyon that the Cheyennes had intended to use as a trap for the soldiers, but which then had become their own prison, is a steep slope of grass with jagged rocks the size of houses. The middle level of the canyon is rimmed by a cliff of tan stone. Above the cliff and at the highest edge, a steep slope marks the start of hills and ridges.

We walk across the mouth of the side canyon and then climb halfway up the far side, above the cliff. The top of the cliff forms a jumbled, naturally paved footpath, and we follow it to the head of the canyon. Andy walks to the far lip directly above the place where the abrupt cleft of rocks starts to form the canyon. Behind him only a gentle swale announces the top of the steep canyon. It was there where the horses had been before the soldiers found them and scattered them. "After this place the hard times began," Andy says. He moves to the lip of a large rock and peers over the edge. Directly below him the overhanging rocks have formed a natural shelter large enough to hold a hundred people or more. Andy stands a long time, studying the space. Many people must have hid here, as the shock of gunfire vibrated throughout the rocks. Their presence here is undeniable, and out of respect, the two of us talk in whispers.

"There must have been reasons to stay here," Andy says. "Important reasons. I think they stayed here not to attack but because they were waiting for something, or someone." The escaping Cheyennes often split into several smaller groups. Independently, these groups would move northward for a time, often fifty or more miles apart, and then rejoin at a predetermined place. This narrow gorge of the Punished Woman must have been one such rendezvous. "They had a good lead on the soldiers after the Arkansas River. They wouldn't have stayed here so long unless it was for a very important reason." Andy talks his thoughts out, scanning from the rock shelter to the canyon and to the far distance beyond. "They must have been waiting for a slower group, maybe the ones carrying the sacred buffalo hat. Only something that important would cause them to wait so long."

We linger here for a while and then roam the hills to the north for hours until at last we see Maddux's car stopped at the terminus of a jeep trail, where a lonely stone marker has been placed to commemorate the battle site. He is a good half mile away, but we can see him talking. He must have returned to town, found the women, and brought them here, for we see him talking to Carol and Phoebe. Barbara is walking along the top of the canyon, looking down toward the rock shelter. We head for them, but before they see us, Maddux has driven them away.

Sam reappears, limping slightly and climbing over rocks on a far edge of the canyon. We cross to meet him and together walk across the open prairie back toward the car.

A graceful movement, like that of a long scarf tied to the grass and undulating in a breeze, catches my attention just soon enough for me to leap over the fifteen-foot bull snake. My reflex carries me several strides further before I slow and turn around to look.

"That's a big one!" Sam says.

"Ahh!" Andy laughs. "Look at the size of him, will you!"

The living blanket of skin flaps in the still air, and my heart is pounding in my throat. Bull snakes are the largest snakes on the plains. The impressively powerful reptile will swell up, hiss, vibrate, and lunge at anything it perceives as a threat. Bull snakes will chase intruders for great distances, and although not poisonous, their bite is painful. They commonly grow to well over ten feet, with a girth as big as a man's leg. I had been lucky. This one is spread out flat. After several days of cool rain it had been soaking up the pale sunlight and had decided to ignore me. Its small head is sheltered by large, triangular scales. A pattern of brown and yellow blotches on keeled scales cover the incredibly wide, flat hide.

"I believe you've found the great-grandfather of every snake from here to Nebraska," Andy says. He is no longer laughing.

It is late afternoon. Mr. Maddux has gone home, and we have spent the last several hours walking from town, retracing on foot the route we drove this morning to Punished Woman Creek. Tired and slow after the long day, we have spread out our sleeping gear on the ground in a dark grove of giant cottonwoods.

There's a powwow going on over Sam. In the slow pace of their own time, Barbara and Andy have been seated on a picnic table, quietly discussing what to do. Carol is sitting in the front seat of Barbara's car. Phoebe and Sam are standing near a big cottonwood, talking. Sam turns away from her and walks over to his sleeping bag. He sits down and then stretches out, bending his thick, youthful arm over his eyes to shield the small speckles of late, hazy sunlight that filter through the canopy. He did not walk after the visit to Punished Woman, yet his limp is noticeably worse.

Barbara, who has walked a good eight or nine miles after the visit to the battle site, finally moves to her car. There is never a rush about things, and slowly – a word here, a check for luggage there – she prepares to leave.

Carol gets out of the car and comes to me. "Well," she says, "I'm sorry I have to go, but you know, things back at home . . ."

"I understand," I say. "I understand, and I'm sorry you have to go. I was getting used to our little community."

She smiles. "Me too. It has been good to see what those people went through. That battle place site today, it was a very powerful place." She shakes her head.

Phoebe has gone to the car. She stands, looking up at the towering trees, and then looks at Sam.

Sam has sat up on one elbow, watching.

Andy comes to where I am seated. He cups a lighter in his hand, lights a cigarette, and takes a small puff. We sit silently until I ask, "Is Sam going back with them?"

He shakes his head. "Uh-uh," he says. Another long silence as we watch the women busy themselves with preparations for the journey, then he begins again. "That Punished Woman place, that's a very special place. I want to go back there with my pipe after they leave." He has not mentioned his pipe since before the Turkey Springs battle site in Oklahoma. It never appeared then, and I have yet to see it. "This Punished Woman, it's a very powerful place," he repeats.

Here, at Scott Lake State Park Campground, a few miles beyond the site of the Punished Woman battle, three female descendants of survivors of that battle are about to return to Montana. Barbara walks over to us. We watch Phoebe a moment and then Barbara says, "She was a very intelligent woman, very smart. She still is; it's just so jumbled up now."

We stand and walk to the car. Sam has risen too and is getting hugged and kissed by Phoebe and Carol. Barbara gives him last-minute instructions on how to care for his leg and what to do if he needs money.

"If you need to come back . . ." she begins, then looks at me. "Well, if he needs to come back, I don't know what to suggest. Put him on a bus, I suppose. I'll be coming back to join you again later, but it'll be a few weeks."

"Me too," Phoebe says abruptly. "Me too!"

Carol shakes my hand. "Nice to meet you," she says.

There's more talk and hugs, and then they get in the car.

Phoebe gets in first. She climbs into the small back seat and then turns to look out at us and wave. Carol sits in the passenger seat, her head down. Barbara looks one more time at us, then gets in. "See you," she says though the open window and begins to drive away.

The last we see of them is Phoebe pressed against the glass of the rear window, her face as calm and ageless as a sculpted goddess. She does not notice me; she has not taken her eyes off her son, Sam.

The haze of the day has faded to a general pall, and the hidden, gray sun is low in the yellow sky. Andy and I are approaching the upper edge of Battle Canyon from the north jeep trail. He carries a long, slender cloth bag. I carry a water bottle, my rain coat, and in my shirt pocket, a plastic bag with the brown tobacco remains of a few bent cigarettes.

Ignited by the depth of Mr. Maddux's knowledge about Punished Woman, we have been talking about the differences between the oral and the written word. "I mean, he seemed to have every single thing ever written about this place," I say.

"He knew a lot about them people who fought here," Andy says, then he adds, "I wrote this book review once."

I wait.

"I wrote this review on a book about Cheyenne religion. I got in a bit of hot water because this book was reviewed all over the country and I apparently was the only one who didn't write a positive review."

In its typical way, our conversation drifts a bit before we come back to the main topic. When it does, we have nearly reached the end of the jeep road and can see the isolated stone marker just before us. "What didn't you like about the book?" I ask.

"The Cheyenne culture is an oral culture," Andy says. "All of our history, all of our stories, all the Cheyenne religion is spoken. Once someone comes and writes it down and says, 'This is what it is like,' it isn't the same anymore. Spoken words are alive. They breathe and change and can't be owned. Once someone writes things down, they try to own those words."

The winds comes up a little, and the approaching dusk is cool. We reach the lip of the canyon. "I know the tradition Mr. Maddux is coming from," I say. "My own history, and my own way of knowing, has all come from words that have been written down."

Andy nods. "I guess I should be thankful, since written words may someday be all we have of the way things used to be."

He stops because we have reached the canyon. Below us is the cave where the women and children had hidden during the battle. We listen to their fear and their courage in the whistling of the wind, then walk along the flagstone boulders to a flat place at the very head of the canyon. Andy sits and I sit beside him. With the careful familiarity of a father for his child, he removes the pipe from its cloth bag. The light-colored wooden stem is long enough to rest on his knee as he shows me the bowl. The stone is carved into a simple, smooth cylinder. The natural coloring of the rock has divided the bowl into lighter and darker shades of red.

"I like to think of this bowl as representing both my Indian side and my white side," Andy says, running his thumb over the colors. Reverent respect guides his motions, but there is no formality to his movements. "I am a Cheyenne," he says, his slender thumb tracing the darker half of the bowl, "and yet I can't forget there are things about me that are of the white world as well." He talks of his religious upbringing, of how he was partially raised as a Catholic. Then a Quaker man who had an association with the tribe made it possible for him to attend a Quaker high school in New Hampshire. In his twenties he had done a sundance. In the last several years he has attended ceremonies of the Native American Church. He talks of the importance to his life of religion and things spiritual. He talks of the holiness of this place and of the things that happened here. He talks, and the wind takes his words down the into the canyon of Punished Woman.

One of the great ironies of the world is that spirituality is the cause of extreme envy. Faced with the contradictions and failures of faith, humankind has raged countless wars to destroy the spiritual bonds of others. When the colonists saw how the Indians' religion provided their strength and unity, they outlawed sacred dances, or forced children into schools where they never heard their native tongue, or took away the tribe's right to determine who raises its children. For five hundred years such religious genocide has been rampant on this continent. The New Age movement, which encourages people to view the Indian culture as a spiritual mail-order house, continues the destruction. Armed with crystals and bone rattles, non-Indians flock to reservations seeking to fulfill a romanticized vision of spirituality. They do not try to gain a genuine understanding of the struggle, seldom try to address the issues of poverty, substance abuse, and violence, and can never understand Indian devotion. Armed with guilt, fueled by their own failures of faith, and driven by the envy of another's spirituality, they continue to usurp and to destroy the Indian religion.

Andy reaches into his coat pocket and removes a pouch of Velvet tobacco and a second pouch of Crown. "I thought I didn't have any tobacco," he says, "so I bought some this morning. Then I found this other. There must be a reason for having them both." He pauses and then hands the second pouch to me. We look into the rocky cleft below us. The ring of flat boulders that form the lip of the canyon spreads out in a V shape. From where we sit, we can see the point of land where the fighting began. "Tobacco is a sacred thing to the Cheyenne. You're welcomed to stay while I smoke, but take that tobacco and leave it someplace you saw today."

I take the tobacco and stand. Without further words I walk away to leave my friend to his own prayers. I know exactly where I will leave the pouch. As I pass near the rock shelter, I pause to remove a broken cigarette from the plastic bag in my shirt pocket. This I roll between my thumb and forefinger so the loose tobacco floats in the wind above the cave. I bow my head and say a prayer to the memory of those who died here, those who fought here to live, both white and red.

I walk on, staying along the upper edge of the canyon until the slope of a small side creek provides a steep scramble to the bottom. I move across the thin grass thick with wildflowers, kicking at the rocks and stomping a bit with my boots. It is the perfect time of day for rattlesnakes. I climb back up the other side of the canyon and walk along the berm of an earthen dam a rancher has built to create a pond for his cattle. The far side of the dam ends at a triangle of land, which is steep enough that I have to grab at handholds of rock in order to climb.

At the top I look to the distant south – the view is of thirty or forty miles across the dry basin land of western Kansas – and then closer, to the green swatch of Punished Woman Canyon, and closer yet to the narrow mouth of the battle canyon. The scouts would have come along just there. I kneel behind a boulder, but the view is obstructed. I try another, then another, and another until finally I discover the place. From the shelter of a little rock wall I can peer almost directly down to where the soldiers were to come. It is an ideal place to shoot at someone. I put the tobacco amid a cluster of yellow flowers on the ground and then stand.

Like the flowers, this tobacco is for the boy who hid here and fired the shot that started the battle. Like the flowers, this tobacco is for his youth, which nearly caused the destruction of so much, but without which the courage to endure would never have been found.

I turn to the north, to the long road still before us. It is for Sam, now, that I pray. For his youth has just as much dangerous pride as it has stubborn and ceaseless courage.

Although it is still quite light, the east is darkening in a low, gray sheet of night. My own youth is there, and I stand a moment at its passing.

I turn back to the west, to the place where some came to die and where the dust and the wind and the rain is all that remains of the people who once crossed this changeless land.

I stay awhile, then climb down the rocks to return.

Andy is standing on the flat stones above the cave when I climb back up to the top of the canyon. We pause a moment. "There's two kinds of religions," he says. "There's what you believe. And there's how you live your life."

We turn to walk away, and it is at that precise moment that I notice the movement. "What's that?" I say, pointing.

Bouncing up the rutted path, a black Jeep Cherokee kicks up a small trail of pebbles and stones. It reaches us and a man sticks his hand out the window. "You're the guys walking north? I'm – "

Two faces pop out from the back seat. "Is that them?" Two boys are clambering over the man at the window. They call out questions while wrestling at one another and for the handle of the back door. "Hey, mister, are you really walking all the way across Kansas? How far have you come so far? Hey, are you walking?"

"Tyler, just wait a moment," the man says calmly despite the tornado of boys at his back. "Ryan, stop interrupting." He turns again to me and reextends his hand. "I'm Rod Haxton. I run the Scott City paper and wonder if I could interview you guys."

I have learned my lesson after the last newspaper article. "Here's the guy you want to talk to," I say and point to Andy.

The car door opens and the two boys spill out. They turn their heads this way and that; their blind eyes peer uselessly into the sky and air.

I am driving, circling around Scott Lake State Park looking for a place to fill my water bottles. The two boys are in the back seat. We have left their father and his assistant seated at the campsite picnic table interviewing Andy and Sam.

Tyler Lane Haxton is three weeks shy of his thirteenth birthday. His words cram up against each other in a nonstop stream of soft, rapid sentences. "Most people can't understand me," Tyler says.

"Most people can't understand him," his eleven-year-old brother, Ryan, says, interrupting.

"I can understand," I say. "Really." For a few moments it was a bit hard, but as soon as I realize the "ums" and "you knows" are all bunched up in there as well, I have little difficulty following his fast speech. Sightless since birth, Tyler attends a school for the blind in Kansas City. It is a boarding school, but every other week or so he comes home for a visit. "My dad drives to come and get me."

"He drives to Kansas City from here every other week?"

"Sometimes every week," Tyler says.

"Sometimes he drives every week," Ryan interprets. "It's eight hours each way."

"At school a bully teased me because of the way I speak," Tyler says.

"Tyler beat up this guy because he was teasing him," Ryan says.

"Yeah, he doesn't tease me very much anymore."

"That showed him," Ryan says.

Both boys are insatiably inquisitive. They ask about my walk, about my life, about Sam and about Andy. "Andy sure has long hair, doesn't he?" Tyler says. Earlier they had felt his face and discovered his hair. "Does he ever get mistaken for a girl?" he asks.

"I don't think so," I say.

"Does he know how to shoot a bow and arrow?"

"He uses a rifle when he hunts."

"Wasn't it cool when he spoke in Indian for us?"

"It was neat when he spoke in Indian," Ryan repeats.

Tyler fingers items from the floor of the car, holds them in the air, and asks what they are.

Tyler loves stories of all kinds. He loves to listen to them, to tell them, and most of all, to read them. He has known braille and used it since he was old enough to read. "Dad taught it to me," he explains. "Dad reads to us a lot too."

"Tyler likes to read, but I don't like it as much," Ryan says. Ryan does like to write, however, which he does on a braille typewriter. "I want to grow up to be a writer, like my Dad."

"What else would you like to do when you grow up?" I ask.

Ryan pauses, thinking a moment. "I want to drive semi trucks," he says. He won't let the slight handicap of being blind get in his way. "I'll have somebody else do the driving," he says. "Maybe Dad will do it." Shorter by a foot than his brother, Ryan will be attending middle school next year. Both boys love to wrestle and have been on a number of teams for the blind. They have been to the state finals as wrestlers. "Our dad is the wrestling coach," Ryan says.

I shake my head. "Wait a minute," I say, "your dad runs a newspaper, drives to Kansas City three times a month, and coaches wrestling? You must have some family."

There is a rare pause of silence. "Our parents are divorced," Tyler says, and Ryan does not translate for him. "Dad got us and Mom kept the other kids. Dad owned a newspaper near Dodge, so we moved there. And now he owns this one here, too. Our grandparents are running the other newspaper."

"Who helps him with the paper here?" I ask.

"Oh, there's people like Curt," Ryan says, indicating the young man we left with the others back at the picnic table. "Dad went to the high school and asked for the smartest English student and found Curt and hired him on the spot. He's always doing stuff like that."

We drive slowly through the empty state park. A dark night has finally fallen, but no one minds, least of all Tyler and Ryan. "Tell us again about the Cheyenne," Tyler says. They listen carefully to how Dull Knife and Little Wolf led their people north. They struggle a little at the geography, trying to grasp the sense of immense distance the Northern Cheyennes had to travel. They want to know all about Little Wolf and how he led the young men in battle, and they quietly contemplate the details of Dull Knife's tragic attempts to protect the heritage of the tribe.

Their father is still sitting at the picnic table talking with Sam and Andy when we finally turn back into the campsite. The high school student, Curt, has placed a flashlight on the table and is busy taking notes. I stop the car and turn off the headlights. The dark night is complete. The boys open the back doors of the car and tumble out. "Careful . . ." I start to say, then stop.

Rod Haxton speaks to them, directing the two boys to the picnic table by his voice. They climb up on the table, chattering and sliding about. Rod clicks off a tape recorder he has been using. The interview is over. "Okay," he says, "we should go on and let these guys sleep."

There is another ten minutes of talk and handshakes before Rod herds his two boys into the Cherokee and he and Curt climb in. The vehicle is a turmoil of coats and jackets and wrestling pads and cameras and tape recorders and sweatshirts and boys.

"You look like you could use a little sleep too," I say.

He shakes his head. "Got to go write up this story. Tomorrow is deadline," he says. "Plus Ryan has a dentist appointment in Garden City – "

"I'm not going," Ryan says from the back seat.

Rod glances in the rearview mirror. He looks like he might respond, but instead says, "Did you guys have a good time meeting these people?"

"It was cool!" Ryan says.

Rod smiles.

"Hey, Dad," Tyler says. "Did you know Dull Knife tried to save all the children of the tribe?"

Rod's smile has not vanished. "He did? Now, that sounds like a good story."

17. The Rattlesnake Way

I have been walking only twenty minutes before I see the first rattlesnake. I jump back, then see that it is dead. An eight-foot western diamondback lies in the dirt road, the blood of its wounds still fresh. Most likely it had been warming itself in the light of the early morning sun when a truck or a car hit it. The ants have already found it. They crawl in and out of the jagged split that runs half the length of the snake's hide. I study its wedged-shape head and, as a last-minute thought, bend over and cut off its rattles as something to take home to my boys.

I am familiar with the way rattlesnakes sound – the dry buzz of bony leaves is unlike any other racket – and yet the first thing I do with the bud of its tail is to close my fist around it and shake. The sound I produce is a puny imitation: the castanets of ghosts, not the sharp report of a living snake. I inspect the rattle. It might be possible to mistake it for the dry seed pods of some innocuous small plant. The dun-colored tail is a series of small round beads. Eight, in this case, although I know the number of beads doesn't indicate its age.

Seeing a snake every couple of hours has been a regular part of each day, but I see this day's second snake, another rattlesnake, only five minutes later.

This one is a young one, only a foot in length. My bootstep may have disturbed it, but the way it races across the road a good two steps ahead of me makes me think it was simply trying to get across without becoming hawk food. Nevertheless, I become increasingly cautious.

There are around eight thousand venomous snake bites a year in the United States. Of those, about fifteen are fatal. Children accidentally picking up a poisonous snake are the ones most commonly bitten. Second to them are men, stomping about in snake country during the summer months. The main reason people die from a snake's bite is because of a lack of adequate medical treatment.

I am forced to ford a stream. I slip off my boots and wade the flood-swollen creek, which brushes against my knees. Ahead, the way north from Scott Lake is a lonely dirt path winding into low, sandy hills. One thing is for certain: if I am bitten by a snake today, even delayed treatment will be pretty hard to find. I am comforted a little by hoping that the snake venom remover in my pack will provide some safety. The gizmo looks like a yellow plastic hypodermic syringe and works like one in reverse. I have practiced placing the small end of the syringe on my skin and pressing the plunger. The intense suction pulls my skin into a tiny plastic reservoir. That suction would have to pull at a snake's poison well enough to save me.

I walk on, up into the hills. No cars had passed me on the asphalt road out of the campground, and none on the gravel road through the big park. Now it is even difficult to find fresh tire tracks on this tiny dirt road. A slender thread of a path slithers down a hillside back to the creek. A long ranch road. I can see the ranch buildings four miles off on the side of a hill.

I see the third snake well in advance. The cream-colored belly of a large gopher snake ripples slowly and stops at a clump of bunchgrass. I walk on through folded canyon land as the creek I am following winds its way down to the Smoky Hill River. I see two rough-legged hawks and then glimpse another, larger bird, perhaps an eagle, just as it disappears over the lip of a hillside.

I had been watching the large bird and daydreaming. I look down; some movement has caught my eye. Twenty feet ahead, the day's fourth snake is another rattler. It sits in a loose coil of loops in the warming morning sunlight. Since the second rattler, I have been walking with a rhythm of kicking steps to toss a small spray of rocks ahead of me. I'd rather alert the snakes to my coming than to hear their rattle, but I am far enough away from this dust-colored four-footer that it simply moves a coil now and then at my approach. I pick up a handful of gravel and skitter it along the dirt. I want to hear its rattle, but my missiles simply cause it to slide a few feet further into the center of the path, forcing me to cut a wide berth around its center-road territory.

Another hour and three bull snakes later, I find Andy and Sam waiting at the intersection of a side road. Both have had trouble reaching our rendezvous. The only road through this place for miles is closed and torn up for repairs. Andy has been walking, but Sam has spent the morning sitting in the car. "Sam says his ankle hurts too much to walk," Andy says. Sam glances up from where he sits in the car. He does not speak.

Andy points with his cigarette. "I was walking here a little whiles ago and I looked up and saw four eagles above me. They came right out of a canyon and circled above me."

I try to sound nonchalant. "See any snakes?" I ask.

Andy smiles. "Lots of snakes. How about you?"

"Lots. Three rattlers."

"I saw a bunch. I found me a good snake stick." He nods at a five-foot-tall branch the thickness of a baseball bat leaning against the car. "I killed one of them just over there." He indicates a patch of taller grass I had just crossed. "He didn't want to let me pass without a fight. He put up a pretty good one, till I whacked him with my stick." Andy smiles. "I put a root from a ground turnip in his mouth so he'd have something to chew on in the afterlife. Ah ha!" He laughs his short cough of a laugh and smiles again.

"I don't like to kill them," I say. "I've just been walking around them." Although we have rested here for ten minutes or better, neither of us is in a big hurry to start again.

Andy takes a short pull on his cigarette, his hand darting up to his lips and back down again. "My grandfather and I were out one time. We'd been riding all day when we came on this big old wall of rocks. Before we knew what was happening, we were racing each other to see who could reach it first. I got ahead of him and rode right up into this little place, right to the wall. I stopped and all around me I hear a buzzing and I suddenly realized I am in the middle of a rattlesnake New York City. There's rattlers everywhere. My grandfather, he just stopped and looked and then he called out, 'What are you going to do now?' I didn't know what to do, and my horse, he was standing as still as a statue. I climbed down and walked out of there in slow motion."

"What did you do about the horse?" I ask.

"He did the same thing as me. He stepped out of there on his tiptoes."

Several factors determine the severity of rattlesnake bites, and the seriousness can vary greatly. If the snake has recently inflicted a bite, it may not have a full load of poisons, and if the snake does not deliver a full blow, or the fangs glance off the skin at an angle, the victim may suffer only moderate effects from a strike. On the other hand, a rattlesnake can release as much as 90 percent of its toxins in a direct hit. The pain, which is immediate, is surprisingly mild at first, but grows to excruciating intensity within the first thirty minutes. The closest extremities, the toes or the fingers, quickly begin to tingle, and the face begins to tingle and become numb. There is a metallic, rubbery, or minty taste in the mouth, and the tongue and lips tingle. Next, tight clusters of dark skin might appear on the face, neck, and shoulders. There's nausea, vomiting, and hypotension as the skin around the bite begins to swell.

I leave my friends and walk on alone. The day is turning into a snake festival. I see two more bull snakes and a garter snake before I reach U.S. Highway 83.

A construction project has left the highway completely and eerily abandoned. The road itself is torn into piles of broken concrete and rocks. I cross the high Smoky Hill River on a partially demolished highway bridge, climb a hill, and turn east into open country at a deserted schoolhouse. The sun is high, but I have yet to see my first car of the day.

More solo miles through growing heat and exhaustion, featureless miles on pathless land or vacant county roads, miles broken only by another rendezvous with Andy and with Sam, who wakes sweating and grumpy from where he has been sleeping in the back seat of the car. They talk not to each other but only to me. Each one tries to outdo the other by telling stories of animals they have killed or seen killed, a competition of killing stories, a gruesome contest of blood tales.

Sam laughs. "One time me and a bunch of kids found this rattler," he starts, then repeats himself, "we found this big ol' rattler back behind some houses. We held it down with a stick and then we cut its jaw muscle, right here." He opens his mouth and places his fingers in the corners. "We cut that snake's mouth open so he couldn't close it, *eh-nah*? He went around trying to bite on things but he couldn't close his mouth." Sam laughs again.

Andy begins to chuckle, then starts his story. He says, "I had a snake-fighting turtle a little while ago while I was walking. I found him and picked him up. Then, when I saw the next rattler, I set him down in front of it." He laughs again. "He gave that rattler a run for his money. I called him 'Bingo.' Bingo the snake fighter."

"Where is Bingo?" I ask.

Andy shakes his head. "Oh, he ran off after getting hit by the snake a time or two, but he fought pretty good, that Bingo did. I had to finish the job with my trusty snake-killer stick." This he thumps on the ground a time or two. "Well, we ready to walk some more? 'Cept for you Sam, you go back in the car and get your beauty rest, *eh-nah?*"

Sam does not answer but slams the door shut and glares straight ahead, silently staring through the window.

I leave them. Through open, fenceless range and down tiny roads, I walk the afternoon away. A single car comes up on a lonely stretch of road and stops. It is an elderly man and woman. The man is a local widower, and he's been showing his girlfriend from Minnesota some of the sights. He knows about the Northern Cheyennes' plight. "Yeah," he says. "They passed right through here. Killed them some pioneers north of here." He drives on. They are the only people I will see all day.

I have already walked more today than on any previous day of the trip. I am exhausted and hot. My water bottles are nearly empty, and twice every hour I am forced to witness death's fanged face. The day has averaged a snake every fifteen minutes. Over half of those have been rattlesnakes.

I cross a flat but high divide between the Smoky Hill River and Hackberry Creek. I stop and take a quick inventory: I am about halfway through my journey. I try to concentrate on the view about me, but instead I drift back in time. I miss my family terribly, and our frequent phone conversations have only intensified my longing for them. I miss my house, the comfort of my wife's sweet arms. I drift forward in time across unknown miles and days until I see them again. I walk on, lost in the imaginings of time past and time to come.

The buzz is immediate, clear, and forceful. A full-grown diamondback sits coiled in the weeds, its arrowhead of triangular, shiny snout pointed at me. I jump away.

Nothing gets your mind back to the here and now better than a rattlesnake in the way.

The rattlesnake's venom consists mainly of proteins that cause the breakdown of body tissues and membranes. Because of the depth of the pit viper's bite, suction, even with the proper venom remover, can take out only a small trace of the poison. As soon as an hour after being bitten, reddish brown welts form on the grotesquely swelled limb. Bubbles of thin skin the size of golf balls form on the wound. The bubbles are filled with pools of black blood. Soon there may be uncontrollable nosebleeds, more reddish spots on the skin, and your urine comes out red with blood. You taste blood, spit blood, and watch your limb balloon dark purple with blood. You suffer from melena – the discharge of dark, tarry stools from a hemorrhage in the alimentary tract.

Some of the complex, poisonous proteins may have an affinity for one organ system, other proteins may be highly toxic to a different organ, and working together they may attack a third and so on, until some eighteen to thirty-two hours later the untreated victim dies. Death is usually the result of attacks on the pulmonary blood vessels: the heart drowns in its own blood.

When the three of us rejoin for a late afternoon break, our words are squeezed out through the exhaustion of too many miles in a day filled with vipers.

"The way to kill a snake is to hop back and forth on each foot," Andy says, waving his snake-killing stick before him. "You keep hopping back and forth and then you land a foot on its head." He stabs his stick at the dry dirt.

What little talk there is is all death and horror. Even the jokes smell of it.

"There was this pig," Sam begins, the low sun shining on his sweaty face. "There was this pig that caught a rattlesnake. He kept eating and eating that snake, and that snake, boy did he get mad. He wanted to bite that pig, but he couldn't reach it. That pig just keeps on eating that rattler until all that's left is the snake's head. The pig spits out the rattler's head and that head is on the ground snapping and biting, still trying to get that pig." Sam can't contain his giggles.

We are resting near a recently abandoned stone house in the sparse shade of two or three lonely trees on a small creek bed. There are still another few hours of light, and we agree to make one more push before setting up camp, but we are so tired that for a long while even this sparse and dark talk is better than walking.

"Today made me think of Sheep Woman," Andy says and then is silent.

After a pause I ask.

Andy stretches out a leg. He is sitting on the ground, his stick beside him. "Oh, Sheep Woman was a woman from the east who must've had a big problem with her family because she came west and found the most remote place to live. She lived way out on the reservation. She came into town only one time a year for supplies. She rode into town on a mule and led another mule for the supplies. She raised sheep. That's how she got her name."

I wait.

"A friend and I decided we would go and see her. We rode all day and then had to sleep out in the open. She lived way out there. The next morning we finally come on her place. We get down off our horses, and she's just as polite as can be. She makes us coffee and all the time she kept talking to this one mule as if was a person. That mule started getting nervous with our horses so close and started pawing the ground and making noises. 'Mind your manners,' Sheep Woman said to the mule. She kept saying things like that – she told it to behave many times, but that mule, he kept right on pawing the ground. Finally she pulls out a rifle and shoots it in the head, dead away!"

Sam bursts out in a staccato of short giggles. "Hee, hee, hee," he says. "She shot that mule right in the head!"

Andy is laughing too. "She talked to it just like it was a person," he repeats.

I am not laughing. The distance between my life and theirs has never seemed as great as it does now. These two men, raised in the open reservation lands of southeastern Montana, swap stories of raccoons chewing off legs caught in traps, of stray dogs shot for sport, of slitting the mouths of serpents, of blowing off the heads of mules, as if talking about the latest village gossip. I do not fault them their lack of sympathy, but I am bothered by how insignificant death seems to them. Granted, my own squeamish, citified, Disney-fed view of life and death is as unrealistic as it is romantic, but their laughter at death, the way suffering is cause for humor, combined with the stressful, snake-filled day is enough to make it seem like I am facing an unfathomable depth between our two worlds.

It is an hour later, and I am walking on a dirt road; there are shrubs of some kind growing in the bar ditch. The sun is low and brilliant yellow; its light stabs the amber hilltops and slices long brown shadows of them across the flats. Three miles ahead, winding in and out of those flats, is Hackberry Creek, where, after the camp chores of food and shelter, I can finally lie down. I have pushed myself so hard today in part because Sam is not walking and I feel somehow the burden of distance is on me. I have been walking for over twelve hours. By the time I reach the Hackberry the day's total will be thirty-two miles. "Thirty-two miles," I repeat out loud to the empty land.

Something is in the shrubs at the roadside. Parallel with me there is a rustling, then movement. This was neither snake nor deer nor bird. A skunk? Getting sprayed would be all I need to cap the day. I stop. The motion stops. A low, flat bundle of muscle slides from the weeds. It is a gray mammal with short, black legs. A long rope of something is in its mouth. It turns to face me. I recognize the unique black-and-white facial pattern. It is a badger, carrying a dead snake in its mouth. Although the snake's head has been eaten off, I can see a tan string of rattles on its tail.

The badger gives me a calm, dull stare and a mechanical flash of calculation: fight or flight? In an instant it is over, but for that heartbeat I face this potentially fierce, solitary animal. In its black eyes rests all of the wilderness of the prairie, all the infinite beauty, and all the harsh indifference.

It scurries across the road and into the far brush. There is no movement or rustling. When I pass the spot there is no further sign of the badger or of the headless rattlesnake in its mouth.

In another hour I reach the campsite. The Hackberry is a small creek here, but there the bowl of the valley will make a fine camp: some protection from storms, a chance to see wildlife, and good exposure to the east for morning warmth.

The car is parked just beyond a small wooden bridge over Hackberry Creek. Andy is in the driver's seat, the door is opened, and his feet rest on the road. Sam is in the back seat. Neither is speaking. I collapse into the front seat opposite Andy and gingerly remove my boots to free my feet, the sheer ecstasy of which silences me for a long moment. My companions still have not spoken. Andy sits smoking a cigarette and staring out the windshield. Finally he speaks.

"You ever see those pictures of Jimmy Carter before he was president and then see how much he aged in four years? The pictures of Dull Knife: he has that same look. I walked today until my pain was pretty bad, but it was nothing compared to them people. And Dull Knife, he had the responsibility of the entire future of the Cheyenne people to carry with him. All those other people who were depending on him . . ."

He falls silent again, and it is my turn to fill it with the story of the badger. I dwell on the rattlesnake and the jagged red circle where its head should have been.

"I lived in New York City for a while and had a job as a security guard," Andy says. "I saw people who had been shot or stabbed. I've seen all sorts of death, but something happens when a person sees the death blood of someone who has been killed. Suddenly it's no more macho and no more act – they change, I don't care who they are. After the way the Punished Woman battle happened, Dull Knife and them changed. Little Wolf was maybe the type who got wilder and more wanting to fight. He wanted to kill more."

"And Dull Knife more wanting to preserve life," I say.

"Yeah." Then a pause. Sam, who only grunted at my greeting, still has not spoken. Even as Andy says the words I want to scream at him to stop, but the words fill the evening like heat lightning in the gray dusk. "Sam, are you going to walk tomorrow, or are you going to sit around like a baby again?"

At first I am simply in awe at how quickly Sam is out of the car and yelling.

"Who you calling a baby?" he screams into the open door at

Andy's side. "I ain't no baby! You take that back." He sputters in Cheyenne.

Andy's voice is cool and smooth, but the words are raw gasoline on an open flame. "What else would you call it? We've been walking and you've slept all day and driven around in the car."

Sam has gone mad with rage. He snatches Andy's thick snake-killing stick from the hood of the car, raises it above his head, and shouts. "Get out of the car you fucker. Get out of the car and fight me! I'll show you who's a baby."

"Andy," I say.

"I'll fight you," Andy replies.

"Andy," I say, "don't."

Sam is dancing about the open door, twirling the heavy stick like a samurai weapon. "I ain't afraid of you. You ever fight my uncle, eh? You ever fight him? What do you say, eh?"

Andy swings his feet out of the open door. "You cannot ride in my car. Get your things out."

Sam flings the stick against the front fender. The sound is like a rifle shot. "I ain't afraid of you," he repeats. "Come on and fight me. Come on. Right now. Fight!"

"Andy," I say. "Stop this."

Instead Andy reaches into the back seat and shoves Sam's gym bag and bedroll out of the opened back door. At this, Sam becomes incomprehensible. He is sputtering and crying and yelling in both Cheyenne and English so that I catch only a few phrases as I get out of the car and cross to where he is.

"I'm walking with this white guy, not with you . . . Fight me . . . Come on . . . I'm strong, stronger than you."

Andy stands up out of the car. I race to stand between them and face Sam. I don't feel the rocks through my stockinged feet until later. He is trying to push past me, barking and spitting at Andy. I shout into his face, "Sam! Stop it. Right now. Stop." I make the most of the pause. "I don't care what happens, there's not going to be any fighting between us. You got that? None. Now go on and cool off." He hesitates. "Respect what I am saying," I repeat. "There will be no fighting. Respect my words."

He grabs at his belongings and throws them onto his back. He storms off, straight into the open range, still jabbering and fuming and yelling.

I turn to Andy. "You didn't have to push him so much. There's nothing we can do but bring him along until he feels like he can walk again."

Andy slowly sits back down in the car and I return to the passenger seat. He lights a cigarette and says, "I thought he could take being pushed like that."

"Look," I say, "feel free to pick on me, I don't mind, but lay off of Sam."

A silence, then, "I keep forgetting the two sides of me. The white way is people want things for themselves, and the Cheyenne way is different."

I can't think about it. I get out of the car and move to set up camp and start dinner. But while I listen to the rattle of bubbles hissing in the pot on my stove, I think how violence and the threat of violence is not bounded by race or time. That my two Cheyenne friends have nearly come to blows with one another instead of with me is an arbitrary result of chance. Circumstances will always arise. Had I been the one forced to ride today, or had I been the only one able to walk, or a thousand other chance circumstances, the venom could have struck first from my own heart. It is a solemn reflection as I wait for the meal to cook: I realize that, as the kicked gravel sets off a snake's rattle in advance, I can only survive anger and hatred by hearing its dry clatter in the shell of my own soul first.

I look up and the sky is deep, twilight blue ringed with towering golden thunderheads.

PART FIVE

Depredations

Ring out false pride in place and blood,
The civic slander and the spite;
Ring in the love of truth and right,
Ring in the common love of good.

TENNYSON, *In Memoriam*

I'm in the glory land way.
I been communin' with the Lord
And I'm in the glory land way.

MARI SANDOZ
in her unpublished notes "Cheyenne Route North:
By bus, Oct. 5, 1945."

18. New Morning (Remembering the Rivers)

Before there were roads, routes across the west were remembered by rivers. Maps and guidebooks for pioneers using the Oregon Trail noted with care and precision the names of creeks, streams, and rivers that would be crossed or that would serve as trail markers westward. Trappers and buffalo hunters found their way through unfamiliar land by learning the names and sequence of rivers from the native people of the area.

For the Northern Cheyennes, as for most Indians, even far distant rivers had names. The name wasn't always the same, for those traveling in distant territory often came to call a particular river or section of a river by a different one, but distances could be noted and a person could find his way as long as he could keep track of the rivers.

Before this trip I had not understood the significance of this information. Maps and descriptions of the exact route of the 1878 Northern Cheyenne trek were few, and the ones that dated from those days were nothing more than a frustrating jumble of lines showing the rivers and their forks. The route across an entire continent, it seemed, could be drawn on a scrap of paper just so long as you showed the rivers. There was no attempt at scale, so that distances of a hundred miles might be squeezed into a half inch, while drawn with great detail across half the page might be a stream only twenty miles long.

But now I understand. Now I too judge my progress by the rivers and streams I have crossed. As I sit making coffee on the banks of the flat Hackberry Creek before sunrise, I can click off their names as easily as the names of the months, and though I

The Northern Cheyennes who were put on trial for the deaths of the Kansas pioneers, in Dodge City, Kansas, April 1879. *Top row, from left:* Tangle Hair, Left Hand, Old Crow, unidentified man, Porcupine; *bottom row, from left:* Wild Hog, George Reynolds (interpreter), Noisy Walker, Blacksmith. Courtesy of Smithsonian Institution, photo no.92-270.

have not seen them before, I know which rivers lie ahead and the direction they should flow. I have come to note my progress and find my own way by remembering the rivers.

For Dull Knife, Little Wolf, and the other Northern Cheyennes, crossing the level bed of Hackberry Creek would have been a familiar experience. This was the southern edge of their homeland. Hunting the massive herds of buffalo that concentrated on this rich grassland, they had crossed these creeks many times before. Now, however, nearly everyone would have been on foot and struggling from exhaustion, having traveled day and night carrying babies, supplies, weapons, still running from the battle at Punished Woman Creek, thirty-five miles behind them.

Andy breaks the cold silence from the night before as I pour the coffee into our cups. "Those people had all they could do not to become desperate," he said. "All them people were on foot. Everything they owned is what they had on their backs. The horses were gone, and the soldiers were everywhere."

Within hours of his death, the telegraph had spread the word about Colonel Lewis and the battle at Punished Woman. Troops were being moved from forts all across the central plains. A noose of blue coat soldiers was closing. As many as thirteen thousand troops were shifted and mobilized to stop a band of Cheyennes that now numbered less than three hundred.

As a perfect dawn arrives, we talk of how desperation could easily lead to panic, errors of judgment, and even bloodshed. No one says it outright, but we know the near tragedy of last night's fight – like the actions of the Cheyennes who were to become reckless with fear and panic – had been out of our desperation and exhaustion. So now in our own much smaller way, we too are trying to survive and endure.

Andy begins joking, igniting Sam's infectious giggle. Two deer pass within a hundred yards of us, munching on the forage near the cottonwoods along the creek. Not a cloud is in the sky, and the heat this dome of cobalt blue predicts won't find us for hours yet. It is a new morning, and with delicate care the three of us are pushing desperation back as best we can.

As we pack up, Sam steps up to me. "Should I apologize to him?" he says.

"I think it would be a good idea," I say. "I know he feels bad about it too." Sam walks away. They do not talk, but I am hopeful that respect has returned to replace melancholy and anger.

We begin to walk, Sam included. Each of us will hike six miles, covering a new stretch of land before we reunite in a couple hours for one of our complex car shuttles.

With the sun still low on my right, I walk north. I am on a better-used road than any of yesterday's, although I have yet to see but a single car in thirty-six hours. The land around me is a big empty: flat land of endless grass, broken only by a few level fields of wheat ready for harvest, or of corn and milo no more than green spears on recently plowed gray earth.

My thoughts jump from one idea to the next. My mind is a monkey that insists on picking up each thought, then quickly tossing it aside for the next. I am thinking of Sam and Andy and of their harsh words last night, then I am thinking of my home and family, and then of the grass and trees. I am thinking of how dire are the acts of people fighting to survive, and then I am thinking of the day's journey ahead. I search the northern horizon for the small rise in the far distance. The Hackberry, where we had just camped, is the last major creek of the Smoky Hill watershed. And the Smoky Hill is the last river of the south. It flows east into the Kansas River, and the Kansas River flows east into the Missouri. The hill in the far distance ahead is the divide to the Solomon River basin. The Solomon, which we should reach by nightfall, is, for me, the first river of the north. It swings sharply northward and flows into the broad open watershed of the Platte River.

On the long slope toward that divide there is a flash, unmistakably that of the morning's sunlight on a car. Although the car is a good five miles away, for some reason I find myself searching the roadside for a place to hide. I stop and laugh. I'm turning into quite a paranoid man if I'm going to hide from the first car I've seen in a day. Five minutes later it crests a hill a mile away and stops. I can see motion – someone has gotten out of the car, stands next to it, then gets back in. It moves again and drops out of sight into a small valley. I can hear it spray gravel, and the dust of its tail floats up into the empty sky. It appears again, now just in front of me, climbing out of the valley and over a small rise. It is a brown sedan with a row of blue lights across the glimmering top. It slows. I stop. It stops. The door opens.

I know in an instant that I will have to be cautious with this one.

"I suppose you're going to tell me you're some kind of fucking Indian too?" The cop is in a sloppy uniform; a white T-shirt shows below his tan dress shirt. He wears no hat to cover his red hair. The freckles on his face are worn dark and cancerous.

"You met my companions, then?" I say.

"I thought they were wetbacks!" He is smiling as if it is a joke. "I didn't believe the boy. He didn't have no identification, so I stuck him in back there and made him sweat while I did a check on him. He said I'd find this white guy eventually he was walking with. Even after I frisked him I still didn't believe it," the cop says, not looking at me now, but off over my shoulder. "Let me get this straight: you're walking a thousand miles with a couple of *Indians*?" He spits the word as if it were an epithet.

I nod.

"Why in the hell would you want to do something like that?"

I give him a brief recounting of Little Wolf and Dull Knife's flight. He begins to smirk well before I am finished. I plow on, and I find myself downplaying the tragedy. "The group who were caught at Fort Robinson eventually tried to escape, and most of them were killed," I say, dismissing the event with a wave of my hand.

"So you hooked up with these Indians and just decided to walk that same way?"

"I started off alone," I say. "These other two guys joined me later." Then I add, "I wanted to see what it was like for those people and for the soldiers chasing them, so I decided to walk the route to find out."

He mocks puzzlement. "Oh. You don't know the two Indians?"

"I do now," I say. "We've been traveling together for two weeks. We're friends."

He smirks again, then leans over and spits to the ground, letting a long slobber of the stuff drift down from his mouth like putty. "Some people always want to talk about what a bad deal they think people get. It don't make any difference, it's all made up. Take that Holy Cost."

"The what?" I say.

"The Jews. They talk about the Holy Cost in Germany. There wasn't no Holy Cost. It just got made up so's the Jews could take over half the world. Same thing with Indians."

"Hitler had millions put to death." I say weakly, "The concentration camps, the . . ."

"There wasn't no Holy Cost for the Indians, either. Indians killed white women and children without mercy and lied every time they spoke to a white man. And what did they get for it? I'll tell you what they got: reservations and schools, which they let go all to hell so they could live off the rest of us by soaking up welfare." His face is inches from mine; his cheeks puff up as he speaks. "Holy Cost my ass. The Indians were just like those bastards in Oklahoma City: killing people and then crying that *we* destroyed *them*.

"You want my advice? Watch those two you're with." He snaps his arm upward, a cross between a salute and a feigned slap at my chest. "Go on out of here." He returns to the patrol car. He has left the motor running and the window is closed. He fishtails the car around on the gravel and drives back over the rise the way he came, as if to spread the truth of his twisted vision was the only reason he had ventured up and out of the familiar rivers of his small world.

19. The Final Indian Raid

It could be called anything: the Wagon Wheel Restaurant or Alice's or Town Cafe. The menu is the same flat western Kansas fare: beef, big red chunks of the stuff morning, noon, and night. I scan the waxed menu: corned beef hash, breakfast steak, sirloins and potatoes; roast beef, patty melts, a fancy reuben, the sandwich choices. Not a chicken nor a dolphin-free tuna. Not even a lowly peanut for a cowboy's boot to grind to butter.

Andy begins to laugh his soft throaty gurgle. We look at him. "I was just thinking of Sam and that Mr. Maddux guy."

I smile. Even though we all have memorized the lines that follow, they still seem funny.

"There's Mr. Maddux talking about eighteen hundred and something or other, and there's Sam a million miles away thinking of that pretty girl who gave him a ride."

Sam giggles short blasts of laughter. "Hee, hee, hee. She thought I was Mexican and started speaking Spanish," he says, repeating his lines on cue. "I say 'No, I'm Indian. I'm Cheyenne.' Then she started speaking English to me."

"But pretty?" I say.

"Mr. Maddux waving his hands in the air, saying, 'Here's this place and here's that place,' and ol' Sam there staring out the window wishing he was with that girl."

We are still laughing when the waitress comes to take our order. "And you?" She could also be the owner, and maybe the cook as well. She is of indeterminate middle age, wears red lipstick and framed glasses you'd see in the 1950s: small jeweled wings flying up from the corners of her eyes.

"I'll have a salad," I say.

"Chef's salad?"

"A dinner salad," I say.

She waits. Waits still. "And . . ."

"That's all, just a salad."

She pauses, tips her head to repeat the order. "One dinner salad," she says and pauses. "Anything to drink with that?"

The room is large. A high tin ceiling painted over a thousand times is a bleak, drab gray. Booths line the long wall, while a half dozen square tables fill the room. We are seated at the table at the front window. We are here to meet yet another reporter for an interview.

Andy can smoke in this place and inhales deeply before taking a long sip of coffee. "I'm losing track of these media people," he says. "Maybe it's time we . . ."

Someone enters the restaurant. She is a doughy woman, her plumpness not disguised by the ill-fitting dark dress suit she wears. Her hair is as red as the ketchup bottle on the table. Her eyes immediately seek mine. They are the eyes of a frightened deer, about to fight for its life against a pack of wild dogs.

"I'm here from the paper," she blurts out.

"I figured it was you," I say, standing. Andy and Sam look at me an instant and then rise as well. She smiles nervously and nods her head but does not shake our hands.

She sits. We sit.

The waitress returns. "Hi ya, Martha," she says and waits.

Martha, the reporter, grasps at the ally. "I'm just doing a story on him," she says. "He's passing through town. He's walking the Last Indian Raid route."

The waitress's eyebrows pop up over the winged glasses. "Ohh," she says, singing the word. "Ohhhh."

"Actually, all three of us are walking the route," I say. "These guys are descendants of those Indians."

"Mmmm," softer, then the waitress walks away, leaving the reporter to fend for herself.

"I brought my camera." Martha the Reporter is fumbling with a tape recorder as well as a pen and a notebook while trying to show me a big, bulky camera stuffed in her oversized purse. "I was so hoping you'd be dressed, well, like an Indian."

I laugh, but she is serious.

"Have you thought about dressing like one while you walk?" She is asking me the question. Andy is staring at the ceiling as his head waves slowly side to side. "You would seem so authentic then."

"Dressing like an Indian?" I ask. "No, I hadn't thought of that." Martha the Reporter starts the tape recorder, switches from pen to pencil, back to pen, mumbles a dozen false starts and finally begins with the standard question. "Tell me: Why you are doing this?" she asks. She means me; she has yet to look at Andy or Sam.

I go on automatic pilot. I repeat dates and names, places and events slowly so that she can write them down accurately. What happens after that is out of my control.

"You know, over in Oberlin they have the Last Indian Raid in Kansas Days the first week of July, every summer," she says suddenly looking up at me. "You could come for the parade!"

Andy pushes his chair back from the table. Sam leans his chin onto the checkered oilcloth and watches her.

"We can't do that," I say. "For one thing, my friends have to get back home." I tip my palms upward and point my fingertips at them. "You should be talking to them. It was their ancestors who came through here."

Martha the Reporter's shoulders grow stiff under the foam rubber pads of her dark suit. She turns abruptly in her seat, then tosses her head toward them like a dog flicking water from its fur. She faces me again.

"What are their names?" she asks.

I stammer. "Ask them."

This time only her head turns. Its pumpkin redness flashes an instant toward them, then drops to her pad. "What? Are? Your? Names?" she barks each word as if talking to men who are deaf.

"Samuel Spotted Elk Junior," Sam says.

"Han-ku-ol Sputty-duck One Ear," she repeats, while trying to write.

"No," Sam says and repeats his name. "I'd like you to include the 'Junior' because my father is Sam Spotted Elk Senior."

Martha the Reporter glances at me. "What's his name?" she whispers.

"Sam," I say. "Spotted Elk – like an elk with spots?"

"Junior," Sam says.

"Junior," I repeat.

She sighs and writes and then, nodding toward Andy, "What's his name?"

"Just ask him," I say.

"Does he understand English?" she asks.

"They speak it better than I do."

She clears her throat. "What? Is? Your? Name?" she shouts again.

Andy appears to be halfway toward Oklahoma, his chair is so far back from the table. He says his name in his usual soft, clear voice.

"Whaaat?" Now Martha the Reporter is screeching, shrugging her overstuffed foam shoulders and wriggling her pen at me. "What did he say?"

Andy stands and walks to the restroom, where he remains a long time.

Martha lets out a little yip, not unlike the sound a poodle might make dancing around on two hairless legs.

For a moment I talk again, tracing the history of events she seems to know only from what she has gathered by standing with ranchers and farmers, housewives and tourists to watch an annual summer parade. When I get to Dull Knife, Sam speaks up.

"Dull Knife was my great-great-grandfather," he says proudly.

Martha the Reporter's face is a cavern of teeth and confusion. Her pen slaps down on the tablet. "I can't understand a word of their language!" she says. I think she is about to cry, but instead she forces air through her nose in a snort of exasperation. "Look," she says at me, "what I really want to know is, What it is like to live in a tepee?"

I stare at her.

Sam stands and walks to join Andy in the bathroom.

"Well," I say at last. "It gets a little hard to find a place to plug in the VCR, but otherwise it's quite nice."

She begins to write, then stops, then writes again. She continues to question me, but I am trying to plot my own escape. Sam and Andy don't return to the table but pass by us and go to the register to pay.

I stand. Martha the Reporter stands. She is fumbling again with her purse. "My, my, my," she says without a trace of irony. "You know so much about Indians!"

Martha the Reporter barely touches my hand when she shakes

it good-bye. Although within feet, she and my friends simply look right through one another.

Only after she has backed from the curb and is driving down the wide, treeless main street of the small border town does Andy speak. "They thought what happened back then near Oberlin was the last Indian raid in Kansas. They were wrong: This interview today was it. This was the Final Indian Raid in Kansas."

20. Depredations on the Sappa

After the calamity at Punished Woman and the loss of their horses, a speedy retreat for the Northern Cheyennes was impossible. Now they traveled in a single large camp, the better to defend themselves. Small bands of men rode out on the few remaining horses in a wide circle around the group. Near a natural formation known locally as Chalk Pyramid, they passed within a mile of a sod house and stopped in sight of the pioneer family huddled in the earthen house. Unaware of the battle that had raged only twenty miles away at Punished Woman, the family watched the Indians pause for a short rest and then move over a low ridge like the remains of a gigantic brown buffalo robe being pulled by an invisible spirit across the yellow grass.

That family was just one of the thousands of hopeful pioneer families who had been drawn to the plains through the combination of railroad expansion and the promise of free land. In Kansas as well as the other plains states the population mushroomed in the 1870s. Because much of the best land of eastern Kansas and Nebraska had already been claimed by 1878, new streams of homesteaders were working their way up the rich bottomlands to the west. Along the banks of the larger rivers such as the Platte, the Kansas, and the Republican, small towns started to rise up from the plains, while even the tillable land on the smallest creeks was being occupied by an increasing number of new settlers. The muddy, twisting Sappa River in northwestern Kansas was one such creek. In just a few years the entire landscape along its winding banks had been transformed from prairie wilderness to farmstead.

That transformation began during the earliest years of the decade with the influx of profit-motivated professional buffalo hunters. Conflicts between buffalo hunters and the Plains Indians were not uncommon. One such tragedy – typical of the brief history of Cheyenne-white relations – happened three years before Dull Knife and Little Wolf crossed the Sappa watershed on their trek north.

In the spring of 1875 the Sappa Valley was largely unsettled and was still a good place to find buffalo. In April Cheyenne Indians and buffalo hunters were both in the area in search of bison. Because of a battle further south in the Texas panhandle, a command of soldiers had been dispatched from a nearby fort to look for Indians. The soldiers met up with a party of hunters, who reported that some Cheyennes had just robbed their unguarded camp. As they led the soldiers north toward the Sappa, the buffalo hunters grew uneasy. Even though no Indians had been seen, they could read the signs: the small herds of buffalo were huddled on high ground, antelope were jittery, coyotes were silent, and the prairie dogs were shy and nervous. The soldiers and hunters cautiously moved on until, at dawn, they came upon a camp of sixty to one hundred Cheyenne men, women, and children hidden in a steep embankment on the Sappa. The Cheyennes, under the leadership of Spotted Horse and others, were unaware they had been followed.

The soldiers raced down the steep embankment and slogged across the crooked Sappa River until they came full upon the camp. The officer in command noted that most of the Cheyennes were sleeping. Many women and children were bedded down in the natural shelter of a large shallow hole. A half dozen Indians moved to protect the horses, while the troop deployed in a skirmish line. At a range as close as fifteen feet, the firing began. The Cheyennes clustered in a semicircle around the largest of the holes, trying to protect the inhabitants while the troop surrounded them. The intense firing lasted only twenty minutes. The troops then fell back until the firing from the hole stopped. After a long silence the troops rushed to the pit, firing as they ran.

Like any event of the past, the portrait of what exactly happened in the next moments of the battle on the Sappa will never be written. The sparse record of the combatants suggests that a limited number of Cheyennes fell that day at the hands of soldiers. Other early accounts, given by men who were nearby but not present, paint a darker picture. Those accounts claim that after the initial volley, a small party of Cheyennes came forward carrying a flag of truce. As soon as they were in sight, the buffalo hunters opened fire; the troops followed with their own gunfire. A little later another group of about a dozen women came forward waving a white cloth. They were all killed. After the soldiers had charged the hole and the people were either dead or wounded, the buffalo hunters built a large fire in the hole. They raised it to a sputtering inferno with tepee poles, hides, and the bodies of the dead and wounded Cheyennes.

This version of events states that it was soon discovered that many women and children had hidden themselves in the sand of another large hole. These were dragged out, "clubbed into insensibility and thrown on the fire." The smell of burning flesh caused many of the soldiers to flee back to their camp. Others remained to loot the camp.

The combatants' story is different. The commanding officer reported that all the Cheyennes were killed, but of the sixty to one hundred Cheyennes reported in the camp, he acknowledged only twenty-seven dead, including "8 squaws and children unavoidably killed by shots intended for the warriors."

The combatants of the battle soon gained recognition and respect for fighting off the dreaded Cheyennes. For years neither the buffalo hunters nor the soldiers spoke much about the battle, which was largely forgotten until one of the hunters, Henry Campbell, and a sergeant named Platten finally spoke at length about the massacre. Platten admitted he had disobeyed a direct order to kill a woman and child and to throw their bodies onto the fire. Campbell said when he returned the next day he counted between seventy and eighty bodies.

After the Battle of Cheyenne Hole, as it came to be known, General John Pope, commander of the Division of the Missouri, said, "It is believed that the punishment inflicted upon this band of Cheyenne will go far to deter the tribe from the commission of such atrocities in the future as have characterized it in the past."

Just three years after the battle at Cheyenne Hole, Dull Knife and Little Wolf's band of Cheyennes reached the same place on the Sappa where so many had died. The change in the landscape was dramatic. Where only a few years earlier massive herds of buffalo thundered across open virgin soil, now black cubes of sod houses were sprinkled over plowed fields.

These 1878 pioneers were so recently settled along the Sappa

that few were aware of the bloody battle that had occurred at
Cheyenne Hole only three years earlier. The Cheyennes, however, had not forgotten. Dull Knife and Little Wolf crossed the
Sappa on September 30, 1878. Instead of continuing the single-
minded march northward, the unity of resolve shattered when the
young men rode out in search of horses. Probably angered at the
memory of the earlier massacre at Cheyenne Hole, and in desperate need of horses, men swept up and down the Sappa in a chaotic
forty-eight-hour dance of rage. Blood was repaid with blood, and
a terrible anarchy was once again loosed upon the land of the
Sappa.

During the next three days, thirty-two pioneers would die at the
hands of the Cheyennes. Later a commission would be appointed
to report all of the particulars of "the murders of citizens by the Indians who escaped from the custody of the United States." The
commission wrote:

> Not only was their stock stolen or killed, their feed and provi-
> sions taken or destroyed, furniture and dwellings broken and
> demolished, wells filled with dead poultry, men shot down on
> the road, or at their homes; but women and girls (in some cases
> mothers with babes in their arms) were taken and repeatedly
> and most horribly outraged by these demons, after they had
> murdered in cold blood their husbands, brothers and sons.
> Others escaped with their children by fleeing and hiding in the
> hollows and bushes, where they remained for days without
> food, drink or shelter, with scarcely clothing to cover their
> bodies.

Thirty-two pioneers would die, including George Simmons,
"colored, from Tennessee," a freed slave working as a cowboy. He
had tried to save his boss's favorite mules when a bullet fired from
one of the Cheyennes struck him in the head.

Still others suffered great loss and then were left to grieve. But
perhaps no one suffered more than Julia Laing, who had immi-
grated from eastern Canada to Kansas with her husband, William.
They had built a sod dugout in Decatur County and had scratched
out the life common to pioneers.

Her husband, William Laing, had been born in Scotland in

1826, the third son of William Laing and Euphemia Grierson. His parents had emigrated to Canada in 1848 and settled in Wellington County, Ontario. While in Ontario William married Julia Ingle, daughter of John Ingle and Catherine Personne. They built a log cabin on a one-hundred-acre plot of land in the Ontario township of Wawanoah – the name is a Chippewa word meaning "peaceful waters." After the accidental death of their firstborn child from a head injury, they moved to the open prairies of eastern Nebraska to stake a homestead on the new frontier. Within a few years Laing listed his personal worth at twelve hundred dollars in real estate and five hundred dollars in personal property. He had six children: three boys and three girls.

William Laing was a stocky, muscular man with broad shoulders and an equally wide jaw. His square chin jutted out, highlighting his oversize lower lip. His eyes, however, were his most arresting feature. Narrowly set with a fold of puffy skin beneath, his haunting eyes seemed to thrust forward as if his entire body would momentarily lunge into the air. His sons' faces mimicked his somewhat dour and stern features. The chin of his son William III was an exact replica of his father's, while the two younger boys, John and Freeman, had the same piercing eyes.

Daughters Julia, Mary, and Elizabeth were spared William's looks. For the most part they took after their mother, whose oval face and sensitive mouth were in sharp contrast to her husband's.

When they moved to western Kansas in 1877 the Laings dug into a steep hillside on a bank just above the Sappa River to create the back half of their sod house. Though surrounded by darkened earth walls, the house was comfortable and well furnished. Outside, William's lifelong skill with stock was evident in the yard full of chickens, hogs, cattle, and horses.

At dawn on September 30, 1878, William and his youngest son, Freeman, along with two neighbor girls, hitched up two of his horses and climbed into a wagon. They were going to the land office in Kirwin, Kansas, to register his land claim.

According to the *Hayes (KS) Sentinel* of November 23, 1878, at about 8:30, as they neared the homestead of Jacob Keiffer, a dozen mounted Cheyennes approached them at a gallop and surrounded the wagon. Within moments the Indians opened fire, killing William and his son. William fell into the lap of one of the girls, and fifteen-year-old Freeman fell forward to the floor of the wagon.

The girls were forced to the ground and made to hold the horses while the Indians ransacked the wagon. They were then taken to a nearby creek, where other Cheyennes were waiting. When the girls stumbled up to the Keiffer homestead two hours later they were stark naked. Their bodies were covered with bruises. Although the report of the girls' being raped at least a dozen times is probably an exaggeration, they had been sexually assaulted and beaten.

Thirty-eight-year-old Julia Laing was unaware of her husband's death when, later that day, some Cheyennes rode up to the Laing dugout. Julia watched from the doorway as the Cheyennes first shot her son Billy and then John. She bolted the door but the Indians broke it down. One source claims the seven-year-old daughter was unharmed but that Julia was raped five times, the twelve-year-old four times, and the nine-year-old three. The Cheyennes trashed the dugout. They smashed their way through all of the Laings' belongings. The stove, its fires still hot from the morning's baking, was thrown over and the stovepipe kicked about the room like a snake. The clock, three beds, dishes and bowls, water pitchers, and pans flew about the room. They were about to set the cabin on fire when an older Cheyenne with thick, long hair – probably Dull Knife himself – stopped them and released the women. Julia and her daughters left the ruined cabin and the bodies of Billy and John and walked eight miles before they reached the Keiffer homestead, where Julia was greeted by the bodies of her husband and youngest son.

Julia Laing collapsed. For the next six weeks she did not eat, or speak, or move.

The next spring the commission was formed to hear claims and recommend monetary awards to citizens affected by the raid. Though too ill to attend, Julia Laing was awarded $1,739.96 to repay items she lost. The list of lost items was an inventory of a homesteader's wealth: one sewing machine, feather beds, four sheets, carpenter tools, $400 cash, seven tons of hay, one plow, quilts, a stove, a clock, and two silk handkerchiefs. The items taken from the Laings were typical of what other pioneers in Decatur and Rawlins counties lost that day. Much of what was taken would provide sustenance for the hungry Cheyennes: chickens, dried fruit, bacon, tea and coffee, potatoes, one stew pan, flour, rye, and wheat. The Laings' list of lost property is also a cold testimony to a day of horror: one wagon, two horses, two pairs of overalls, a shot gun, a revolver. The commission awarded Julia Laing $5.00 for underclothes.

As soon as she could travel, Julia and her daughters returned to Ontario to live with Julia's brother John Ingle on the Bruce Peninsula. Julia died in 1931 and is buried at Eden Mills, Ontario. The longest-surviving daughter lived until 1961. All three daughters are buried in Ontario.

Seventeen men were killed in Decatur County that Monday, and thirteen were killed the next day in neighboring Rawlins County. Others survived. One of the last survivors of the Cheyenne raid was Charlie Janosek, who had been an infant in 1878. When the Cheyennes reached Charlie's parents' homestead, his father grabbed him and ran from the dugout. The slug that passed though his father's brain cut a deep path in the skin on Charlie's forehead. For his entire life Charlie bore a dark purple slash just below his hairline, left there from the bullet that killed his father. Charlie Janosek died in Kansas in the 1970s.

In 1932, on a recently exposed muddy bank of the North Sappa River, a rancher stumbled across the white bones of a human skeleton. The rancher who found it did the only thing he could think of at the time: he rode on in to nearby Achilles and found someone who had a telephone. From there he called the physician in Oberlin. The doctor came out the next morning and recovered the remains. He found the skeleton of a mature Indian woman of short stature, about five feet tall. He estimated the body had been buried fifty or sixty years earlier, or sometime between 1872 and 1882. It was found about six miles below the site of the Cheyenne Hole Massacre of April 20, 1875, and very close to where Dull Knife, Little Wolf, and their band of three hundred Cheyennes crossed the river on September 30, 1878.

21. The Pride of Oberlin, Kansas

Penn Street in Oberlin may be the most beautiful entrance to any small town in America. First of all, it is a brick street, and the bricks are a deep, earthy red, polished to a glossy sheen from a century of use. Penn Street marks the north entrance to town. The street begins at the top of a small ridge above the pretty Sappa — pronounced "Sappie" by the locals. From the highway it drops down into the river's valley and then widens to include two shaded blocks of calming and green boulevard.

Just there stands the pioneer memorial statue. A woman and a man stand back to back; to one side is a young girl, to the other, a boy. The man is looking up, the woman down.

The boulevard shelters clean, neat houses and inviting yards, graceful reminders that the true value of a place is always a matter of the heart. And there is a reverence here for the artifacts of history.

Beyond the boulevard of homes is downtown Oberlin. At either side of the two downtown blocks are tidy brick storefronts and bank buildings of a gray local limestone. Cars are parked diagonally along the curb. Wooden portals cover the walks that line both sides of the meadow-sized street, and folks stroll down the portals in an easy, unhurried pace with plenty of time to stop for friendly conversation.

At the end of Penn Street is a jewel in the bright crown of this lovely town: the Decatur County Museum. It would be easy to miss the modern, shingled storefront except for the collection of historic sheds, farm implements, and structures in the lot next to the building. Inside, Director Fonda Farr listens carefully to Andy and Sam tell their stories.

I head for the "Last Indian Raid in Kansas" room just off the main entrance. The room is a tasteful and informative display of the tragedies that befell the white settlers of the area, and a fair representation of the plight of the Northern Cheyennes.

We spend delightful hours at the museum. A reporter arrives, and despite our latest escapade, Andy says he is learning how to speak to these people and he and Sam sit down for an interview.

Fonda Farr talks to me of the unusual visitors she has gotten over the years. "A great many descendants of pioneers who were killed have stopped here," she says, "but this is the first time we've had relatives of Dull Knife's."

"Oh, no, it isn't. We've had others," her assistant curator, Cyndy Dolan speaks up from a nearby desk. "Remember those people a few years ago? The older man?"

"It might have been Ted Risingsun," I say.

"Yes," Fonda says. "Yes, I remember." Like any good historian, Fonda wants to find an artifact to prove or disprove the theory but resists the urge to start flipping though the thick pages of signatures and dates of the guest register perched on the barred wooden teller's desk nearby.

"This is quite a pretty town," I say.

Both of them smile. "Yes," Fonda says, "people take a lot of pride in this town."

Sam and Andy are finished with the reporter, and after we linger awhile more at the museum, it is time to move on. Outside, the midday sun is bright and warm. We walk back up Penn Street to the top of the ridge. Although neither Sam nor Andy seem anxious to do so, I want to see the cemetery and convince them we have to stop there.

While most of the through traffic on U.S. 36 zips right by Penn Street and never turns toward the lovely downtown, the highway goes directly past the inviting hilltop of flowers, trees, and tidy rows of white stones that mark Oberlin's cemetery. The cemetery at Oberlin is as pretty as the rest of the handsome town. The cool, manicured trees might be mistaken for a park.

Close to the highway a pale white memorial rises from among a square of low white tombstones. In 1900 the state legislature appropriated fifteen hundred dollars, and the citizens of Decatur County two hundred dollars, to build a monument to the pioneers who died during the Cheyenne exodus. The monument was dedicated on September 30, 1901, twenty-three years to the day after the county was ravaged by the Northern Cheyennes. On each side of the base of the monument are the names of the seventeen men and boys killed in Decatur County that day. Many of them are buried within feet of the marker, their identical, ancient white markers melting back into the earth. A few days after the massacre the names were carved into these tombstones of local, soft limestone by the man the tiny town considered best qualified: the barber. Some stones are so worn the names are nearly gone.

I turn to say something, but my companions are not there. They stand at the entrance to the cemetery. "You should see this," I call to them, but they do not acknowledge my shouts. Sam is leaning against a tree with his back toward me, and Andy stares off toward the south as if he is somewhere far away. I begin to call out again, but stop myself. Clearly, they have made a choice not to enter this ground, but whether it is to honor the pioneer dead, or to respect the memory of their own ancestors, is not certain. When I walk back to them all Andy says is, "The Cheyenne warned there would be violence, and it happened."

We walk out of the cemetery. "Pretty town," I say.

"Yeah," Andy says. "It's clear the people here really look after things."

I nod in agreement. In addition to our talks of distances, jokes, weather, stories, and simple grunts of acknowledgment, we have established a continuous dialogue of ideas that we seem able to resume at a moment's notice. Lately the three of us have been talking about how pride so affects the deeds of humankind. Most of the time the effect is negative, but not here. There seems to be a lot of "good" pride in Oberlin.

Towns like Oberlin survive and flourish on dignity, not vanity. The difference lies, in part, in how such self-awareness affects others. Almost without exception people who live in Oberlin spend a great deal of thought in how their homes look. Whether a house sports a thick carpet of suburban-style lawn or a natural arrangement of prairie grasses and carefully tended wildflowers, this community of six thousand is a charming, inviting place to live because of this good kind of pride. "There is a difference between eating and drinking for strength and from mere gluttony," Thoreau says, and so it is with pride. The best kind gives us strength to endure an otherwise cold wilderness of arrogance, conceit, and immodesty. Good pride is glory taken in appreciation of our humble place in the world. It is how we preserve what is beautiful, whether town or wilderness, artifact or culture.

Dull Knife, Little Wolf, and the other Cheyenne leaders understood. So too did the Laings and the other pioneers of Oberlin. They understood that the future was a matter not just of survival but of survival with dignity. The very future of the Cheyennes depended on how many could survive the march north, and though constantly challenged, the Cheyennes seldom let that future be compromised by desperation. Through the bloody Sappa Valley Dull Knife moved the people northward across a world that had changed remarkably during his lifetime. While some Cheyennes and some pioneers lost control and grew desperate with arrogance and self-righteousness – the very heart of "bad" pride – Dull Knife let the vision of a future for the Cheyenne people guide him. He continued to move his people north in order to find a place where the Cheyennes could pay homage to the land they knew as home.

Little Wolf too knew the good pride of survival with dignity. The chaos of the journey brought out the best in him as well. His strategic skills helped save the people at Turkey Springs, it helped them escape from Punished Woman, and it would serve those who would survive the coming long, icy winter when he hid 120 of them in an invisible canyon in the midst of an entire army. With calm, clear authority, he directed movements and battles; with a leadership that never faltered over vainglory, never was clouded by ego, he earned the greatest honor of all: survival.

The great problem with the world is that pride comes most often as righteous indignation falsely born of self-importance. Such pride festers in the soul until we grow desperate with desire for money, power, and immortality. The outward manifestation of such false pride is displayed in civic pomposity that pretends that a blighted strip of neon-emblazoned fast food shops represents progress. Worse: it is the glimmering casinos that pour money not into the hands of the poorest families on reservations but into the gaping gullets of the most corrupt.

Such desolate landscapes are communal manifestations of the bad pride found in individuals. Dull Knife and Little Wolf had such pride as this too, and it surfaced often in their human lives as it does in us all, but for a precious time they and many others triumphed over the power of this other, this darker pride. When it mattered the most they suffered with great courage and strength in order to preserve life for those who would come later.

I am hiking west from pretty Oberlin. The land is in long, alpha-wave hills, and where those hills grow deep enough, abrupt twenty-foot banks open on flat, grassy draws: green and golden chutes sliding south down to the Sappa or to Beaver Creek on the north. The Beaver is a tree-lined thread four miles distant. It is easy to see how warriors could ride up and out of the Sappa and down to the Beaver, where the Northern Cheyennes killed additional pioneers. Andy thinks they rode single file, although these valleys are wide enough for several riders to move abreast of one another.

I cross Hundred Head Draw. A mile off the highway and near the top of the draw I search and locate a stone marker. It reads:

> October 1, 1878. A party of Northern Cheyenne Indians from the Indian Territory crossed the Beaver Creek on the way North between what is now Atwood and what is now Herndon. They killed 12 white men on the Beaver. . . . An Indian boy about 18 years old was wounded and left behind by the Indians on what has since been known as Hundred Head Draw near where this stone stands. He was killed on this spot on November 13, by Abbott and Harney who were herding cattle here. The body was never removed except by coyotes.

At the bottom are the initials of the superintendent of the railroad who had the stone erected in 1900. The boy, who was probably closer to fourteen, had been shot in the leg or hip and couldn't travel. Hastily, he had been placed in the shelter of some rocks where there was water. A beef cow had been killed and dragged near. He had been given a knife and a blanket and then the rest rode quickly on. If they managed words at all, his parents could only speak briefly. There was no time for tears, none even for grief before the boy was alone. Dragging his immobile torso, he could move only by pulling himself along the ground on his elbows. He moved only the few feet from the shelter of rocks to the rotting beef or to the dribble of water nearby.

For six and a half weeks the paralyzed boy was alone here. Imprisoned in this grassy cell he fought the demons of chronic pain, loneliness, boredom, and the most devious devil of them all: fear of death. There would have been precious little hope to cling to. No one was coming back for him, this he knew, which meant his only salvation was to be discovered by whites whose punishment would be quick.

Alone, he waited.

One cold morning he watched as the two cowboys edged closer and closer to his hiding place. Later, the men said the boy had cried out and brandished a rifle. They shot him dead and discovered the "rifle" was simply a leg bone from the cow.

It is not the accumulation of details that make a thing real, nor the artifacts, for they serve as evidence only to events. It is rather the words from another time that are carried in the wind; it is the whisper we hear in that breeze, the murmur of voices who knew of us long before we were born.

History is the sigh of pride on the wind.

PART SIX

In the Time of the Buffalo

Each blade of grass has its spot on earth whence
it draws its life, its strength; and so is man rooted
to the land from which he draws his faith together
with his life.

JOSEPH CONRAD, *Lord Jim*

22. In the Time of the Buffalo

On the flat divide ten miles north of Beaver Creek are a series of sharp canyons dipping abruptly northward to the Republican River and the border of Nebraska. In October 1878, with the hope of finding fresh horses and the memory of the bounty of this area, the weary Cheyennes climbed down those canyons into the great buffalo land.

With no imagination it could be buffalo land yet. I have crossed the Republican and am north of Benkelman, Nebraska, where the prairie rolls as far as the eye can travel. It is short-grass prairie: big patches of golden-white tips throwing sheets of light across the darker shades of other grasses, silver-green sage not yet in bloom, the sandy edges of countless rolling hills thick in forests of yucca, until with distance the jumble of grassy hills flattens to a single vast horizon, its enormousness only dwarfed by the immeasurable sky, the ceaseless wind.

I hike along the major creek of this part of the county, the route the Cheyennes followed as they headed for a camp on Frenchman River. The Frenchman River was a familiar place for the Cheyennes to camp, for often they had come here for buffalo. Now, however, they had been running for twenty-three days; they had traveled 450 miles mostly on foot, eating what little they could find on the once buffalo-carpeted prairie. They stopped only for a day on the Frenchman.

In the morning, warriors reported seeing troops nearby, so the Cheyennes split up into small groups. Some moved twenty miles further to a small river whose very name foretold the disaster that by then was spelling the end of the old ways of life. Flowing through the heart of what had once been the richest buffalo grounds on the

Lieutenant W. P. Clark, the man who kept his word to Little Wolf and saw to it that the Northern Cheyennes could remain in Montana. He is pictured here in 1879 with the Sioux chief Little Hawk, who was not involved with the Cheyenne Exodus. Courtesy of Smithsonian Institution, photo no.365-K.

continent, the Stinking Water Creek had been named for the thousands of buffalo carcasses left to rot on its banks by non-Indian hunters.

With the demise of the buffalo, Indian culture on the plains changed forever. A new life would have to be shaped where once the buffalo had held the center. From the sacredness of the buffalo hat to the practicality of the buffalo chip, Cheyenne culture, like that of all Plains Indians, had evolved from a long association with the bison.

The Cheyenne tribe is made up of the descendants of two ancient tribes. Perhaps as late as 1700 the Cheyennes lived in more permanent villages further east, near the Mississippi River in present-day Minnesota, cultivating fields and occasionally venturing out in search of buffalo. Around 1700 the Cheyennes joined together with another tribe in that region, the Suhtais, who spoke a similar language, to form a single tribe. While there were distinctions in language, custom, and heritage, enough similarities existed that the two groups easily melded together. With the arrival of the horse, the Cheyennes moved further west to occupy the great buffalo lands of the higher plains. The distinction between Suhtais and Cheyennes is still a matter of tribal discussion, and most Cheyenne families are aware of variations in vocabulary as well as the lineage of their own ancestors. The current division of Southern and Northern Cheyenne tribes is more an arbitrary result of geography rather than a cultural distinction; in the 1830s they had broken into northern and southern bands for convenience of trading and hunting. All Cheyennes were to be kept on a southern reservation until some, like those who escaped north with Dull Knife and Little Wolf, gained a reservation in the land they preferred.

When the Suhtais and the Cheyennes came together, tribal stories were reconciled to incorporate the two traditions. Each tribe believed the power and mystery of the great spirit was embodied in a sacred object. A group of four sacred arrows – called the medicine arrows – were given to the Cheyennes by the cultural hero Sweet Medicine to protect the tribe and bring them strength. For the Suhtais a powerful covenant – a sacred buffalo hat – was the incarnate object of the Most Powerful One. Both objects were always in the care of selected individuals whose job it was to see to their safety and to ensure their proper handling.

Inside a special crescent-shaped sack trimmed on all sides with buffalo tails, the Sacred Hat remained hidden almost all of the time. On the most special of occasions or to bring good luck in a battle, the hat was removed from the bag. The thick fur of a cow buffalo served as the main covering of the sacred hat, and spectacular, shining blue beads adorned the sides. Slender, long horns came from the sides, and each horn was decorated with a pattern of red geometric shapes. On those rare occasions when the hat was taken out to renew the people's power, or to bring blessings on a great hunt, or in times of tribal crisis, it was placed on a bed of buffalo chips and adorned with sprigs of sage.

Objects from the buffalo also played an important role in the Cheyenne version of the sundance, a midsummer ritual that has been practiced continuously for centuries by the Cheyennes and other Plains tribes. In the old days the individual dancer, who had found himself in a dangerous situation, or who was threatened by something, or who wanted success at some great endeavor, promised to make a sacrifice by performing a special dance in the sun. While some of the cultural aspects of the ceremony have vanished, the buffalo remains an important spiritual aspect in the modern continuation of the sundance.

Such devout respect also was evident as the Cheyennes prepared for a buffalo hunt. Medicine men were consulted, dreams were discussed, and rituals to lure the beast toward hunters' weapons were performed.

Often small parties of hunters would spread out in search of buffalo. If a large herd was located, signals were sent back to the main camp and final preparations were made. Before the arrival of the horse, Indians often would surround a herd, hoping a shift in the wind would not give them away. Slowly those participating in the surround would move in, trying to form a human fence around the herd so that those men most skilled in the use of the lance or arrow could kill a number of beasts. Likewise, this method was used to drive a herd into a box canyon, or over a cliff, or – in winter – into deep snowdrifts or onto thin ice, where the weight of the huge beasts would cause them to fall into the water and thus become easy marks for a hunter's arrow. Other times the Cheyennes used a combination of wooden and human fences to impound the creatures in a natural or man-made trap. Another method was to set prairie fires to drive the buffalo toward waiting hunters. This method was always at risk of going awry. Some fires set for hunting changed direction or raced off across the prairies for miles.

When the horse arrived, its value in hunting the buffalo was so great that virtually overnight it took a prime place in Plains Indian culture. At first the horse was used in the surround, where its speed and agility made it ideal in herding buffalo. As Indians became more proficient and skilled with horses, the buffalo hunt became a contest that matched the skill of a horse and rider against a twelve-hundred-pound bison. It is no wonder that the Plains Indians quickly became some of the world's foremost equestrians, and the Cheyennes, it is commonly agreed, were the foremost horsemen of the plains. Quickly the horse became the most valuable commodity in tribal culture, and the number and quality of a man's horses was a mark of his wealth. More and better horses meant more buffalo, which meant that a man not only could afford a large family but also required additional wives in order to tan and prepare the hides and meat.

Meat from a crudely field-butchered buffalo was wrapped in its hide and loaded onto a horse for transport back to camp, but if the kill was large, or close enough to the camp, the people came to the kill site for butchering and returned to the camp for preparation of the meat. Strips an inch thick were dried in the air and sun into jerky; bits of chokecherry might be pounded into the strips to give the jerky a different taste. Pemmican was made by pounding jerky into long strings with a rock, placing it into leather bags about the size of grocery sack, and then pouring hot fat into the bag. It was then sealed, pounded flat, and stored. The contents, which were considered a delicacy, remained edible for years. Such bags of pemmican were often cached under specially marked rocks as insurance against hard and lean times, or stored away for the winter months. While pemmican provided a reliable long-term food supply, fresh meat was prepared in all manners, and the Cheyennes ate it raw or barely warmed, made it into thick stews and soups, or roasted it over a fire of glowing hot buffalo chips.

Occasionally a great deal was wasted, as in mass kills or when whole animals could not be butchered on the spot or dragged back to camp, but generally Indians used most parts of the buffalo. The Cheyennes used the hide for tepees, clothing, and tools; they used the hair as rope and ornamentation; the horns were glued together to make superior bows, used as spoons and ladles, arrow tips and cups, or ground into medications and potions; the bones were worked into versatile tools and weapons; the marrow was eaten, or it was dried and used as sponges and paint brushes. Occasionally the teeth were used for ornamentation on special dresses, while the sinew was prepared as sewing thread and bowstring. Parts of the buffalo were ideal waterproof containers, and stomachs, bladders, and scrotums were useful ready-made pouches. In winter children used the beasts' ribs as runners for sleds, and year round they used them as sticks for games or whittled them into whistles, dice, or drums.

The lowly buffalo chip was renowned as a source of fuel. First off, the properly sun-dried chip is nearly odorless and, when burned, gives off a faint incenselike smell of cinnamon and citrus in a nearly invisible smoke. The chips can be broken up into small slivers, which serve as kindling, and then larger and larger pieces can be added to the fire. They do not flame up as wood, but rather glow red much like charcoal. They give off a strong, constant heat without flaming up to sear the cooking meat. They continue to glow for a long time from the center of a nearly pure white ash. In the morning a buffalo chip campfire is nothing but a pile of white ash, still retaining the shape of the original chips.

The bison was so integral to the life, culture, and health of the Cheyennes and the other Plains Indians that it is easy to see why some military leaders for the U.S. government understood that the best way to eliminate the Indian was to eliminate the buffalo. When the demand for buffalo hides and meat reached its peak, the most shrewd military strategists saw ultimate victory over the Indians.

Grazing buffalo might give the impression of being clumsy and slow, but the animal is an excellent runner, capable of outlasting even a relay team of horses. When in a hurry, the buffalo gallops much like a horse, each leg pounding the earth in succession; but for fastest speeds the gallop gives way to a uniquely powerful, bounding leap. The bison throws out its skinny hind legs until they are well beyond the front feet, and then it leaps forward, all four legs suspended in air. At full speed of thirty-five to forty miles per hour, the leaping rear legs fly up high on either side of the huge head, a bluish-purple tongue wagging from an open mouth.

A tightly packed herd of these running beasts can flatten anything in its path, leveling fence posts and trees six inches in diameter. In his unmatched masterpiece on the animal, *The Time of the Buffalo*, Tom McHugh describes a stampeding herd:

> [The lead animals,] alarmed by some disturbance, dash off in headlong flight. . . . Following by the others is virtually automatic. . . . At the beginning of a stampede, the buffalo rush headlong into a tight bunch, massing together with a herding instinct so powerful that the group can seldom be divided. This same stubborn tendency to bunch thwarts ranchers attempting to drive a buffalo herd onto a different range. No matter what technique – pushing with a line of men, chasing with jeeps, or encircling with horsemen – the task is so difficult that many drives end in failure. Sooner or later one buffalo manages to outmaneuver its pursuers and squeeze through a minor break in the line, whereupon the rest of the animals quickly slip through the opening like so many links in a chain, and the drive falls apart.

On a trip across the plains in 1862 a group of travelers were stunned one morning to see an enormous stampede of these bounding beasts. The herd was at least ten miles wide. For well over an hour the ground was a seemingly solid mass of buffalo as they raced past the observers.

Reports like these seemed exaggerated to people who had not witnessed the enormous numbers for themselves, but the vast quantities were truly beyond measure. One traveler on the Santa Fe trail took three days to pass through a single herd. The entire horizon was "so thickly covered with these noble animals" that he could not see the bare ground. He calculated the herd to cover 1,350 square miles, an area roughly the size of Rhode Island.

Clearly, it would take more than hunting parties to wipe out these numbers. It would take more than tourists shooting from trains, more than Sioux and Cheyennes and Arapahos and Pawnees and dozens of other Plains civilizations. Motivated by greed and inspired by money to find ever more efficient means of slaughter, it would take a few hundred professional buffalo hunters a handful of years to bring the buffalo nearly to extinction.

New breakthroughs in the tanning process, combined with an increased demand for the flexible, tough hide of the bison, spurred the initial wave of non-Indian hunters. The market-economy demand for hides brought on by railroad expansionism and the need to feed the populations of growing frontier towns resulted in staggering numbers of bison kills. As late as the Civil War the bison herd was estimated to be as large as fifty million, but by the early 1870s the methodical slaughter by professional hunters was well underway. During the 1873–74 season the Santa Fe railroad alone shipped 459,453 hides. As many as four million were killed in a three-year period ending in 1875. The slaughter was so widespread and wasteful that pioneers let their hogs roam the prairies in order to feast on the buffalo meat left behind by the hide hunters. The decimation of the buffalo was so complete that in 1883 the discovery of a single hidden herd of twelve hundred near present-day Bison, South Dakota, was so monumental that it made international news.

The annihilation of the bison coincided with an increased demand for beef cattle. As the railroads pushed west, new towns along the routes served as shipping terminals to send beef east to a growing population. Nearly wild herds of cattle, fattened on grasses so recently vacated by the demise of the bison, were driven northward to savage railroad towns like Dodge and Ogalalla by gangs of rough-edged cowboys. Dull Knife and Little Wolf's route paralleled – and sometimes followed – the Western Cattle Trail north through Kansas, to the Nebraska border, and across the buffalo land. Remnants of the cattle trail can still be seen near the Frenchman and Stinking Water Rivers.

By the time the Northern Cheyennes were crossing the buffalo land between the Frenchman, the Stinking Water and the Platte, news of Colonel William Lewis's death at the Punished Woman and stories of the brutal deaths of the pioneers in Rawlins and Decatur counties was everywhere. The full might of the U.S. Department of War turned to stopping the Indians. From Texas to the Dakotas, from the Missouri to the Rockies, troops moved across the Great Plains like chess pieces trying to stop the three hundred Cheyennes. Many feared the Cheyennes' actions would cause widespread revolt among other Indians being held in the newly developed reservation system. Others worried that Oglala Sioux under Red Cloud would flee their new South Dakota reservation. As in Indian Territory, rations were short on the Oglala reservation. Thousands of troops moved into positions along the Nebraska–South Dakota border. Rumors of a general Sioux uprising were rampant.

Because of those fears, a band of Oglalas were nearly wiped out in early October. Traveling from the Missouri to the White Clay River, the Oglala panicked when they came upon 250 soldiers along the South Dakota border. They didn't believe the story of the Cheyenne outbreak and believed, instead, that the soldiers were after them for having left the Missouri. The soldiers faced the Oglala, and the Indians took cover. The chiefs had trouble holding the people together; the soldiers called for reinforcements. A group of chiefs and officers met all night long to prevent fighting and to talk over the confusion. After the tension eased in the morning, the Sioux moved off in one direction and the soldiers in another. One tragedy was averted, but far greater bloodshed awaited the border area.

By the first of October Captain Mauck moved through the buffalo land south of the Platte with his heavily armed troops. Mauck had recently been transferred from elsewhere in the West to this place so troubled by the Cheyennes. He now was in charge of five companies of infantry and thirty-five cavalrymen – over three hundred men – completely outfitted with two weeks' rations. He was confident that he would stop the Cheyennes before they reached the Union Pacific railroad tracks at the Platte, one hundred miles to the north. Meanwhile, to the south, Captain Vance with seventy field infantrymen and twenty-five cavalrymen was moving across the headwaters of the Little Beaver and toward the Republican. Another one hundred troops under Major Dallas were on the lower Republican, headed west. Orders were for the three groups to converge at the Republican and to engage the Cheyennes.

It was 9 A.M., October 2, when the Cheyennes crossed the Republican River five miles east of the forks and moved north to the one-day camp at the Frenchman River. That day a rancher on the Republican named Connor lost forty-five horses, two mules, and about eighty-five cattle killed; a neighbor named Wilson lost twenty-seven horses. The Webster spread on the Stinking Water lost about twenty-five head of horses and seven or ten head of cattle killed. In total the Cheyennes captured sixty-four horses from local ranchers, and although the body of a slain rancher was found some weeks later, after crossing into Nebraska there was no more bloodbath.

They now had restocked the horses lost at Punished Woman and had as many as 250. They could move much more rapidly. According to two Cheyennes, Wild Hog and Crow, it was when they camped at the Frenchman River, and Cheyenne scouts saw the troops in the distance, that the band split up into numerous smaller bands and moved north. Besides confusing their pursuers, splitting into smaller bands was effective because the organization of the U.S. military made it nearly impossible for troops to scatter into small units to follow every trail.

Racing northward toward the Platte across the now nearly lifeless buffalo land, the Cheyennes hoped to avoid another head-to-head confrontation like Punished Woman. The new supply of fresh horses made their travel swift, although the cries of the wounded and sorrow for the lost ones resounded with every hoofbeat.

All around me are the tall spires of soapweed yucca, which thrust skyward from a bouquet of dagger-thin leaves. The massive taproot of the soapweed yucca is a foot-thick appendage that slams five feet deep into the earth.

There are at least 720 species of tubular plants growing without cultivation on the prairies of western Nebraska. Of these an astounding 670 are native species in a land that to some appears to be nothing but a monotonous carpet of grass. The golden-white flags throwing sheets of light across the darker green near the yucca are the seed tips of buffalo grass, the dominant species, unique because it grows in mats and not isolated bunches, and because it produces both male and female plants. The taller male plant is responsible for these one-sided spikes I see everywhere before me.

While the climax bunchgrass community remains largely unchanged for a long period of time, other areas change in composition from year to year. Often the reason for the fluctuation is soil disturbance. In the time of the buffalo these plants thrived in the wallows where bison rolled dust onto their hides. These days, after the soil has been disturbed by erosion from cattle, wind, or human activity, a hearty, fast-growing group of grasses and plants known appropriately as the pioneer plants establish themselves. Blowout grass, a plant typical of this community, sends out slender shoots in all directions, stabilizing the soil. It can be buried under wind-blown sand and still survive, but eventually gives way to other species that take hold of the soil it has helped to stabilize. While these plants grow quickly and can produce a lot of seeds, they cannot tolerate competition from other plants and so disappear once their rapid growth has stabilized the shifting soil.

Blooms are everywhere around me in this land of the buffalo: the bold white flowers of sand cherries pepper the hills; purple fireworks of lacy-leafed asters grace the ground, while amid grass and daisies, milkweed and flowering cacti, I nearly fail to notice the slender poles of the delicate palespike's bluish-white flowers. I follow a dirt path alongside the coolness of the wet creek bottom and pass a thick, dense thicket of Arkansas rose. I smell the sweetness of the bloom just before I see its pink flowers opening in the sunlight. In the tiny valley are thickets of wild plums, framed by an abundance of leadplant, prominent because of its hairy blue flowers. Near the ground where cattle have kept the grass cropped close to the earth, bush morning glory forms a spray of white flowers. By fall it will dry up, break off at ground level, and roll away in the autumn wind like a tumble weed, scattering its seeds across the entire length of the creek bed.

At the center of the small valley is a wet meadow where taller grass and more flowers are blooming. A few trees are here: cottonwood and ash, box elder and hackberry. Out here trees survive only near water; seldom does one thrive on the dry uplands. Stands of cottonwood and ash sometimes can get a few acres in size, but the ground below such small woods usually is barren as a result of the cattle that have congregated in the shade. It is not clear how trees found their way into these drylands. Whether or not human attempts to control prairie fires contributed to their growth, they have established themselves in these wet lowlands and in the fields now long abandoned.

Although we have killed off the buffalo, tried and failed to plant our crops, and finally sent our cattle out onto these plains, grass steadfastly resists our repeated attempts to leave a mark on the prairies. Grass covers the bloody pools left from battles with Indians, and it masks the horrors of lynchings, suicides, and deaths in fiery gun battles; grass hides the shame of the surrender of pioneers, and it grows through the concrete slabs of the hundreds of nuclear missile silos that are scattered over the land of the buffalo. Over and over it wins battles fought only by us, yet we continue to rage against it: the mushroom blast of death and horror in downtown Oklahoma City was created with a bomb made of fertilizer. The dust of its deathly destruction now enriches the soil where a grass-covered memorial will be built.

In their time the buffalo were so numerous, the grassland so vast, that men thought nothing could ever change. Although I have walked for miles without seeing much change to this landscape, I have as much chance of looking into the inch-long, pear-shaped iris of a buffalo's eye as I do of seeing one of the giant tortoises whose petrified bones are often unburied by the perpetual wind of this lonely land. In their time the tortoises were countless. The tortoise, the buffalo, the human: all so numerous in their time on this sea of wind-whipped waves of grass.

PART SEVEN

Sand Hills Sundays and Others

Some saw it as a great sea caught and held
forever in a spell and were afraid of it.

MARI SANDOZ, *Old Jules*

Thou hast been in Eden the garden of God;
every precious stone was thy covering.

EZEKIEL 28:13

God is able of these stones to raise up children
unto Abraham.

MATTHEW 3:9

23. White Tail

Her rich melodious whistling never echoed in the big house when there was company, but on sunny, bright Sunday mornings in the warmth of endless childhood, the reverberation of my mother's joyful, tuneful whistling from the kitchen was a sure sign of a happy day. We would awake early enough some bright June morning so that the mourning doves' coos would still be coming from the eaves, but she'd already been awake for hours.

Awake and whistling. Or singing. The fluted notes of her rich songs wrapping around the diamond flecks of dust in the colored shaft of sunlight though an open door.

Each song of the countless she knew was from some corner of her life. Folk songs her Romanian parents sang long before World War II, love songs from the scratchy radios in the hospitals where she spent the war working as an army nurse, and jazz songs from after the killing had finally stopped. Sometimes they were songs we had never heard before, and other times old favorites we knew by heart, "Merry Widow Waltz," say, or "They Call the Wind Mariah."

I am trying to whistle the latter on this cool, bright Sunday morning, but the ceaseless wind grabs each note and runs away across the prairie grass with it before I can savor its memory. Another car is approaching. For the past hour an occasional car has passed, each carrying a neatly dressed farm family on their way to church. This one slows. A man in a dress shirt is driving. A window full of kids' faces presses toward me from the rear seat. The woman in the front is the only one who does not look at me. She is staring out across the open space as if watching for the notes of my mother's song on the invisible wind.

Group portrait before the march into Fort Robinson. *Standing, from left:* Barbara One Bear Spang, Beatrice Small, Annie Brady, Martha Wolf Name, Rose Killsontop, Josie Sootkis, Phoebe Spotted Elk; *seated, from left:* Samuel Spotted Elk Jr., Alan Boye, Andrew Sootkis, Hubert Seminole.

As the family drives by, I wave. The persistent wind knocks the dust of the passing car flat to the ground. A last-season tumbleweed stomps across the narrow bar ditch and slams solid against the barbed wire of the fence line. Beyond the fence, plump seed heads of winter wheat stand with tails turned in the gale.

The wind has not let up for days, and although the sky has been clear, the sunlight strong, and the open rolling prairie just south of the Platte beautiful, the wind has kept me from fully appreciating my surroundings. Instead, there is the relentless breeze. The expectation I have that there will surely come a break in the howl, some instant of silence and stillness, however brief, is never satisfied. No break comes from the maddening whistling. The constant drumming against my ears has driven me inward, trapped me with nothing but my own thoughts for company.

When the non-Indians first scattered themselves across these hills, they built low-slung soddies and dank dripping dugouts with backs to the northwest, the direction of the merciless wind. I don't think it was the solitude that drove some crazy, but the unending wail, for the wind so entombs a person that there is nowhere to turn and nothing but his or her own dark thoughts to use against that roar. The women had it worse, for they had nowhere to hide from either the roaring wind or the anger of men gone mad from it.

During the same week that Pawnee Woman and the other Cheyenne women were carrying their children north through these windy hills, a posse found the bodies of a white woman and her four children buried in a haystack behind their Platte River dugout. Pinkerton detectives later captured a man named Samuel Richards. In jail he bragged how he had used a flatiron to kill three of them; he boasted how he had strangled the fourth, and how he had dangled the baby by his feet until he too was dead. His swift trial led to a sentence of death. The following spring, on the same April day that the last of Little Wolf's band were captured in Montana, Richards died swinging from a noose.

The wind and the men gone mad by it in the tunnels of these hills.

In the dry winds of October 1915 a ranch hand scribbled the words "I won't tell what the trouble started over but you will find our bones in the ashes," and pinned it to a bridle in the barn of

Mrs. Nellie Heelan of Valentine, Nebraska. He then went inside and killed Mrs. Heelan and knocked another woman to the floor. He poured kerosene over the still-breathing second woman and set her on fire. The fire destroyed the wooden house and everything in it.

It wasn't just the twisted actions of men such as these that women had to face. Driven from the lonely dugouts by dust, darkness, and the fifteen-foot-long bull snakes that continually slithered into the black chamber home, most women essentially lived outside in the unquiet air. Every moment of every day, again and again through day after countless day they were out in that wind. The voices of women at isolated homesteads who fought against the madness that wind could create fill diaries and journals; their voices fill yellowed letters, and their hollowed-out voices endure in the tinted photographs of survivors: wizened old women with eyes that are round, vacant windows on the landscape of this lonely, this perpetual, immeasurable wind.

I stop. Surely there was happiness here, too. Surely there was the laughter of women and men. Even the Cheyenne women who fled through here nursing their wounded and comforting the children, even in the midst of such anguish as theirs, must have sung. Even in the wind. The song-robbing, ear-drumming wind.

Another car approaches. In it is an ancient ranch couple. The old man is behind the wheel; although his face is wrinkled, the skin is taunt and tight from a lifetime spent in this wind and sky. He doesn't wear a baseball-style feed cap or a cowboy hat, but a dark, formal dress hat. His suit is brown, the tie narrow. As he passes he solemnly lifts three fingers off the wheel as a greeting. His wife is next to him in the front seat in a blue print dress, a narrow-brimmed yellow hat pinned to her silver hair. Her face is round and full and lively. Her eyes catch mine just as the car passes, and she gives me a warm smile.

They have come up out of a long thick line of trees three miles ahead: the South Platte. Just beyond the river a dark edge is on the distant horizon, a sudden line jumps into the big sky: the Sand Hills. I stop to look at them. When the army troops in pursuit of Dull Knife reached this point, young men in the infantry who were seeing these hills for the first time claimed they were as abrupt and as towering as a mountain range. That was a bit of exaggeration, but the way the massive, undulating hills crowd away into the busy horizon worries me. All along I've known that these hills would provide my biggest challenge.

The Nebraska Sand Hills, twenty thousand square miles of grass-covered dunes, are a unique geological area. At least 250 miles wide and 100 miles across, they are the largest sand dune area in the Western Hemisphere. Dunes as high as 400 feet are often 20 miles wide. The 25 percent grade on some slopes explains the soldiers' contention that these green and tan hills of grass easily pass for mountains.

The hills were created after a great inland sea dried up some 100 million years ago and wind and water erosion began to shape the sand. Much more recently, perhaps just ten thousand years ago, the great ice sheets further transformed the area. Imagine a vast Sahara of frozen waves of sand, the parallel made even stronger by the wind-driven motion of a thick carpet of short prairie grass.

The wind-rippled hills are wet enough to support a lavish texture of native grasses, but the pioneers soon learned that – instead of providing a bed for crops – breaking through the grass with a plow caused the perpetual wind to blow out an ever-enlarging cavern of sand. Farming was soon confined to sheltered areas, and most of the few who chose to remain on their homestead turned to raising cattle. Just like the thousands of buffalo that once roamed here, the cattle feasted on the rich grasses of the delicate hills, so that today the Sand Hills constitute one of the most productive cattle ranges in the world. Sadly, over a hundred years after those early pioneers learned how best to use the land, the lesson has to be relearned by a new generation of those who insist on breaking through the grass and sand, this time to plant gigantic irrigated circles of croplands.

For the next eighty miles or more I will face this maze of identical round hills. Although there are a few freshwater lakes, most of the lakes are white with slick alkali. There are infrequent roads and fewer trees, and sparse human occupation is limited to clusters of ranch buildings every twenty miles. If I'm lucky, one out of every three will not be abandoned.

I cross over the sudden busyness of Interstate 80, metallic streams of east-west refugees from distant metropolises, and a half mile later, the swollen South Platte River. I chat with two men who are taking readings of the river with a strange scientific box they wheel along the length of the narrow bridge. "All the rain we've been having, combined with all the snowpack that's melted here this last warm week, has got the river this high," the younger one explains. They are from the Army Corps of Engineers and are trying to determine whether the narrow bridge where the three of us stand should be closed because of the rising swirl of chocolate water just beneath our feet. The Platte, they tell me, hasn't been this high since 1965.

I walk on, through the quiet Sunday noon of the tiny burg of Roscoe, its few once-busy storefronts empty and faded since the Interstate pulled away the last lifeline of economic health. Just to the west of town are Alkali Flats, where midmorning on October 4, 1878, Dull Knife, his family, and probably 120 others crossed the South Platte and continued north through a wide notch in the Sand Hills. I stop and face the long slope of the first hill. Below this wall the persistent wind cannot dip low enough, and I am in the sudden quiet, the birdsong and whisper breeze through grass stem the only accompaniment to my own whistled tune.

Up and over the hills and two hours later I hike down into the North Platte Valley at the small, friendly, and clean town of Keystone.

We are together again, and after we briefly share the stories of our mornings and eat a lunch of store-bought sandwiches, Andy, Sam, and I start knocking on doors trying to find directions to our next destination: the head of White Tail Creek.

It doesn't take long. Three houses later we are standing talking to the town's unofficial local historian and geographer, who carefully sketches the route in the soft sand at the edge of his neatly trimmed lawn. He listens with interest to our story. "And what is it about the White Tail Creek?" he asks.

"We think Dull Knife may have camped there," I say. I begin to explain how the troops had found the fresh trail at Alkali Flats and had followed it northward until they came upon Dull Knife's camp in a little round valley somewhere near the head of White Tail

Creek. "There's a story that Andy and Sam's great-great-grand-mother was fatally kicked by a horse at a spot just like it," I say.

The man nods. He listens with great interest and then nods again. "Pretty area up in there. Could just well be the place for a camp," he says. "But I don't know – isn't much up there – maybe a few stray cattle, but not a drop of water for a good distance once you leave the creek."

An hour later we are headed north off the paved county high-way west of Keystone and up the faintest track of a trail into fence-less tufts of buffalo grass and yucca, climbing hillsides turned yel-low with tiny starlike flowers.

"This is definitely where Dull Knife camped," I say as we move ever up into the hills, following the ridges above the twisting White Tail Creek. "I recognize this area from something I read." I take Andy and Sam's silence as encouragement, so I go on.

After the depredations in northern Kansas, and moving quickly on fresh horses, the Cheyennes raced through southern Nebraska traveling northward toward the Platte. While five hun-dred troops searched to the south on the Republican, hundreds of additional troops under Major Thornburgh were stationed on the South Platte River with orders to intercept the Cheyennes as they crossed the Union Pacific tracks.

Somewhere south of the Platte the Cheyennes split into two groups. It was a parting of major consequences, for the two bands would never rejoin again. Much has been written about this split, but just as the exact location will forever remain a mystery, the rea-sons for the separation will remain honored by silence.

An old Cheyenne man who was captured in Kansas after the Cheyennes passed through there told a reporter with pride that his people had been evading the entire army with fewer than sev-enty men over the age of eleven. When they split, many of the strongest of these men, the warriors loyal to him, went with Little Wolf. The remaining Cheyennes, including many women and children, several of the walking wounded, and men loyal to Dull Knife, stayed with him.

Although the Cheyennes no longer traveled in a unified band, their tactics were still somehow precisely coordinated. Little Wolf sent small groups of men westward to plant tracks in sandy washes so the military would think they were headed toward the towns of northeastern Colorado. Major Thornburgh gathered the reports, telegrams, and gossip on the location and numbers of Indians and sent out small observation groups in order to keep the bulk of his command ready to move once the band was finally sighted. Little Wolf's cunning tactic of placing tracks all over a hundred-mile-wide path largely kept the troops immobile, even though the Union Pacific Railroad provided a special train that stood ready to transport Thornburgh's 250 men at a moment's notice.

That notice came when Dull Knife's trail at Alkali Flats was discovered only a few hours after his band of Cheyennes crossed the South Platte River. Troops, horses, carts, and supplies were loaded onto the train at Sidney. At thirty-five miles per hour the train covered in an hour what it took the Cheyennes a day to travel. The soldiers reached Alkali Flats before dark, unloaded the train, and immediately started north. By dark they had reached the North Platte River and were only two hours behind the Cheyennes; thick quicksand and an even thicker fog, however, slowed the troops to a crawl. They were all night just crossing the North Platte.

At four o'clock on a Sand Hills Sunday morning, Thornburgh's scouts galloped back to the column to report that they had found a trail going up White Tail Creek. Thornburgh left the last of his supplies – the heavy ambulance wagon – and marched his troops forward through the dark and fog in the predawn hour.

"Just after daybreak the column was riding through extremely rough country," I say as we move higher into the hills. Andy nods. "Coming up this very canyon. See how narrow it is? That meant Thornburgh's troops had to ride single file."

It was a perfect spot for an ambush, and there was no way for the army to form a skirmish line. All of Thornburgh's scouts but one became so nervous that they abandoned the lead and dropped back to the end of the line. Disgusted, Thornburgh himself rode to the front of the troops. When they reached the head of the creek they found a fresh camp below a shadow line of semicircular sand hills, on the crest of which the Indians had dug forty to fifty rifle pits. Had it not been for the fog and the dark, Thornburgh and his men would have been trapped and attacked as they came up the steep canyon. As it turned out, it was the Cheyennes who were surprised and forced to quickly abandon the camp. When Thornburgh arrived at the head of the canyon the camp was empty, but the grass was still matted down from where people had slept. In the distance they could hear some Indians calling for help, trying to mimic the sound of white men in distress. They were trying to lure small groups of troops in order to attack them.

A confusion of several trails led out of the canyon, but after a time the trail of the main body of Dull Knife's Cheyennes was located. It headed back toward the southwest. Although the Cheyennes had another head start, Thornburgh took out after them, leaving a few men behind to wait for the ambulance. As soon as the main body of troops was out of sight, a rifle shot from a Cheyenne took away the trigger of one of the remaining soldiers' rifle. The soldiers who had been left behind were held at bay for an hour while a few Cheyennes took shots at them from the surrounding hilltops.

Thornburgh would ride for days until, with exhausted provisions and weary troops, he met up with Colonel Caleb Carlton on the South Dakota border. He would never get close to Dull Knife again. Thornburgh carefully gathered mementos of his near-miss of the Cheyennes. Tucked away in the files of the Colorado Historical Society is his fragile, faded scrapbook. In the scrapbook is this clipping from an unidentified newspaper:

> Those Indians marched through an organized force of 20,000 soldiers with little loss. Say that the whole western army has been demoralized by a few wild Indians, but give Thornburgh just credit, he gave them the hottest and longest chase.

We are climbing steadily now, and I am out of breath. A long hillside has cut off our view of White Tail Creek to the west, and we are scaling its edges while moving ever deeper into the hills. "Lookouts had seen the troops coming up the canyon and had alerted the camp," I say, panting. "It was then, as she hurried to pack her pony, that Pawnee Woman was kicked by the horse." I am so excited with my idea that I do not hear the silliness of my next words. "Dull Knife was so distraught over the accident that it made him slow down. That's why he was caught."

I pause, and before I can fill the silence again, Andy speaks.

"I don't think so," he says simply.

"Why not?" I stammer. "Everything fits perfectly."

He does not speak for nearly a full minute, and then begins. "The more I think about it, the more I think Little Wolf and Dull Knife split up in order to survive. Winter was coming on, and they didn't have anything to feed the people. Little Wolf took the strong ones and maybe went way east of here to avoid the army."

"And Dull Knife?" I ask.

"I think Dull Knife was trying to get to the Sioux, because they were close with the Sioux, and the Sioux would help hide them."

As is always the case, the three of us are instantly caught up in one of our frequent speculations. Sam says, "Dull Knife took the weaker ones, and they made it up into this place here. Maybe he was acting as a decoy so that Little Wolf could slip through."

Just then, as if by design, we reach the top of the long hillside. Side by side the three of us crest the ridge together. In the green, narrow valley at our feet two grayish-red coyotes are loping along the creek. They freeze for a split second, their pointed noses working the air, then, catching our scent, ford the stream in a single leap and trot up into a side draw, becoming invisible in the camouflage of colors.

"Coyotes," Sam says, not as an announcement, but as a commentary on this special place. We sit on the grass and look about.

Below us and stretching back to the far southern horizon is the steep V shape of the draw where Thornburgh's men rode single file. If I had to, I could climb down the slope, but it would not be easy. From here, the course of the White Tail is a line from south to north. Like all of the Cheyenne camps so far, this spot provides a grand view, and we can easily see at least forty miles to the south. Such a view, however, would not have been any use to the Cheyennes in the thick fog that choked the canyon that early morning long ago.

The steep sides of the draw become easier to climb only a quarter mile to my right, where the slopes at the head of the draw are much more gentle. You can see why the Cheyennes chose this place to camp. There would be grass for the ponies and a good view to the south, and while it would be difficult if not impossible for the soldiers to climb out of the canyon, escape from the top of the draw over these low hills would be easy. At the head of the valley is a round, spring-fed meadow with an arc of low hills behind it. The spring creates the lush green of the level campsite and provides water for White Tail Creek, which sparkles in the afternoon sunlight.

For a long, long time no one speaks. Because of its remoteness not many have visited this inconsequential valley in a wilderness of sand hills where Thornburgh and Dull Knife came within an eyelash of each other's destiny. The wind blows easier on our hillside, and in the cloudless sky two red-tailed hawks slide down chutes of vapor.

Into this silence, Andy's words float not as an interruption but as a benediction, as a prayer.

"The prophecies of the Cheyenne religion were always told to a younger man by an older man. It would take the older man four days of nonstop talking to tell all of the revelations. The stories had been handed down like this for centuries." Andy's words pause and the hawks bank on an updraft just above the green circle of the camp. "Sweet Medicine had a prophecy that there'd come a time when the Cheyenne tribe would be so small that people would have to marry into their own families in order to survive. To marry into your own family is forbidden by Cheyenne law and is about the worse thing you can do. Once the Cheyenne started to marry into their own families, Sweet Medicine's prophecy said, a naked woman would appear and run alongside of the camp." He stops again, and when he starts I am jolted by the overpowering sadness in his voice. "This woman would give birth to a baby who would be born with a full set of teeth. That baby would cause the destruction of all of the Cheyenne people."

The hawks have disappeared, but somewhere in the valley below us a prairie grouse's tremolo vibrates the air. When we stand and walk away, each of us leaves a small offering of tobacco to the grass and the rocks and the sky.

On our way back down to the county highway we try to understand. We talk about the difficulties that now faced the people. We talk about mothers and children, and about the strength of Dull Knife's and Little Wolf's good pride, and about the strength Pawnee Woman must have had. Never simply trying to save just themselves or their family, as they frequently had the opportunity to do, the strong ones forsook their safety because they saw as their duty the protection of the entire group.

"Along with the good kind of pride," I say, "there has to be something like decency as well."

Andy nods. "Yeah," he says, as always cutting the word off in his throat, "Dull Knife could have killed those pioneer women – the Laings – back in Kansas, but he didn't; he saved them. Even though they were the enemy, he let his decency guide him."

Andy's words bring back the horrors of those days. After leaving White Tail Creek, Thornburgh's soldiers found ponies abandoned by Dull Knife's band, their tongues swollen with thirst; the trail led to the southwest across a wide, waterless expanse of hills. "Imagine how hard it must have been on the children," I say and fall silent, overcome by a painful longing for my own sons.

"The Cheyenne learned from animals how to best raise their children," Andy says. "Kids didn't just have the parents they were born with. Everybody acted as parents. If you weren't supposed to be doing something and some older person saw you, they had every right to discipline you."

I am considering this, hoping my wife has found a similar kind of support for herself. "Animals do that?"

"Yeah," he says. "That's the way elk raise their young: all of the older ones look after all of the young. Like elk, other people would have urged the slowest kids on. They would have kept everyone moving." Uncharacteristically, he suddenly stops. When he speaks again, his voice has an odd quality to it, as if he is holding something terrible in his words. "I've been thinking a lot about that boy they left back there in Kansas: the one that couldn't travel on, so they killed a cow for him and left him in a good spot. They hoped for the best: that some decent white might find him and take pity on him."

I say, "I can't possibly imagine the anguish of the mother who had to say good-bye to that boy."

Andy nods, but he is not looking at me. "I've been thinking about that boy for a long time. You see, I was laid up for about two years with a bad back. I'd given up all hope until I met a good man who threw away all of my pain killers and told me I couldn't dope myself back to my life, I had to work myself there with exercises and hope."

Sam and I wait. Andy continues.

"That man saved my life. But this boy, he was all alone; even his mother had to leave him. He couldn't move. There must have been so little for him to hope for, and yet he survived and he held on until the cowboys came and killed him." Andy's voice breaks. "I think of him lying there for six weeks not moving, so alone, so hopeless."

A reverent silence, then Sam speaks. "My mother, Phoebe, would like this place, *eh-nah*? My grandmother would be proud that I'm here at this place."

There is nothing left to say, and we remain silent even as they leave me at my stretch of highway to resume my solo walking west.

There is much for me to think about.

It was through my mother that I came to love the outdoors. My mother insisted on recognizing the absolute presence of nature in our lives. She never diverted in her steadfast resolution to draw attention to nature at every chance. Even before its call had died out she would shush us and say, "You hear that? A purple finch is somewhere nearby." While walking she was just as likely to jump to the ground and pull our faces close to the white flowers growing there. "Lilies of the valley. Look how delicate!" The bloom of sunsets, the contour of clouds, the music of wind, and the scent of rain were her great lessons, and she taught them daily with nothing but awe and joy. Through her I learned that in nature I could find, if not reason, at least all of life's power, horror, joy, and balance, and that if I listened to it close enough I might hear on its prairie winds the lingering songs of her own loving motherhood.

Of the way my mother's musical mornings nurtured me I can only say that like her joy of nature, her singing and her soulful whistling enveloped my childhood. Unlike my father's straight-ahead conversations and sermonlike guidance, my mother spoke to us with every action. Her exuberant love of the outdoors, her dancelike movements, every facial expression and action imparted some lesson, some love on us. I owe this precise moment of insight, freedom, and perspective to the unmistakable joy and the loving caress of her musical, sun-drenched, mornings.

I watch the far horizon for a moment, then begin to whistle one of her soft, melancholic tunes. Now not even the ceaseless prairie wind steals the song.

24. Walking

It's a free country, so they say, and yet there are great differences in freedoms. Dutifully, during the darkest months of late winter, New Englanders trudge through gray streets to sit on hard metal chairs in town halls so they may exercise their freedom to vote on matters most civil and civilized. Champions of culture and guardians of education defend budgets and debate motions, while the vast silent populace of the town listens carefully, tapping the rolled paper tube of the town meeting agenda against their knees. Three, sometimes four hours later, the room finally exhales and the masses rumble out into the winter again, having discharged their freedom. But there is another freedom, an absolute independence and wildness, in contrast to mere civil liberties, a freedom found not in the orderly expression of individual members of a society, but in the envelopment of nature.

One way to get to that freedom is to walk.

I never appreciated the art of walking before this trip. Now, having walked eight to ten hours a day, every day, for over a month, I am becoming at least a minor authority on the subject. Before now I never understood that to simply get myself out the door of my house or my office, or up from the television set, or even away from a good book, in order to actually start was not really taking a walk. To truly walk, to amble, is to accept the knowledge that there is no real destination to reach.

The seemingly endless string of cops who stopped me as I walked across Kansas must have seen my lone, backpacked figure walking down a road miles from nowhere and thought of me as a vagrant: a man without land or a home. But the truth is that people who sit still in their houses are much more vagrant than I. In walking these distances I have learned to be equally at home everywhere. Before – leaving the security of the frame of milled lumber I call home – I simply took a tour, coming back to my house, my office, my television. I simply made a circuit, confident that half of my trip would be in the comfort of retracing my steps back to the familiar. Ah, but if you set out on the most mundane of strolls with the belief that nothing is for certain, prepared never to return, confident only that you are leaving your family, your spouse and children, never to see them again, only then you are really ready for a walk.

This morning I woke well before dawn to list in my journal what it has been like to do nothing but walk for a month. While a family of white-tailed deer grazed a few feet away in the shadow light of stars and dawn, I wrote "missing my wife and children" next to a big number one on the page. There followed heat, cold, heat with no wind, wind, and an assortment of ticks, flies, deer flies, bees, hornets, ants, mosquitoes, strange weird crawlers, tourists, and rattlesnakes. The sameness of freeze-dried food, the layers of dirt and grime on my body, the cramped tent, and fear. Walking on asphalt road. Walking where there are no roads. On and on the list continues, created, I tell myself, to record the not-so-romantic realities of long-distance walking. What is most significant, however, are the near thirty items listed under a separate category called "body check." First among these is a notation of "incredible pain in the soles of my feet after about twelve miles with the backpack." There follow several additional complaints regarding my poor feet: blisters, toes on occasion scraped to raw bloody pulp from the insides of my boots, deathlike aches, and no relief from pain after two hours of massaging the soles of my feet. Then sunburn, chafing, a strange majestic pain from my waist to the tip of my toes, my thighs beaten to senselessness, nerves deadened from the cinch of the heavy backpack's belt; splinters, cuts, scrapes, peeling skin, burning eyes, blistered ears, burned (I always forget to sunscreen it) nose, shooting back pain, and a piercing side pain, eased only by the awkward act of swinging my arms in wide arcs like a hairy ape as I walk.

But my discomfort is far from the limit of endurance. Last night as Andy, Sam, and I sat around my little stove, we compared the difficulty of our journey with that of Dull Knife and Little Wolf. We concluded that they walked until it was very painful, and continued to walk until the pain burned red hot across their entire bodies, and yet continued to walk beyond even endurance; and still on further until even many of the strongest reached the place where such an iron human will can no longer help and they simply died in their footsteps.

Still, there are those who sit all day on legs that were designed for walking, who pass hours, days, lifetimes without so much as a glance through a window. Some may make their way to gyms and even don running shoes for a regular jog around the neighborhood. This repetitious motion becomes their most adventuresome activity for the week. Pity those whose view of the wellspring of life is in the religious repetition of habit while the very essence of true adventure goes unsought.

The basics of walking are these: place the left (or right) foot a single easy stride in front of the right (or left) foot, then bring the weight of the body forward, lifting the right (or left) foot up off the ground and forward. Repeat as necessary. All else is secondary.

For my comfort however, primary among those secondary items are my boots. I bought big, thick, meaty, leather monsters – long-distance hiking boots with soles so stiff my step is like walking on a wooden board, so that my toes, not my heels, leave deep imprints in the path behind me. I don't know how Andy, with his pair of worn cowboy boots, can make it, or worse: Sam with his thin tennis shoes and tendinitis ankle. That they have come so far without complaint on such meager footwear is just short of miraculous.

Preparedness helps, too. I'm packing Band-Aids and blister aids, bug repellent and sunscreen, snake bite kit and Ace bandages, aspirins and Maalox, extra boot insoles and extra shoestrings. I've got a watch, a compass, a pedometer, a chunk of rope, a needle and thread, a compass and maps. I carry sunglasses, three pairs of wool socks and three pairs of thin silk inner socks, short pants, a raincoat, three T-shirts, a single sweatshirt, and a pair of slippers for around camp. My food is freeze-dried, and ten-day supplies of it are sent by my wife to post offices along the route. Oh, and tent, and sleeping bag, and a comfortable, lightweight camp chair.

Rest is important, critical. In the mornings, fresh from sleep and with the day cool and full of promise, I walk a full three or four hours without a break. This morning distance is rich with thought, ideas, speculations, introspection, elation, praise, prayer, and plans. It is in the morning that I am least aware of my surroundings. I walk bodily but am not there in spirit, for my mind is too busy with activity to match the slow pace of walking. After nine or a dozen miles, however, I stop and sit. I drink a long draft of water and eat some jerky or nibble on an energy bar. By then my mind has slowed to the rhythm of my feet.

Today's morning walk has taken me from the North Platte Valley and into the heart of the Sand Hills up the banks of the beautiful Bluewater Creek. When they reached here, the Dull Knife band would have walked forty miles from the close call at White Tail without water. The clear, cool, and reliable waters of the Bluewater were a familiar and, as they are now to me, a welcome sight. My wandering mind is drawn to the inverted cone of a valley along the banks of the creek where a different page of violent history was written: the Battle of the Bluewater. Here, in 1855, Little Thunder's band of Brulé Sioux was attacked and hundreds were killed in retaliation for the deaths of thirty soldiers who had been killed a few months earlier. All of this human carnage came as a result of a single missing cow.

In August 1854 a young and brash lieutenant named John Grattan had been sent out to find and arrest High Forehead, a Miniconjou Sioux who had allegedly killed a stray cow belonging to a Mormon caravan. When Grattan and his thirty men located High Forehead among Conquering Bear's band of Sioux, he demanded the Miniconjou's surrender. When it was not forthcoming, Grattan opened fire on the Sioux, killing Conquering Bear. The outraged Sioux swarmed over the soldiers, killing them all.

In retaliation for Grattan's death, General William S. Harney and a force of one thousand men moved against the Sioux. Harney discovered Little Thunder's band of Brulés camped at this place on the Bluewater, and during the night hours of September 3, 1855, soldiers surrounded the camp and prepared for a dawn attack.

The Brulés had seen the soldiers coming but had been cut off from retreat. With the morning's light a line of soldiers opened fire, wounding the leader Little Thunder and killing two women and a child. The Brulés fired back until the smoke was thick as fog, but they were far outnumbered. The death count for the Sioux was exceedingly high. Dozens of children lay in mounds of bloody pulp, trampled by the charging horses of the soldiers. A few hours after the battle, the great Sioux visionary warrior Crazy Horse, then about thirteen years old, came upon the ruined village. He led the single survivor he found – a Cheyenne woman – back to safety. Some believe that Crazy Horse's shock at seeing the mutilation here helped to shape his life and led him to become the great warrior and spiritual leader he eventually became.

The patch of shade offered by a thick chokecherry bush is the perfect place to take my first break of the day. The clear, sandy-bottomed Bluewater still reflects the blue sky that earned it its name. The battle site is before me, a conical indentation in the hills near the creek, the entire area about two acres in size. There is nothing about this pretty place to suggest its brutal history, and no trace of human activity at all beyond the tiny dirt road that meanders up the distant hill.

Roads are for vehicles, not walkers. Roads don't lead toward freedom but away from it, toward the centers of commerce, village, town, metropolis; the ground before me has likely not seen a human footprint for decades, and despite the bloody history of this place there is no need for commercial or political freedom here. There are few fences, save those to prevent cattle from wandering where they shouldn't. I am not worried about trespassing. The further away from towns I travel, the more the land becomes ownerless. Much of the wild land around me is in public trust, or held by large cattle companies or, I like to think, by ranchers who understand the fleeting nature of ownership. Here people understand that to value a thing exclusively is to exclude yourself from the true value of it. Roads, however, lead back to places where the giddiness of gain and the slavery of ownership blinds us to the real value of the natural world. Or so my morning mind believes.

My break has ended. I rise and walk. A century ago walking west meant walking toward the unmitigable future and away from the European influences of the east. Now I walk northward, following spring's bloom of yucca and wildflowers up the continent. Far ahead, over these hills and beyond, is the great tundra wilderness, the great empty white road, the road to sacred whiteness. If I simply kept moving, placed foot beyond foot, I could follow this path to that frontier. I have the time.

Last winter, in preparation for this hike, I often walked the twelve miles to my workplace. I would have to leave my home quite early in order to make it to work on time, but once I determined that walking was easily as reliable as traveling to work by car, and far more pleasant, the early mornings didn't bother me. In fact, I always reached work calmed and peaceful, with a much broader perspective on life than I had after driving there. Even with such a purposeful stroll as one takes in getting to work on time, such a walk can still provide a lesson. For me, walking narrows the gap between time past and time yet to come. I walk without a past or a future, for the truth is we have neither, and nothing but the present to repair. The art of walking is to learn that walking takes time, but that in time, it gives it back again.

While I can hike for three or four hours before the morning's break, the second stop comes only two hours later. My rest stops for the remainder of the day will be as regular as clockwork, though I do not judge them by my timepiece but rather by the distance I travel. Once every three miles – roughly once an hour – I will stop. Often I remain standing, while other times I'll sit for a leisurely five- or ten-minute break. I sip water, munch some goodies, study the map, and give my feet a break. I study the land ahead, contemplating the route Dull Knife was likely to have taken across these empty hills.

My next stop is where I am to meet my companions for a midday break. I reach the faint T intersection of two lonely ranch roads near a bubbling creek and sit to wait for their arrival. The map tells me that these roads – vague pathways, really – are the only auto route through this part of the Sand Hills for forty miles in either direction. Just as I am recalling that I have yet to see a car all day, I hear the low rumble of a large truck moving slowly over the rutted crevasses of the path to my right.

Andy is seated on the back of a flatbed ranch truck. My first thought is that he has been hurt, a rattlesnake bite, perhaps, and is being rescued. Instead, as the truck stops, he jumps down and nods to the driver. The driver only stares a brief second at me before dropping the gear shift and moving on down the road. Beneath his window are painted the words "Sand Hills Natural Water." A sign on a post announces Johnson Ranch.

"He says there was no way through north here," Andy says by way of explanation.

"No way through?"

He nods.

I state the obvious: "That's ridiculous, of course there's a way. We can walk anywhere."

"I think they saw me and didn't want me on their land," Andy says.

"Their land!" I scoff. "They won't let us walk through 'their land'? Half of this land belongs to the BLM, and the other half hasn't anything more valuable than a few scattered head of cattle."

Andy has seated himself down on a comfortable slope. He pulls his hat across his eyes to shield himself from the sun. He does not answer, and by the time Sam arrives a few moments later, he is fast asleep.

I cannot rest. My speculations on the nature of ownership in these vacant hills of the American West has been rudely shattered. For the first time in over five hundred miles, I will have to detour from Dull Knife's route. It doesn't matter that this means we will miss only four or five miles of his route, the point is that no man has a right to stop the peaceful passage of another simply because he does not like the color of his skin, and it is precisely because of Andy's dark sun-brown skin, I believe, that the rancher has demanded we turn back.

Before Sam falls asleep too, I wake Andy and we build a shade shelter, propping two of the corners of a tarp with sticks and anchoring the other two with rocks. After a midday meal of freeze-dried soup and jerky, the two of them crawl under the tarp and are asleep in seconds. I rest by writing in my journal. This break is the most important, for the heat of summer has come full force from the high sun overhead, and we need to be out of it while the hottest hours of the day pass by.

I wake them two hours later, but there is no hurry to move on. Instead, we exchange stories of the morning's walk.

Andy tells how he was walking and noticed something moving in the grass ahead of him. The wind had been in his favor. "I walked closer, and I saw a big ol' head pop up out of the grass. A buck had been sleeping there, but he didn't see me. He was looking straight ahead. I got close enough so I could take my walking stick and touch that guy right between the ears. His ol' head jerked around and he saw me and jumped up and was out of there real quick."

Sam laughs and then tells his story of how he nearly stepped on a rattlesnake, and how a hawk he had seen seemed to circle him four times as he walked, and then he talks of the landscape. "This is finally starting to look a little bit like Montana, *eh-nah?*" he says. "It feels good to be closer to home."

"More cattle, too," Andy says.

"No matter how long I stare at these range cattle, I can't imagine them as buffalo," I say.

"Cattle are stupid," Andy says. "They're easy to dominate, which is why the non-Indians got rid of the buffalo. Now we have these filthy, stupid animals. Men always want things they can control, and they couldn't control the buffalo."

Notwithstanding the detour we must now make, we slowly rise, stretch, check our water bottles, and then finally collapse the tarp sun shade. Although it is now midafternoon, the heat is still strong. It slams down on the emptiness of short-grass hills, unhindered by a few pale white wisps of clouds.

Then I am alone again in the wild land. I am following a ridge up a series of long, undulating hills, blazing in the towering light. There are a few nearly invisible cacti at my feet, but mostly I walk on short grass full of blue and yellow flowers. The wildest things seem the most alive, and everywhere in the heated light, life abounds. It is in such a light that we see best our civilized communities. Like heat lightning shattering a dark night, the wilderness illuminates our methodical human world. The Greeks' word for the world – Order – seems inappropriate for the apparent randomness and utter fecundity of nature. After centuries of human alterations, chaotic nature has been hammered into an ordered box. For us today, "order" – the world – is defined as having been modified by humans. In our abhorrence of natural order, in our scorn of the dirt and grime of wilderness, with our the fear of the sharp prick of cactus and sting of snakes, or the threat of mammoth storms, we can see only chaos. Order resides in the comfort of our regulated liberty, our paved city blocks, or our predictable walks from car to mall and from car to home again. Give us our civil liberty or give us death, but never mind the fenceless field and never mind the open land.

By late afternoon my hourly breaks are longer, and my pace has slowed. While the morning is full of dreaming and scheming, the afternoon goes from a comfortable acceptance of walking's labor, to a rhythmic monotony of steps, to the dulled ache of overwhelming exhaustion. I have walked twenty-two miles so far today and all of it through this nameless landscape.

Well past the turn of the twentieth century a farmer in northern California went out to see what had disturbed his chickens and found a strange, nearly naked man huddled in a shed. After some time the sheriff's department handed the man, who was dressed only in a hide breechclout, over to a man of science. The scientist labored to communicate with the strange man and eventually unlocked the man's mysterious tale. Ishi, as he called himself, was the last survivor of an entire race of Indians. He had eluded the modern world for the better part of his lifetime; he was, for all practical purposes, a prehistoric man who had finally stumbled into the modern world.

Eventually Ishi found a home as an exhibit in a museum, where he calmly worked arrowheads from stone and sandals from reeds while tourists stared at him. Rather than embrace the orderly world he suddenly found himself in, Ishi lived his last years in a simple microcosm of his natural world. He died in 1916. Since the tribe never uttered their own names, or the names of the dead, and were careful how they spoke the names of others, Ishi never spoke the names of his family or friends from long ago. Nor did he ever tell anyone his own name, for Ishi simply means "man."

So I reflect as I rise from a rest, stretch, and begin to walk up the slope of yet another hill. Out of respect for Ishi I try to quiet my unending need to name everything around me. To place a name is to claim ownership; in naming our environment we begin to force a false order on the wilderness of nature. Instead, I will simply walk ever northward through the nameless world.

Then I crest the rise and see before me the flooded lake that blocks my way.

For a long time I do nothing but stare. The rainy spring has raised the level of Crescent Lake so that its shores are far wider than what my maps have led me to believe. Instead of a lakeshore stroll, I am now faced with another detour, albeit a natural one, of a couple of hard scrambling miles over a rugged terrain. Then I find my courage. I remove my boots and put on my camp sandals and step directly into the water. I wade out into the refreshing coolness, and with splashing steps follow a mile-long contour through waters of Crescent Lake until I emerge on the far bank.

Another three miles, another rest. Another, another. At thirty-one miles this is already among the longest days of the journey, and I still have another three miles before I rejoin my friends and stop for the night.

Sunset this stop. I am seated on the banks of Goose Lake, another in what locals call the Lake Country of the Sand Hills. Although natural lakes abound in this region, the size and density of the lakes in this area of central Garden County make it the most obvious of sand hill wetlands. I have walked past gorgeous turquoise jewels set in amber and emerald hills: Hackberry and Crane, Blue and Swan.

A pair of widgeons float unconcernedly before me in the magic, long light of dusk. I remove my boots and massage my numb feet. I am as sore and as tired as I have been the entire trip. A new, minor inconvenience has plagued me as well. Because of the great distance and the heat, the insides of my upper thighs have been chafing most of the day. Now that chafing has worn irritating raw wounds, and for the last mile blood has soaked through my pants. The sticky trail of blood that runs down each leg has added to my complaints. When a person becomes this bone tired, there is a tendency for the brain to quiet down in order to conserve its energy and to avoid the risk of foolish desperation. Rather than that, however, I am oddly giddy with a thousand thoughts. In sharp contrast to the sluggishness of my weary body, my mind has reawakened with the twilight. I doctor my wounds, massage my feet one last time, then replace my boots and stand. I have to conscientiously command my dull-witted legs to begin to walk, and yet I am acutely aware of everything around me. The low-bent yellow sun on a million tips in a vast sea of deep brown grass is unlike anything I have ever seen in this life. It is such a light as I could not imagine a moment ago. Because of its mystical angle, the light illuminates the amber hills on one side and shadows them purple on the other. I am poised here between them. Such a moment will never happen again, and will happen forever and ever an infinite number of evenings. I stop after only a few steps and turn to the east. A full moon is rising. I can see the lip of the earth fall gently across the brilliant face. Dove call. Coyote howl. My heart soars, then is lost in the vastness of night.

It is remarkable how few experiences we have had. We know well our history of wars and kingdoms, of events and crises, yet our lives are limited by our quiet desperation. We fight such desperation in our ordered acts of civility, in our gathering as a society, at liberty and free. Yet in nature there dwells a different freedom, one to which I would gladly pledge all of my allegiance, but no widgeon or dove call, no frog chorus or whippoorwill, comes to show me the route to the dwelling of this wild and independent liberty. Nature is so vast and incomprehensible that we can never see the features of its face. I walk in a land foreign to any I have ever seen. I walk though a world that changes constantly, yet the momentary picture fades from the glass and this instant leaves no trace. Even now I struggle to recall the experience of the day, but it fades irrevocably from of my mind.

Tomorrow I will walk again.

25. Good Reporting

Because of the fiasco with the reporter in northern Kansas, all three of us were hesitant about talking to this man, but Sam thought we should try one more time. Both he and Andy are cautious, stealing quick glances at the man across the big table from us.

We are sitting in the employees' lounge at the *Alliance Times-Herald* newspaper offices. The reporter, Tom Huddleson, is the Associated Press bureau chief and managing editor of the paper. Huddleson pops a cigarette into his mouth, fires it up with one hand, and jots in a notebook with his other hand.

"Spell your names for me," he says.

We oblige him.

"You two are both are from Lame Deer, Montana?" he reaffirms, and then looks at me.

"Vermont," I say. I hold my breath waiting for him to start with me instead of my companions, but he doesn't. Tom Huddleson knows where his story is.

He turns to Sam. "Why are you doing this walk?" he asks.

Sam speaks as he always speaks: in little half sentences punctuated with pauses and soft inflections, his voice oddly flutelike and round, his words clear and confident. "I'm making this trip for a lot of reasons. But I'm mainly making it for my family. For my grandmother." Usually Sam would stop with that much, but today he speaks on, his words stronger than I have heard before.

"I'm doing this for my mother, Phoebe, my grandmother, and the Cheyenne people," he begins. "My grandfather, August Spotted Elk, raised me in a traditional way, but my generation is losing the traditional ways. We are losing something important." He pauses, and I think he is finished, but he speaks again, the words strong and passionate. "The Cheyenne people ain't like themselves anymore. The people have lost what our ancestors like Dull Knife all had," he says. "Grandma told me lots of stories about him. About Dull Knife and how he was a good leader. She wanted us to know, she wanted us to tell others, she wanted us to pass those stories on. That's why I'm doing this."

Tom Huddleson does not look up from his furious writing. "Refresh my memory of what happened to your great-great-grandfather Dull Knife as he passed through here."

Once he hit the Sand Hills, Dull Knife and his half of the remaining Cheyennes slowed down. Whether it was out of necessity for the elderly and children who were with him, or whether it was tactical, is uncertain, but the action gave the Cheyennes one more escape from the soldiers.

After he nearly caught Dull Knife's half of the people at White Tail, Thornburgh followed them up the Bluewater until their trail ran out in the dissipated sand hills of the lake country. He found the trail only a few times after that. According to Thornburgh, each time he found tracks, the trail would come up to the top of a grassy hill and then "scatter like quail."

Still Thornburgh marched quickly on, determined that the Cheyennes were headed for Sioux country to team up with the Sioux leader Red Cloud. The soldiers gave up on their maps, which were so inaccurate they were useless. They watered their frantically thirsty horses at the few freshwater creeks and lakes they could find and marched through sand hills "sometimes as high as mountains," through country with "no water except salty lakes and no vegetation except grass and weeds." In a few days Thornburgh's supplies had dwindled so much that the men ate nothing but fresh game, and "everyone is so loose in the bowels the saddles are empty much of the time." They pushed northward now simply to survive. They pushed northward into the Sand Hills, terrain that one man described as "the worst country I ever saw." After another week they reached the Niobrara River, in northern Nebraska, without finding any additional trace of Dull Knife. The only trail they found was that of a military party, which they followed until they met up with men from Colonel Caleb Carlton's command.

Colonel Carlton had been telegraphed while he was at Fort Robinson, in northern Nebraska, with the news that the Cheyennes had made it across the Platte. He set out immediately with nearly three hundred men, traveling roughly parallel with the Nebraska–South Dakota border. Convinced by his Sioux scouts that the Cheyennes would travel rapidly northward, Carlton moved to head them off. He traveled with small parties of fifteen to twenty men to his front and rear, and sometimes the soldiers were spread out for fifty miles in any direction. After traveling as much as thirty-five miles a day through unusually hot days, they regrouped and made dry camps during the cold October nights. When Thornburgh's half-starved soldiers showed up, Carlton listened to their report of the fruitless trek across the Sand Hills.

Carlton grew worried. If the Cheyennes had crossed into South Dakota and were on the Sioux reservation as he suspected, he didn't know what to do. The reservation was supposed to be protected and safe from the military. General Sherman himself replied to Carlton's questions by telegram, saying that if the Cheyennes had in fact made it to the Sioux reservation, then it was a problem for the Office of Indian Affairs, not the army. But, Sherman added, he hoped that they could be stopped before they joined up with Red Cloud, for otherwise the entire reservation system might be put in jeopardy.

On Wednesday, October 9, Carlton's scouts spotted smoke to the north. Soon "the atmosphere was thick with smoke," and a heavy column of it rose from the northwest. Carlton assumed the smoke was from ranches the Cheyennes had set on fire along the South Dakota border. He turned northward to head off what he thought would be the main body of Cheyennes. Instead he found nothing but a prairie fire, probably set by lightning from one of the big, late-season storms that passed through the dry country. There were no Cheyennes.

Carlton then sent his scouts to find Red Cloud and to ask him to come and talk. Red Cloud promptly responded, arriving with twenty-five of his men, nearly all carrying powerful Sharps carbines and revolvers and knives. All except Red Cloud were in paint and feathers. They sat on the floor of a building at Camp Sheridan and smoked. Most were ready for war, but Red Cloud seemed anxious for peace, and the absence of paint and feathers meant that at least Red Cloud was done with war.

"My young men are angered by so many soldiers here," Red Cloud said when the smoking was finished. "The young men have been watching your soldiers night and day. They are ready to fight."

Carlton said he thought the Cheyennes were already with the Sioux. He asked Red Cloud to give them up.

Red Cloud sat silent a long while before he answered. When he finally spoke, it was in a deep voice. His hands rose in graceful gestures. A young man named Billy Garnett interpreted, repeating the words in English with a small, frail voice.

"The wind of the grave is blowing around me," he said. "I am not afraid. My young men would not defeat the whites, but they will fight them to the death if I told them to do so. I have seen nothing of the Cheyenne. The Cheyenne are my friends. Their young men have married our young women and the pipe will always pass between us. If they come, I will take them, feed them and let you know they are here, but I think they have already passed through here and are beyond the Black Hills."

Carlton said he had heard rumors that the Cheyennes were already in Red Cloud's camp.

Red Cloud was angered by the remark. He said he did not lie when he spoke. "I speak with one face. The Cheyenne have been treated poorly by the whites," he said to Carlton. "That is why they are running,"

The anxiety among the Sioux brought on by all the soldiers in the area meant that any little spark could set off a general battle. Carlton was keenly aware of the situation, so after receiving another assurance that Red Cloud would hold the Cheyennes should they come to be among the Sioux, Carlton decided that he and Thornburgh should return to Fort Robinson. They reached there October 15, having traveled 265 miles in nine days, and averaging over 40 miles a day for the final four days. Except for Thornburgh's close encounter on the White Tail ten days earlier, no one had seen a trace of Dull Knife or Little Wolf.

The *Chicago Times* reported that a Sioux had boasted to Carlton that the Cheyennes were quite happy to have baffled the troops, and that "one Cheyenne was equal to a Company of cavalry." The paper also reported that the only casualty of Carlton's was a man killed when a loaded gun accidentally went off in his hands. Finally, they dryly commented that they never expected Thornburgh to capture the Cheyennes but were rejoicing that the Cheyennes didn't capture Thornburgh.

The late afternoon sun is shining through the window and turning Tom Huddleson's cigarette smoke from gray to blue. The newspaper man lights another, inhales deeply, makes a quick aside about how one day soon he's going to quit the damn things, and digs in again.

"So where exactly was Dull Knife?" he asks.

Andy too lights a cigarette and inhales before he speaks. "I've been thinking about that," he says. "I think maybe Dull Knife was a decoy to lead the troops away from Little Wolf's band."

Andy explains how Dull Knife's best bet was indeed to try and make it to Red Cloud's people, where he might find help to survive the winter, but he crossed the Sand Hills slowly to keep the troops on a wild goose chase so Little Wolf's half might pass undetected.

Once the Cheyennes divided into two groups, Little Wolf and his band, unhindered by as many weak and wounded, were once again able to travel in familiar fashion of splitting into smaller bands and spreading out. In this manner Little Wolf and his half of the people moved deep into the Sand Hills. Rather than cross north into South Dakota as everyone had expected, Little Wolf's people halted. They set up camp in a remote, hidden valley on Chokecherry Creek where there were plenty of deer, pronghorns, and cattle to help them make it through the winter. They kept a careful lookout, watching white soldiers and ranchers from a distance. Remarkably, for the next four months no one would come close to discovering their canyon hideout. They would spend the winter safely camped in the midst of the army.

The military, meanwhile, initially had no idea that the Cheyennes had split into two main groups. Thornburgh noticed from the trail he followed to the Bluewater that the Indians were traveling without lodge poles. He assumed this meant there were mostly "braves" and few women and children left among the fugitive Cheyennes. In fact, what it really meant was that the Cheyennes with Dull Knife were traveling without much protection from the wild vagaries of the autumn weather on the high plains. Across the undulating hills of grass and sand Dull Knife and his people moved slowly, probably hiding out, then moving, then hiding some more. It was unlikely that they took many cattle for food, as few ranchers reported missing stock. More likely, they hunted the pronghorns and deer that even today roam these hills in great numbers.

Because so many were hungry and weakened by the six weeks of running battles, and perhaps because Dull Knife was arguing with the young men against further bloodshed, the group was inclined to avoid fighting. With the diminishing numbers of men fit for fighting, and with the departure of Little Wolf, a new hierarchy for the warriors had to be established in the Dull Knife band. Others were needed to lead the warriors now that Little Wolf was gone. One of the young men who stepped forward to speak for the warriors was a giant of a man known as Wild Hog.

Wild Hog towered over all the other Cheyennes; his wide, meaty face, his huge hands, and his broad shoulders made him stand out from all others. Later, after the tragedy at Fort Robinson, and after being acquitted of murder charges for the Kansas killings, Wild Hog would rise to prominence in the tribe, eventually playing a key role in obtaining the Montana reservation. But in October 1878, with the Dull Knife people struggling northward, he added his voice to those of other leaders. His importance was in defending the remaining Northern Cheyennes. Wild Hog sent out scouts a day or two ahead of the main body to keep a lookout for soldiers and ranchers. He spoke forcefully, encouraging the people not to give up. Everyone knew that Wild Hog was prepared to die for freedom, and by his example, others were inspired. Should the need for fighting come, even this decimated group of ragged men, women, and children would be ready to defend themselves.

Nevertheless, the rigorous pace, the long journey, and the magnitude of the physical trial was taking its toll. Many were weak and sick, particularly children. There were barely enough healthy men to ride as scouts, much less defend the band against a large number of soldiers. Each day's journey was shorter than the previous day's. It seems likely that Dull Knife won the argument to slow down in order to rest the people and to give Little Wolf a chance to escape. "This is our country," he was reported to have said. "Nothing bad has ever happened to us here. Let us rest. The soldiers will leave us alone, for we are in our own country." Despite this, Wild Hog and other young men remained ready to fight to the death should soldiers appear.

While Dull Knife's people were moving through the Sand Hills, Little Wolf's people slipped into the secret canyon. And while soldiers under Carlton and Thornburgh were returning to Fort Robinson so as not to enflame the Sioux, the officer who had first engaged the escaping Cheyennes in Indian Territory, Joseph Rendlebrock, was placed under house arrest. He spent three days in a drunken stupor while being held at Lockwood House at Fort Sidney, awaiting trial after being charged with retreating under fire at Turkey Springs.

Tom Huddleson looks over his notes through a cloud of smoke. His seasoned reporting skills show as he tosses a seemingly simple question to Andy. "What have you discovered this trip?" he asks, tapping ashes into a crowded ash tray.

Andy takes a deep breath, pauses, and says, "The entire trip has been a voyage not of answers, but of questions. It was unexpected what would happen each day. Every day I wonder what new things we'll find about the old history. All of these questions, and all of this information, I hope to take back for the descendants as well as for the tribe." He nods to Sam. "Like Sam says, maybe for the younger generation, maybe they will better appreciate their homeland."

It sounds like a good way to end, and Tom Huddleson flips his notebook shut, then pauses and reopens it again. "One last question," he says. "Who is the leader of this group?"

It is Sam who answers, his voice as strong and soaring as before. "We have no leaders," he says. "We work together to move the group further on."

26. A Table Community

I crest a hill above the Niobrara River and decide that this long valley with cliffs in the flat distance and sand hills above is the most beautiful river valley I have yet to cross. Cheyenne bands traditionally camped at particular rivers at particular times of the year, often returning to a favorite location. This perfect thread of blue glimmering in the late afternoon sun must have been such a favored place.

Above the Niobrara is a flat pancake of grass twenty miles across. Around here they call it simply "the Table," this level, featureless plateau surrounded by sudden sharp buttes, a crinkled southern horizon of the Sand Hills, and, although yet invisible to me, the sharp escarpment of Pine Ridge to the north.

The Table is home to a dozen ranches, a cemetery, one church, one school, and one 4-H club. The members of the Highland Huddles 4-H Club have placed a sign at the edge of the Table. Hand-painted bold letters announce "Table Community," and below it are listed the names of all the community's ranchers with simple directions to each. "Anton Wohlers," the sign reads, "5w 1.5s 1.5w." And, "Table Center School 5w 3s." It takes me a moment of staring before I figure out the system: to get to Table Center School I would need to travel five miles west, then three miles south, and so on, each place located by this east–west–north–south designation.

I study the sign again. The residents on the Table are tied closely together. Family blood lines cover the Table like a finely woven cloth. Among the small handful of names are two Gregorys, two Bruns, and three Scherebarths. Although I cannot see a solitary dwelling from where I stand, and houses are miles apart, there is more of a human community here than exits with people placed side by side on the same floor of a triple-locked suburban apartment complex. Here, certainly, flourishes the protective and nurturing impulse of our human desire to gather together in a band of kindred souls.

Some archaeologists have recently suggested that one reason *Homo sapiens* flourished and ultimately survived, when our other erect cousins the Neanderthals did not, was because of a crucial innovation. While the Neanderthal used tools and possibly built simple shelters as did *Homo sapiens,* the latter also developed strong social ties of family, clan, and tribe. With the formation of communities, our human ancestors were able to band together and thus expand their means of survival to include farming and trapping. Only by living in communities were humans able to flourish and give voice to creative impulses of art, music, and language.

We talked of just such things earlier today at lunch as we sat at a picnic table in the pretty city park in Hemingford for our midday break from the heat. Shady old cottonwoods protected us from the blistering sun, and across the way the air filled with laughter and shouts from children packed into the city pool. We sat at our picnic table and talked about how, without community, the Cheyenne people would not have survived. The topic of conversation combined with the shouts of the playing children had me longing for my own sweet and distant family.

Andy has stepchildren but no children. His home is located in a small compound of houses where his sisters, brother, and parents all live. A scattering of half-brothers and sisters, cousins, children of his stepchildren and friends live close by. I live in a house with my wife and two children. We say hello to our neighbors and exchange pleasantries. My mother and my brothers are over a thousand miles away.

"The struggle to stay alive does a lot of damage to a community," I said, thinking of my family and then of how the venom injected by the spreading jaws between poverty and wealth threatens even my little region of Vermont. My brothers live far away because our jobs and the modern way of life forced us to move apart. We are lucky, at least, to have jobs, and the money to travel for visits. In Vermont many people have been hit hard by a New England economy that has been sluggish for decades. They're out of work, and many are in poverty. It's hard to maintain a sense of community under those conditions.

"It's desperation," Andy said. "People get overcome and then they get desperate. On the reservation there is a lot of desperation where money is concerned, but there are some very poor families who never get desperate. They stick together and manage to deal with all of the problems, and they survive those problems."

"There's desperation everywhere," I said. "People get desperate for things: money, or fame, or power."

Andy lit one of his cigarettes, and the smoke drifted lazily in the sunlight toward the diamond splashes and shouts from the pool. "I think desperation is always related to money."

"Maybe," I said. "Or fear of death. When people get desperate one of the first things to go is that sense of community. They revert to primitive ways of doing things; they react out of pure self-interest, without a thought for the community."

Andy nodded, pushed out a "yeah," then said: "One big problem is, desperation causes people to panic. It leads them to take advantage of situations for the wrong reasons. The Cheyenne are famous for being generous, but there are many Cheyenne who have gone broke giving away money and possessions, only to realize that other Cheyenne have simply been taking advantage of them. Still, like I said, I know a lot of very poor families who have nothing, but they manage to deal with all of their problems and they manage to survive without growing desperate for money."

"Maybe that's because of the good pride again," I said. "Bad pride causes people to grow desperate for even more money, or fame, or whatever riches people hold dear."

"Yeah," Andy said again. "I think bad pride and desperation can kill a community just like it could harm a camp in them days. You could be a good hunter, or tracker, or storyteller, or whatever skill you have. You can take those skills either as a way of serving the community, or take them as something you get to boast about."

"That boy they left in Kansas with a broken leg, what do you think: Would he have grown desperate?"

Andy inhaled slowly on his cigarette before he answered. "If he had enough good pride he would have said, 'Go on, leave me and save yourself.' He could have been desperate, though, and said, 'Save me!'"

"Surely the survival of the entire community would have been at stake if they had tried to take him along," I said.

"I think it would have been wrong for him even to have

shouted, 'Be sure that my family is looked after,' for that would have been desperate too.'"

I thought about that for a moment. It was difficult to accept that the best way for him to have served the community would have been not to request preferential treatment for his family. "Either way," I finally said, "it must have been hard for his family to leave him there."

There was a silence. Sam rose up and walked off to find a good place for a long nap.

Andy laughed then. "There was this guy who went around camp in them days collecting stuff off the ground and tying it on a long rope; wherever he went he kept tying more on to the rope and then would drag it behind him all over the place and wave it in the air. He was a little crazy, but people just said this was what he did and let him carry on.

"Then one day the cavalry appeared on a hillside next to camp and no one knew they were coming so the people were running about trying to get their stuff together to escape. Well, this guy, he just went about his normal thing, pulling his long rope behind him and dancing all around at the edge of the camp. The officer in charge of the cavalry watched this guy and thought he was a medicine man putting a curse on them in case they crossed where he danced and so they decided not to charge.

"The officer got down off his horse and called to the chief and they talked and said they wouldn't attack this time, but they wanted them out of the area or else next time they would attack. So the camp was saved all because of a guy most people thought was crazy."

At that we both got up from the table and sought out our own shady spots for a nap. Andy chose a place near a cottonwood, with the curve of a root for a pillow, and mine was flat out on the green mattress of mowed grass. Our small community of three formed a rough triangle about the picnic table; ragged and worn, dirty and sun-black, we must have presented quite a sight to the townspeople who strolled past. But they need not have worried, for we were as nonthreatening and content a group of men as this modern, desperate age is likely to produce, wanting nothing more than to nap through the heat of a summer's day.

Just before I fell asleep Andy said, "There was this saying as I was growing up that if it hadn't been for coffee we wouldn't be here. That's because the few who managed to escape from Fort Robinson were able to get away because the soldiers who were chasing them had to stop to make coffee all the time."

I closed my eyes and wondered if in Dull Knife's time the heated summer air shimmered with such priceless silver sounds when children played in cool pools of blue water.

It is now seven in the evening, and although we slept a good long while at the park this afternoon, my thermometer says it is still one hundred degrees. I walk past the "Table Community" sign and climb up a long hill above the Niobrara River. It is hot enough that I keep rationing my water supply so I don't drink it all at once.

At the top of this hill the land flattens suddenly out to form the broad table. Just as I approach the top of the hill and am about to step onto the flat expanse of the Table, I spy a gigantic dark shape on a fence post. The golden eagle has been watching me for a long while. It sits with its head cranked parallel to the ground – it is eyeing the sky or something beyond the lip of the hill – then snaps it upright to steal a glance at me. It does not fly off even as I approach closer, though something in its agitated stance assures me it is about to explode into flight. Finally it leaps off the post, dark wing feathers pounding the air, and flies off away and low across the flat tableland.

Somewhere in the distance, where the eagle is a fading shape flapping wide wings to soar, is the place where Dull Knife and his people were finally captured.

I stop to watch the black speck of eagle. Here are spirits: Cheyenne ancestor spirits. Still, I can't help feeling that the essence of my own great-great-grandparents has joined me here in spite of the foreignness of this grass-covered tabletop and these strange pronghorn plains and the cry of that distant eagle. Maybe what I am to learn from this study of history is that while the events of the past are bound to specific times and places, the human essence of those events is free from such constraints. The intricate details of this Cheyenne history have become less and less important the more I learn, until they have fallen away before the reality of the human story. Now even that reality fades before the resurrected spirits – the living, breathing reality – of all the people who have come before me. In coming to know the tragedy and triumph of the Cheyennes on these prairies, my ancestor spirits have been set free to speak to me with their own human voices. My ancestors and parents, like all people before me, felt the anguish of war, the suffering of loss, and the joy of life's delicate balance. It is their sound, that community of voices, that I hear in the eagle's cry.

I jerk to a stop at the top of the hill. A hundred yards ahead, near a car and seated on the flat grass at the side of the dirt road, is a human being. He sits motionless, hatless, his back in the full sun. Although he may well be in trouble, I know enough to realize that I won't be much good to him if I invite heatstroke by running the last of the distance between us.

When I am closer he speaks first, shouting, but not rising up.

"It's my damn bad luck," he says. "I didn't bring any water, because I was just headed into town."

I remove my full quart bottle as I walk to him. He takes it without looking at me and without rising, his eyes fixed on the contents. He gurgles a good half of the quart before he comes up for air, gasping and drooling like some prehistoric pale ape, suddenly awakened in a strange world.

He wears a mechanic's steel-gray shirt. "Mel" is sewed in yellow over his left shirt pocket. He is probably in his early or midfifties, chubby and with pasty white skin in little droopy folds on his chin. His mid-1970s model Buick has a series of dents and creases, and it lists starboard, the right rear tire a pool of flattened rubber.

Mel does not thank me for the water but instead begins to talk in a childlike excited chatter. "I'll be all right. I'm here visiting my friend. My best friend, actually. That's his ranch over there." He nods and I pick out a cluster of trees and buildings across the flat Table two miles to the northeast. "We were on our way into Hemingford for a drink or two. He's walking back to his ranch and is going to drive back in his truck with an air compressor to fix the flat."

"You live around here too?" I ask.

"I was born not far from here, but I moved to South Dakota.

Biggest mistake of my life," he says. He rests the hand that still holds the open water bottle on his knee and waves it as he talks.

I want to steer the conversation away from desperation, so I nod back toward the distant ranch. "How long have you known your friend?"

"We were very best friends growing up here on the Table. Still are, even though I live somewhere else. I come and visit him as often as I can. We're the same age. We were always exactly like each other. We had a great time as kids. Always together. Always doing things that were exciting and creative. We always have done things together. Why, we even both gave our first horses the same name."

"How about that," I say.

"Rusty," he says. "We both named our horses Rusty. If it weren't for him, I don't know what I would do because my life has been one long downward spiral since 1986."

I wait. He still holds my water bottle.

"In '86 my house in South Dakota got ruined by a hailstorm. My wife had spent all of her free time making that house beautiful, and then, suddenly, it was in ruins." He chatters on; even the heat cannot warm the Ice Age words. "She began asking what all of her work in this life had been for. Wasn't too long after that she became codependent and started going nuts. Just plain nuts. She treated me like dirt, drank, yelled all the time. It was living hell, I tell you. I never thought my life could get that bad. Then we separated. I didn't think I would stay alive without her." He stops, then makes a noise somewhere between a laugh and a curse. "Now things are even worse: I never have any money, and no girlfriend — you know how it is without a girlfriend, and always broke."

It is not the heat, nor the lack of water, but the desperation that shows in the wild eyes of his face. He says that except for his youth on the Table his life has been nothing more than a long series of primal acts of survival.

"I don't even feel human," he says.

I am at a loss for words. "Help yourself to the water," I finally say.

He looks at his hand as if he just now has noticed it holds an open water bottle. He tips the bottle back once again, gulps another mouthful, and hands it back to me.

"You sure your friend is coming for you?"

"Oh, he'll be along here in a bit. He had a ways to walk." Mel looks out toward the distant ranch but does not smile.

I walk away. While the Table raised him, Mel no longer gives voice to the creative impulses it once instilled in him. He holds desperately to the faint memory of the humanizing social fabric of families, clans, and friends in his visits back here to the Table Community where he grew up with a very best friend.

Dusk. Andy and Sam have found me, and we have located a phone. I am standing in a phone booth built into the side of a brick building, speaking in turn to Linda, then each of my children, then Linda again. When Linda comes on the second time I describe the dark wall cloud and fierce winds that are blowing the grit of the tableland hard against the glass of the booth. She describes the Little League baseball game they just returned from. I tell her of Mel and of the Table. She tells me how much she misses me. How the boys miss me. Lightning and stronger winds.

"You're my family," I say stupidly. I expect a chuckle, but instead she answers softly, "I miss you so."

Then I am standing alone outside the booth, waiting for Andy and Sam to finish their calls and watching the darkest clouds sweep off and away to the east. By the time we reach our campsite even the lightning no longer seems a threat, distant on the southern horizon.

After our late meal we sit for a while at a picnic table to talk before sleep. After a few stories of the day, I tell them about Mel and then our conversation returns to talk of Dull Knife and his Cheyenne community that was about to be captured.

"Did I tell you one of the soldiers at Fort Robinson wanted to marry one of Dull Knife's daughters?" Andy says. "After they were captured and taken to Fort Robinson some soldier wanted to marry one of Dull Knife's daughters, but Dull Knife refused. He could have saved himself from the tragedy that was coming. He could have made it real nice for his family, but he had to try and save all of the people, not just his family."

"I wonder who the soldier was," I say.

"As many of the group as possible had to survive. That was what was critical," Andy says. "Dull Knife knew that his duty was to the entire group. The tribe was his family."

The waning moon has not yet risen, and tonight's darkness is black and full. In such darkness my eyes simply give up and other, more sensitive senses take over. It is these that tell me exactly what Andy has before he even speaks.

"Here," he says as he reaches something toward me across the tabletop. "I found this today out there on that flat land."

I fumble for what he hands me. The weight is soft and warm and rests comfortably in my hand. My fingers close naturally around the shape as if acting on impulse or paternal reflex.

"I looked down and there was this rock," Andy says. "It just seemed like a good rock, so I picked it up and I started carrying it in my hand. I was walking and walking and holding this rock and then I realized why I kept holding on to it: it felt just like I was holding someone's hand."

He is right. Although I am holding a stone, it is warm from my touch and smooth and soft and perfectly sculpted so that instead of rock, my fingers insist that they are grasping someone's small, living hand.

"I walked all day holding that stone," Andy says. "And I imagined it was a child's hand. Dull Knife and Pawnee Woman and all them other adults would have held many hands on this journey. So today I was holding one of those child's hands too."

I pass the stone to Sam. The stars blanket the black dome above us, while lightning illuminates the furthest horizon. In a while Sam gives the stone back.

I hold it once again. It is the hand of a child who long ago walked here on a terrible and frightening voyage home; it is the hand of one of my own sons, as we hold one another up and give to the other our courage; it is my own hand in that of my mother or held in the guiding grasp of my long-dead father. Hand to stone to hand again.

In this way we fall silent to the night.

PART EIGHT

All Is But a Beginning

Did the dignity of the government require removal of these
Indians back to Indian Territory without a full investigation
into the merits of their complaints?

Question posed at the *Proceedings of Board of Officers*, January 25, 1879

Home is where one starts from. As we grow older
The world becomes stranger, the pattern more complicated
Of dead and living. Not the intense moment
Isolated, with no before and after,
But a lifetime burning in every moment
And not the lifetime of one man only
But of old stones that cannot be deciphered.

T. S. ELIOT, *East Coker*

What we call the beginning is often the end
And to make an end is to make a beginning.
. . . And any action
Is a step to the block, to the fire, down the sea's throat
Or to an illegible stone: and that is where we start.
We die with the dying:
See, they depart, and we go with them.
We are born with the dead:
See, they return, and bring us with them.

T. S. ELIOT, *Little Gidding*

27. Witness Tree

In the end it came down to a simple act of God.

The night before they were captured, everyone in Dull Knife's camp had seen the Evil Moon, the yellow crescent low in the sky. An Evil Moon meant a hard snow was coming down the White Road of the North.

The next day, Wednesday, October 23, the lingering warmth of summer vanished. The coldest of winds started at noon, and by midafternoon the snow had started. It was the beginning of one of the plains' severe and sudden autumn blizzards. Soon a thick wall of white blew horizontally and no one could see beyond a few hundred yards.

At dusk, Dull Knife and his people were somewhere on the Table, coming down a hill toward a creek in order to make camp. Suddenly, out of the white, they saw some soldiers riding down to the same creek.

According to a dispatch sent by Captain John B. Johnson, who was the officer in charge of the soldiers of Companies B and D of the Third Cavalry, he and his men were just arriving at a small stream during a violent snowstorm when he saw a band of about 150 Cheyennes in a thicket some three hundred yards away.

Because of the snow, neither side had seen the other coming. The meeting between the soldiers and the Northern Cheyennes was pure accident.

Some of the Cheyenne leaders had wanted to fight the soldiers, but Dull Knife is reported to have told his young men, "We are in our own land. We have reached our home ground, and from now on we will no longer fight the *veho*." Despite the presence of the soldiers, the Cheyennes set up camp on a wide flat area that offered some protection from the wind and snow.

The soldiers, startled by the sudden appearance of so many of the elusive Cheyennes, began to deploy in a skirmish line before cooler heads prevailed. Dull Knife, Old Crow, and Wild Hog met Captain Johnson at the creek and shook hands. Dull Knife said,

"We have come back home to go back to the Sioux agency; you can return at once. We shall go to the agency as soon as we can get there."

Johnson was not so sure. He believed that the only way to proceed was not to let the Cheyennes out of his sight. He commanded his troops to set up camp near the head of the little creek within easy sight of the Cheyennes.

Through the bitter night the two sides huddled about fires. In the morning the soldiers gave the Cheyennes some boxes of hardtack and a few blankets. Now nearly a foot deep, the snow continued to fall. Johnson said he knew of a better camp not far away and suggested they all move there for protection against the storm.

The Cheyennes agreed to move to this better camp.

No one knows the location of the creek where the two sides stumbled upon one another that night in the storm. Johnson himself simply said it was on some nameless creek somewhere up on the Table, but the next morning an uneasy parade moved across the Table through the gray air: the soldiers marching single file or in twos, breaking a wary trail through the deep snow, the Cheyennes following in like manner some distance behind. They came to the head of Chadron Creek, where it jumps suddenly off the abrupt edge of the treeless flat land, spilling trees down the wall of Pine Ridge into the White Clay watershed. That night they reached the new camp, ten miles below the lip of Pine Ridge on a horseshoe-shaped hillside. After the Cheyennes unpacked their horses, the soldiers rounded up the Indian horses and drove them to the far side of the hill.

Second Lieutenant George Chase rode into the Indian camp and discovered a few horses hidden in the trees. "I rode back to report to Captain Johnson and he demanded the Indians deliver these, allowing them to keep one horse they said belonged to a wounded man who could not walk," he later testified. "There was considerable trouble over these last ponies. One Indian drew his bow on a soldier leading the ponies from camp. Excitement with different officers prevented us firing into the Indians. All of this in a frightful snowstorm."

The Cheyennes camped in the protective arms of the semicircle of hills amid a thicket of cottonwoods. The soldiers camped nearby. Late that night the Cheyennes were given more rations, this time sugar and coffee in addition to the hardtack. Johnson noted that the Indians looked "more ragged and dirty than generally, with poor moccasins, bad bed quilts or some thin sheet-like cloth for blankets."

Johnson and some soldiers approached Dull Knife and the other Cheyenne leaders. They met for an agitated two hours. Over and over again Dull Knife spoke of the bad conditions in Indian Territory and of how poorly they had been treated in the south. Johnson made no reply to this and instead repeatedly demanded their weapons. After a long while, the Cheyennes agreed to give up their weapons. The Indians went into camp and soon returned with the oldest and least efficient of their few remaining guns and threw them in a pile next to the soldier. In total there were probably no more than fifteen weapons, among them two shotguns, one barrel-loading rifle, one Spencer carbine, and a handful of muzzle-loading rifles. Correctly assuming that only the men would be searched, the Cheyennes hid the few remaining pistols and rifles amid women's blankets and jewelry. "I had a carbine hanging down my back," one woman later recalled.

The storm raged for two straight days. On the morning of the twenty-fifth the storm broke, but it left long, deep drifts of snow on the rugged land. Although Fort Robinson was nearly twenty miles away, Colonel Caleb Carlton, who was in charge of the post and had been telegraphed about Johnson's lucky accident, arrived at the camp with more artillery. With Carlton's fresh soldiers were some Sioux who told the Cheyennes that Red Cloud's agency, where they had been heading, was no longer located at Robinson but had been moved several miles further to the north. The Sioux told them that the soldiers planned on taking them to the fort, which had since replaced the agency and the small military outpost that had been located there.

The *New York Times* reported that when the Cheyennes learned they were to be taken to Fort Robinson instead of Red Cloud's agency, they scattered over the hillside and began to dig rifle pits through the drifts of snow. The Cheyennes correctly believed that being taken to Fort Robinson was the first step in the military's plan to return them to the south. They would rather die in battle in the north than to return to Indian Territory.

Carlton, who was now in charge of the Third Cavalry, set up the heaviest artillery on the lip of the horseshoe above the Cheyennes. The soldiers had the Cheyennes surrounded. New artillery pieces – including a twelve-pounder Napoleon gun and more howitzers – arrived and were placed into position. More soldiers arrived from Fort Robinson. At least three hundred well-equipped soldiers with heavy artillery were in a tight circle around the Cheyennes. The Indians' few knives, bows, and hidden pistols would be no match for weapons the army had trained on the small valley.

About 3 A.M. a Sioux by the name of Two Lance reported that the Cheyennes were saying they would start toward the new Red Cloud Agency in South Dakota in the morning. Two Lance had spent the night in the Cheyenne camp. He had been promised by Carlton that his daughter, who was married to one of the captive Cheyennes, could leave with Two Lance and not have to be taken prisoner if he spied on the Cheyennes.

Carlton sent no message in return to the Cheyenne insistence that they were leaving for Red Cloud's people, but only kept his soldiers ready for battle. "The Indians threw up breastworks, cutting down some trees," Carlton later testified. "I knew in a fight we would have to kill most of them and then be accused of disarming and dismounting and murdering them."

At 10 A.M. Saturday, October 26 – forty-six days after he left Indian Territory – Dull Knife walked through the snow drifts that covered the flat area near the cottonwoods and met with Carlton and Johnson. Here, and forever after, the stories differ.

Carlton testified: "I showed them the display of troops, told them they must go to their people, and all be ready to go to Fort Robinson in an hour. All this time they demanded to know what was to be done with them. I said I could promise them nothing. This, if correctly interpreted, must have been clear."

Dull Knife, however, told George Bird Grinnell that one of the officers kept saying, "We just want you to come into the post and surrender there. Then you shall have plenty of rations and we intend to send you down to the new Red Cloud Agency." This was

said so often, Dull Knife claimed, they at last believed it. The Cheyennes agreed to go to Fort Robinson.

Second Lieutenant Chase was ordered to move on ahead with
the horses. He started toward Fort Robinson with 138 head, but
shot 14 of the weakest and most troublesome on the way to the
fort.

Wagons then came forward for the women and children. At
first they refused to ride, choosing instead to walk through the
deep drifts of snow behind the Cheyenne men. Wild Hog stood up
on a wagon and made a long speech to the men, but no interpreter
was nearby and so the soldiers never understood what he said.
When the speech was finished, all the Cheyenne men began to
sing.

Carlton arranged companies in front, to the rear, and on both
sides of the Cheyennes, and in this manner the last remaining free
Cheyennes of Dull Knife's band were marched to Fort Robinson.
Just before they reached the fort, Buffalo Hump's wife rolled herself up in a blanket and threw herself off the wagon into the deep
snow. Sioux scouts gathered quickly about her and did not report
her escape.

I am standing at the base of a hill just behind the Dawes County
Museum on U.S. Highway 385, a half dozen miles south of Chadron, Nebraska. This is the site of the standoff between Carlton's
Third Cavalry and the Northern Cheyennes, the place where Dull
Knife and the other leaders agreed to go to Fort Robinson, the
spot where the long Cheyenne era of nomadic tribal life ended
and the new reservation life began.

Sam, Andy, and I are with several others. We have been re-
joined by Barbara One Bear and Sam's mother, Phoebe, who
pulled into our camp late last night at Chadron State Park. Now a
growing number of other Cheyennes have appeared in order to
walk the hill where Dull Knife and his people surrendered to Carlton and Johnson.

Barbara says the people who have joined us are just the first of
many Cheyennes who will arrive from Montana. She says the Associated Press story was everywhere in Montana and thinks there

will be quite a few others coming to walk with us into Fort Robinson tomorrow.

Andy's aunt Beatrice is walking near us. She is a solemn-faced woman whose clear eyes and rocklike profile reflect the respect others show her. She tugs at a scarf she wears to cover her hair. She stoops to a plant near a yucca.

"Turnip," she says.

"A turnip?" Mary Irving asks, peering at the plant curiously. "Can you eat it?" Mary is a freckled blond woman who, with her husband, farms this land and is fixing up the old historical farmhouse. She stands staring at the turnip, then calls her ten-year-old daughter, Missy, to her side. Both women's straw blond hair and fair skin shine in the sunny afternoon. Mary is originally from Minnesota but has lived in northwestern Nebraska since 1971. She once taught elementary school but mainly has farmed all over the area and, even though she hates snakes, thinks this spot is the loveliest of all the places she and her husband have worked.

"Good to eat!" Beatrice says. "Someone should pick it. Have it for dinner tonight."

Sam is in front of our group in a cottonwood thicket with Horse Small, an older Cheyenne man whose face is never anything but smiling. Horse just today purchased his first pair of sneakers, believing they will be more comfortable than his cowboy boots for walking into Fort Robinson. He is using a stick to measure the girth of two gigantic cottonwoods along the banks of Chadron Creek. When I ask him, he tells me that judging by their size these two trees had witnessed the Cheyennes in their last free camp.

Sam and Horse discuss the most likely spot for the Cheyenne camp and decide it must have been just here, where the creek bed would provide a place for the women and children to hide and the protective arms of the hill gave the best shelter from the wind, even today blowing ceaselessly from the north.

The group of us begin our climb to the top of the hill. Several are walking ahead, up the tall finger of the eastern half of the hill. Beatrice and Horse are a bit slower and linger behind while Andy's sister, Rubie Sooktis, and a friend scramble everywhere, shouldering video cameras for a film they plan to make about all of this.

We reach the highest point and look down at the cottonwoods a quarter mile distant. This is the place where the soldiers had put some of the big artillery. The exact shape of the hill is now clearly evident to me, and I am struck by how this final hill is so similar to the red dirt bluff outside Geary, Oklahoma, where I started this long walk, the hill where Dull Knife and Little Wolf and all the others camped before they escaped northward. Both hills are in the shape of a wedge. The flat, inner valley of this one is bordered on three sides by slopes, and on the fourth by Chadron Creek, very much the same configuration as the Oklahoma hill. The difference from Oklahoma is that here the soldiers occupied the high ground, and escape for the Cheyennes would have been impossible.

Even if the winds would not take them away, our words are few and somber. "So this is where his luck ran out," Andy says, surveying the distance about us.

I disagree. Dull Knife's luck didn't run out here. Whether the Northern Cheyennes had escaped or been captured here, nothing of history would have changed. The modern age, with its wars, nuclear weapons, holocausts, and environmental threats – its own long history of holocaust and refugees – would still be with us. No, his luck didn't run out despite the passing of a great era of nomadic life, for the simple fact that Dull Knife and Little Wolf and Pawnee Woman and Wild Hog and all of the others had the strength – had the courage – to survive. They survived and they endured. With the inspiration of such leaders, and the lessons of history to guide them, Cheyennes like Andy and Sam and Barbara and Ted Risingsun and Rubie and Beatrice and Horse Small are stronger, wiser, better educated, and better able to lead new generations of Cheyennes into the uncertain and threatening future we all must face.

We climb down off the hill. Loose plans begin to form for tomorrow's walk into Fort Robinson. Then the others drive off, leaving Andy, Sam, and me to walk the few miles into Chadron.

In the warm shadows of late afternoon we talk. Although no one says it, we know our time together has passed and that from now until we part will be a busy time filled with the demands of other people. The simple but added details of trying to coordinate our walk with an undetermined number of others has sucked us back into the world of schedules and timetables.

We savor walking together, aware of the fleeting nature of time. After a bit Andy softly acknowledges that our time together has ended. "Traveling together like this has been so easy," he says simply. "We made decisions well. Someone would suggest something and the others would go along. We worked as a group. I think it was how we made it all this way without growing desperate." Unspoken, we all understand it is the only way any of us will ever make it.

As it always has done, our conversation turns and turns again. "Tell me," I say to Andy. "What does a fairly traditional Cheyenne from Montana, who was raised Catholic, and who went to a Quaker school in the east, think of the afterlife?"

Andy laughs. "I think when it ends . . ." he begins, then starts again. "When I was little, I had this toy. It was a windup metal bug that when you twisted the key and set it down it went around collecting everything it bumped into until it wound down and stopped. That's how I think of life. It's the things you collect in this life, the things you leave behind for others to see, that are important." He tells a story of how once, when he was a teacher trainer, he met an old man seated in the shade of a tree drinking a bottle of pop. They talked, and soon it became clear that the old man knew a lot about tools. Andy showed the old-timer a tool he had found. The old man told him the antique had been used to fasten milk cans in the old days.

"If that man hadn't been there I never would have known what that strange tool was used for," Andy says. "That old man grew sad then. That tool was a reminder of what had been wrong in his own life. He told me how he had been a handyman who could fix anything until suddenly there were transistors and color televisions, things he didn't know how to fix. He said technology just passed him by. That old man said he was once a jack of all trades but wasn't anything anymore. And if that old guy had cried, I would have cried with him right then and there."

Our footsteps are the only sound for a long moment, then:

"As a kid I was always taking things apart and trying everything that came my way to the fullest and then going on to the next experience. I wonder if I'm like that old man: just a jack of all trades who masters none of them."

"We can't relive those mistakes," I say. "All I hope for is that my children won't make the same mistakes I've made."

Footsteps again. The sound of our weeks together, a clock's gravel ticking to mark time's passing. Then Sam breaks his usual silence. "What we leave behind is what the children pick up from us and carry with them," he says.

28. Fort Robinson

Andy's mother, Josie Sooktis, leans forward in the chair and crosses her hands in the air in front of her to emphasize a point. She had been silent for much of the time we have been together, but a moment ago as we sat for breakfast, without any formality she took the seat next to mine and began speaking intently.

I am bending forward to hear the soft syllables she delicately sets like puffs of a dandelion seed onto the air. Her head nods and bobs as she speaks, her eyes flicker and look backward to another time. Her mouth does not smile when she tells the old stories; her lips stay turned slightly earthward. giving weight to meaning.

On and on her words flow, soft round stories punctuated by sharp pinpricks of names and places. She well remembers Buffalo Hump, Dull Knife's son. He lived to be a very old man, 105 years old or better. She was thirteen when he died. Buffalo Hump told her the stories of the hard times from Indian Territory and told her that she should put it up here – Josie taps her head – and to keep it there. And now she is old and talking of the hard times herself, but remembering Hump and her parents and the others she so misses, and her eyes well up. Her hands are always working, and it is a long moment before I realize that her slight movements are a dance of visual message: deliberate stops and graceful parades of fingers, a ballet dance of arms – sign language.

We are seated at a table in a small cafe just to the rocky west of Chadron, Nebraska. There are a dozen of us walkers: kids squirming and eyeing the pancakes floating in syrup, Andy's sisters, wife, brother, aunts, uncles, and parents. Some kind of magical, invisible Indian telegraphic system has apparently been used to make arrangements for the day because, although no one is certain how many people have arrived from Montana, they all assure me that everyone will gather at 9 A.M. near Crawford for the three-mile walk to the fort.

Andy's father, Charlie Sooktis, is at the far end of the table, silently watching the group talk and laugh. Charlie, who is well into his seventies, has an immense but calm and friendly face, with eyes that do not focus right, a large round nose, gigantic ears, and a short, neat Indian school haircut. He politely and discreetly takes a small pinch of snuff and places it under his front lip. At his side is his aluminum cane. I had forgotten about his recent amputation.

His wife, Josie, is the oldest remaining grandchild of Dull Knife's daughter. Josie was twice married, and four of her children are at the table: each built on a tall, thin frame of muscle and bone, just like their mother. Her adult children talk and laugh and occasionally glance at the two of us seated at the furthest end of the table. Josie continues to talk to me. Her voice is full of breath, like the wind in water some quiet night; vowels the shape of lakes, consonants the waves on their shores.

Despite the early hour, the cafe is busy. Josie pauses, and because of the din, it is a moment before I notice that Charlie has bowed his head and has begun to recite a long grace in Cheyenne. One by one the others at our table fall silent and bow their heads. Charlie continues to pray. I have never seen anything like it. As he speaks the entire room begins to hush, a strange silence falls as others all about us grow quieter and quieter until the voice of the old gentleman is all that is heard in the room full of people. As he finishes, there is a momentary stillness, then the room bursts back into the normal chatter of private conversations.

Josie does not miss a beat, and as our meal is served and we eat, she talks on and on, pausing only long enough to take a quick bite of food or to sip at cold coffee. She tells of the times before and of the events at Fort Robinson. Her words are not meant to be made into artifacts of printed words, for the true chronicle of passions exists solely in spoken words.

An hour later we are seated at picnic tables near the roadside three miles from Fort Robinson. Despite my earlier doubts, one after another Montana car has magically appeared off the road and pulled to a stop. Andy is doing his best to make certain I am introduced to every person, but before long the group has grown to over forty and I am having difficulty remembering many names.

This gathering must be much like a gathering one hundred years ago, with people arriving from different points to come together at one central place. People are reuniting, exchanging embraces, telling stories, and – a constant sound at any gathering of Cheyennes – laughing. Our "camp" of three has grown considerably but is no less a camp.

The elders sit on lawn chairs or at picnic tables, upon which are boxes of doughnuts. In between animated conversations in Cheyenne, Andy and Sam introduce me to this cousin or that uncle. Andy points out a shorter man with gray hair and tells me he has been one of the main chiefs ever since he was a little boy. Andy's niece Jade has arrived with her friend Kayla. The two young girls buzz about on Rollerblades, zipping in and out among their parents and grandparents and great-grandparents. Other children are playing, and there is much standing and talking. Almost all of the conversation is in Cheyenne.

"I was telling Whiskey Man here all about your coffee," Andy says, laughing. "I's telling him how one cup of that stuff in the morning would keep us going all day long." He turns to the others, and although he speaks in Cheyenne, I can tell from a few words he is describing sites we have visited along the way: Turkey Springs, Punished Woman, White Tail. The men are very interested, listening to Andy's words and asking questions.

The morning is still new, and a thin layer of clouds has kept the heat of the sun at bay. People slowly begin to move as if by some invisible signal. I count fifty of us before I lose track. They are gathering in smaller family groups, packing away food, cleaning up the tables. There is no hurry, but there needs to be some organization in order to get this large group headed down the road. Finally Andy gets them all going. Although he and Sam have walked since Turkey Springs, Andy steps aside and allows the old chief to lead. Someone nearby lets out a long, high-pitched tremolo. Another and then another join in. The groups begin to move.

I turn toward Whiskey Man's Oldsmobile 88. I will drive the car slowly behind the group to provide a ride for the older folks when they need a rest. Almost everyone, even Josie, wants to walk. They are adamant in their refusals when I offer to take the oldest of them in the car. Because of his amputation, Charlie can't walk well and so he alone is seated in the car, waiting for me and watching the others move out onto the highway in a long, broken line of old and young alike. He does not see me coming. As I approach I hear him singing a low, wavering song.

I hop in and start the motor of the big Olds. People file past us, their conversations and laughter drifting out onto the asphalt. We watch the line snake its way around a short curve toward the high bluffs that form the northern border to Fort Robinson State Park. Rubie and her friend zip by in a car; one of them leans far out the window focusing a camera, recording the walk for their film.

Charlie and I follow behind the last of the Cheyennes, and we occasionally stop to give one of the elders a ride. After a mile Josie joins us, and together she and Charlie sit in the Olds and watch the others. They both cry and laugh.

In this way the descendants march toward the place where so many had suffered so long ago. Every person who is here today, except for me, had an ancestor imprisoned at Fort Robinson.

SATURDAY, OCTOBER 26, 1878

It was sundown when the captives reached Fort Robinson. They were led into a long building and were counted while food was being cooked for them. There were 149 "ragged and starving" Cheyennes: 46 men, 61 children, and 42 women. The names of leaders were written down: Dull Knife, Bull Hump [another name for Dull Knife's son Buffalo Hump], Wild Hog, Tangle Hair, and Strong Left Hand. Of the men, possibly as few as thirty were capable of fighting. The post surgeon inspected the prisoners and found most were near starvation and almost all had chills and fever. One man had a fresh gunshot wound in his leg.

The building where they were held had been a barracks. It was a large, open space about the size and shape of a present-day tennis court. Lieutenant Chase, who had been in on the capture of the Cheyennes, was put on duty, and he and half of his company guarded the Cheyennes that first night. Chase ordered the prisoners into one end of the building, away from their bundles. After a search, about six additional guns and two or three pistols were found. "I then personally inspected all of it," Chase said. "I found some lead, powder, caps and bows and arrows. A sergeant reported seeing a pistol drop from a Young Medicine Man's wife. I went to Dull Knife and demanded he get it from her. He did, but said she told him it belonged to her husband who was killed on the way north and she was keeping it as a relic."

Chase placed two sentries inside the building with orders to keep enough light on the prisoners to watch what was going on at all times and to keep an eye out for weapons. No one was allowed in the building without written permission, and under no circumstance was anyone to be allowed in with arms.

SUNDAY, OCTOBER 27, 1878

The next day some soldiers and Sioux scouts came in to talk to the prisoners. Buffalo Hump's wife, disguised as a Sioux man with her hair braided and wearing men's leggings, was among those in the group.

Colonel Caleb Carlton spoke to Dull Knife. "Now the fighting is over. We are friendly with one another," he said. "You must stay here while the Great Father decides whether to send you south or to send you to the Sioux." After a moment the commanding officer continued. "While you are here nothing bad will happen to you. You will have the freedom of the post and may even go off into the mountains, but each night at supper time you must be here. If one man of you deserts and runs away, you will not be treated like this any longer. You all will be held responsible for him."

Dull Knife answered him. "We are back on our own ground and have stopped fighting. We have found the place we started to come to."

TUESDAY, OCTOBER 29, 1878

The next night about midnight, two Cheyenne Indians were discovered in the bluffs north of the fort. Two of the army's Sioux scouts, Little Big Man and Fire Coal, captured one of the Cheyennes. Carlton immediately wired Sherman: "I picked up a Cheyenne last night of Little Wolf's band. Lt. Chase and Hunter are out with details east of here, looking for 10 to 12 Indians he claims to have been with him." Later a small camp was located, but it had been abandoned.

From the beginning, the government never intended to allow the Cheyennes to remain in the north. In his telegram about the new captive, Carlton outlined the army's plan. "If prisoners are to be taken south," he wrote on October 29, "I recommend they not be told. I have few men to spare to guard them." The commander of the Department of the Platte, General George Crook, said he wanted Carlton's forces to be kept up not only to search for Little Wolf but also to be ready to escort Dull Knife's Indians south. Carlton replied that since the Cheyennes said over and over that they had been starved in the south and wanted a northern reservation, he believed the prisoners would have to be tied and hauled to get them south again.

WEDNESDAY, OCTOBER 30, 1878

With Lieutenant Chase out in search of the renegades from Little Wolf's band, Carlton ordered Lieutenant George Baxter to watch over the prisoners. Baxter was told he might be called to escort the prisoners south, and like any good soldier, he began to consider how he might best fulfill his duty. "I tried various plans in my mind in case I had to take Indians south," he said. "I don't believe I could have ironed them without injuring men. I couldn't take their knives from them, for they needed them to eat." After a bit, Baxter realized the best way to deal with the Cheyennes: "Only by trickery could it have been done. I first decided to separate the bucks from the rest, but to no avail. For one thing the building wasn't strong enough, and it would also mean providing a double guard. Besides, the Indians would be more content if they thought their presence here was for indefinite time."

Inside the prison building there was no fuel for the single small stove. Women were allowed outside to gather horse droppings to use for fuel. Some furniture was dismantled, and by this feeble fire the Cheyennes warmed themselves.

So began the ten-week captivity of the Cheyennes: with assurances that the government had not yet decided their fate, and secret plans for their transportation back south.

EARLY NOVEMBER, 1878

The Cheyennes were easy to care for. Their only complaint was that there was not enough meat in the soup; they liked the mush the army cooks made for them and the soup made from beef bones. According to testimony from a number of soldiers, they were fed well with plenty of rice, coffee, and sugar. The Cheyennes were allowed to go out into the surrounding hills in groups no larger than three and to hold an occasional dance. They were quite cooperative: they said they would do anything that was asked of them except to return south. If they were allowed to go free, the Cheyennes told their captors, they would willingly leave behind all of their possessions and depart naked.

Although the conditions were somewhat better than they had faced on the hard journey from Indian Territory, the Cheyennes still had nothing but the clothes on their back to ward off the cold winds of November and but the single stove to heat the large room.

Early in the month a solitary old Cheyenne man was captured at a nearby ranch. He was so badly frozen that the army decided he was worthless as a scout in the search for Little Wolf. With the capture of this man, the single captive from Little Wolf's band, and the release of three captives into the care of the Sioux scout Two Lance, the total number of captives held at the post was now 148.

MID-NOVEMBER, 1878

The main obstacle to the speedy removal of the Cheyennes to the south was an ongoing dispute at the highest levels. The management of the reservation system was in the hands of the often chaotic Indian Bureau, which had been under the Department of the Interior since 1849. The theory was that civilians would best know how to civilize the Indians. This often resulted in the appointment of Indian agents who filled their own pockets at the expense of their wards. If and when Indians became troublesome, however, the War Department stepped in and took over temporary management of tribes through the use of the army. This split in responsibility made it difficult to carry out a consistent policy. With the ever-increasing publicity about the small band of Northern Cheyennes who had outmaneuvered three departments of the military, serious questions began to be raised in Congress and in the press about the wisdom of the system. In addition, neither the army nor the Indian Bureau was willing to take full responsibility for what might yet happen to the Cheyennes. Neither agency wanted to bear the brunt of responsibility for them.

As the bureaucratic wrangling raged, General Philip Sheridan, commander of the Division of the Missouri, complained that there was an unnecessary amount of sympathy in the Department of the Platte for the Cheyennes and suspected they had some encouragement to come north before they started. He believed that someone had encouraged the Indians to act against the government's official reservation policy. "The condition of these Indians is pitiable," he admitted in a mid-November telegram, "but it is my opinion that unless they are sent back to where they came from, the whole reservation system will receive a shock which will endanger its stability. Most of the Indians on reservations are dissatisfied and if they see they can leave without punishment or fear of being returned, they will not stay long." Sheridan had cause to worry, since some of the Spotted Tail Agency Sioux, farther north in South Dakota, had apparently left their camps and were moving to the edge of the reservation. Indian agencies at other reservations on the high plains reported similar movements.

Part of the strategy to move the Cheyennes safely back south included separating the most troublesome leaders from the rest. To do this, authorities accused several of the captive Cheyennes of masterminding the murders of the pioneers in northern Kansas. The order came to arrest several of the Cheyennes and take them to Kansas for trial. While the government's resolve to take Dull Knife's band back south stiffened, the Sioux leader Red Cloud warned that should the Cheyennes be forced to return south, even their hunting knives should be confiscated to prevent mass suicide.

FRIDAY, NOVEMBER 22, 1878
The secretary of Interior, Carl Schurz, determined that all of the captive hostiles should be returned to Indian Territory.

LATE NOVEMBER, 1878
Tangle Hair was given a horse for hunting small game, which was all that was left in the hills about the post. One day Buffalo Hump used Tangle Hair's horse to ride north to the Sioux country to visit his wife. Two days later, while counting dishes from the evening meal, a soldier realized that Buffalo Hump was missing. Immedi-

ately the Cheyennes lost all of their privileges. The doors to the single room were bolted and the number of sentries increased. No one was allowed out of the building except for a call of nature, and then only in small groups of women and children, who were allowed out only at certain times and led to a spot behind the horse stables. Most Cheyennes assumed that such strict treatment was because of Buffalo Hump's actions, but they did not blame him when he and his wife were recaptured and returned to the prison several days later.

Once again Carlton tried to persuade them to go back south voluntarily, and once again the Cheyennes refused. Dull Knife said, "We will not go there to live. That is not a healthful country, and if we should stay there, we would all die. We do not wish to go back there, and we will not go." When Carlton persisted, Dull Knife grew more insistent: "No. I am here on my own ground and I will never go back. You may kill me here; but you cannot make me go back."

WEDNESDAY, DECEMBER 4, 1878

Captain Henry W. Wessells Jr. replaced Carlton and assumed command of the post. A short, bushy-haired man, Wessells immediately tightened the army's grip on the Cheyennes. First of all, he intensified guard duty on the barracks building and tried to unnerve his captives by having soldiers barge into the room unannounced at all hours of the day and night. He himself visited the building as often as twenty times a day, often after taps, slamming open the doors and flooding the room with lamplight that he might keep the prisoners on edge.

EARLY DECEMBER. 1878

"On bright days I made the women work," Wessells later bragged. "I had them policing and unloading grain wagons for exercise." The women worked through bitterly cold days without gloves and considered it more slave labor than anything else. At least once a soldier struck at one of the women with the butt of his rifle.

"They asked daily about food, which was all right. They got more than the soldiers and even full rations were ordered for suckling children," Wessells later testified. "They seemed content and good natured." Contrary to this testimony, Wessells was send-ing telegraphed pleas for more food almost daily during the month of December. A squaw later said that the women stole corn and hid it in their dresses during these "exercise" times, and this extra food helped feed the children.

James Rowland, a mixed-blood interpreter, said of the Chey-enne women, "They were afraid of the soldiers, particularly at night – probably they were just timid."

According to a rancher who claimed to have witnessed the event, one day in early December Red Cloud was brought from South Dakota to speak with the Cheyennes. A great council was held with Red Cloud, American Horse, Red Dog, No Flesh, and other Sioux. Wessells and other officers sat with the Sioux and Cheyenne leaders in the middle of a tight circle at the center of the barracks room, away from the window. Red Cloud spoke first. "Our hearts are sad for you," he said, "but what can we do? The Great Father is all-powerful, his people fill the whole earth. We must do what he says." Red Cloud said he hoped the Cheyennes would be allowed to come to live with the Sioux, but even so, there was little the Sioux could do to help; their own food supplies were low and the winter was very harsh. "You cannot resist, nor can we. . . . Do what the Great Father tells you."

There was silence, then the nearly sixty-year-old Dull Knife rose to his feet. Thin and pale, his canvas moccasins and single blanket worn threadbare, he nevertheless was an imposing and powerful sight. "We know you are a friend whose words we may believe," he said to Red Cloud. "All we ask is to be allowed to live, and to live in peace. I seek no war with anyone. I am an old man and my fighting days are done. We bowed to the will of the Great Father and went far into the south where he told us to go. There we found a Cheyenne can not live. Sickness came among us that made mourning in every lodge. Then the treaty promises were broken and our rations were short. Those not worn by diseases were wasted by hunger. To stay there meant that all of us would die. Our petitions to the Great Father were unheeded. We thought it better to die fighting to regain our old homes than to perish in sickness. Then our march was begun. The rest you know."

Dull Knife turned away from Red Cloud and addressed Wessells. "Tell the Great Father that Dull Knife and his people only wish to end their days here in the north where they were born. Tell him we want no more war. We cannot live in the south; there is no game. Here, when the rations are short, we can hunt. Tell him if he lets us stay here we will hurt no one."

Nothing ever came of the council with Red Cloud.

THURSDAY, DECEMBER 12, 1878

The search for Little Wolf's band had yielded nothing. Under Carlton, troops of the Third Cavalry examined most of the panhandle of Nebraska and found no Indians and no fresh trails. Carlton reported that he thought the Cheyennes had divided into three groups. One, under Dull Knife, was captured, one returned south, and a third, under Little Wolf, was now somewhere north of the Black Hills. General Crook, commander of the Department of the Platte, was not so certain. He ordered Carlton back to the post so the Indians who remained at large would become less alert and perhaps show themselves.

In the sheltered, hidden valley of Chokecherry Creek, seventy miles due east of Fort Robinson, thin, nearly invisible plumes of pale smoke rose from the small fires keeping Little Wolf and 120 other Cheyennes warm through the dark, bitter month.

SATURDAY, DECEMBER 14, 1878

A report from Fort Reno, Indian Territory, arrived in Washington DC outlining the reasons for the distress of the Cheyennes who had been brought to Indian Territory in the summer of 1877. Before the end of their second week, the report claimed, the Cheyennes had complained about insufficient food and supplies. They repeatedly asked that their complaints be taken to a higher authority so as to ensure results. Their objections were not only about the small quantity of bad beef but also about the sickness among them. They said the country had been misrepresented to them: there was little game, no food from the government, and few supplies. The report said there was no known instance when the Cheyennes got what they had been promised. By winter they had been destitute. There was so little to eat that they had to trade their winter

robes for food, and as a consequence, many of them froze or became ill. The report concluded that the Cheyennes had often
asked why the government insisted on bringing more Indians to
Indian Territory when so many of the ones already there were
starving and dying.

FRIDAY, DECEMBER 20, 1878
Wessells sent another telegram east, this one with an increased
sense of urgency, pleading with General Crook for clothing for the
prisoners. "Cannot clothes be issued by the Indian Department
from annuity goods at other agencies?"

MONDAY, DECEMBER 23, 1878
The commander at Fort Reno, Indian Territory, was impatient
and nervous. He telegraphed the War Department asking when
he might expect the arrival of the Dull Knife Cheyennes.

TUESDAY, CHRISTMAS EVE, 1878
It was a very cold, dark day. The bitter, subzero temperatures
lasted through the daylight hours and made the night air feel like
shattered glass.

Early in the day Wessells sent yet another request for clothing.
"Didn't you see my telegram from the 20th?" he wrote. In response, Wessells later said, he received orders that he would soon
be told to move the Cheyennes south, "but never any instructions
as to method." He fired off another telegram. "It is inhumane to
move Indians as ordered," he wrote. "Carlton says the men must
be handcuffed when moved." The response from Crook was methodical: then handcuff the men and "issue such military clothing
as could be made available," but, he ordered Wessells, be prepared
to move them "without difficulty."

WEDNESDAY, CHRISTMAS DAY, 1878
A trader on the post gave the prisoners a box of cigars.

TUESDAY, NEW YEAR'S EVE, 1878
General Crook received confidential instructions from the military headquarters in Chicago "relative to the removal of those

Cheyenne accused of the depredations on the Sappa." The orders originated from no less an authority than the commissioner of Indian affairs, who wanted several Cheyennes sent to Leavenworth to be identified and tried for the crimes committed in Kansas. About this same day the final orders to remove all of the Cheyennes to Indian Territory were jointly issued by both the War Department and the secretary of the Interior.

The arctic, subzero temperatures at Fort Robinson continued for the sixth straight day. The Cheyennes, said several soldiers, "are in rags unsuited for travel."

FRIDAY, JANUARY 3, 1879

Major P. D. Vroom arrived at Fort Robinson from Fort Sidney with orders to take Wild Hog and others to Fort Sidney and then on to McPherson, Kansas, to stand trial for the murder of the pioneers in Rawlins and Decatur counties.

With careful forethought, Wessells finished his preparations for the transport of the prisoners. He telegraphed Chicago. "Ready to move when clothing arrives," he wrote. He then had the Cheyenne leaders brought to his office. After Wild Hog, Crow, Dull Knife, Tangle Hair, and Left Hand were seated on the floor of his office and guards stood ready on all sides, Wessells announced that the Great Father had decided they must all return immediately to south.

Dull Knife was the first to rise. "This is the home of the Northern Cheyenne, our fathers are buried here, our children have been raised here. There is not enough to eat in the south. Fifty eight of our people died there in one year."

Wild Hog stood and repeated the same message.

"I must obey orders," Wessells is reported to have said.

Major Vroom spoke. "I will go as far as Sidney, on the North Platte," he said. "I can assure you I will see to it that you are well cared for."

Dull Knife spoke a final time. "No. I am here on my own ground and I will never go back. If the Great Father wishes us to die, we will, but here, where we are. You may kill me here, but I will not go back."

The Cheyennes walked from the room without speaking further.

Immediately Wessells removed the sentinels from inside the prison building and increased the number of guards on the outside.

SATURDAY, JANUARY 4, 1879

At midday Wessells toured the inside of the prison building. Neither he nor any of the Cheyennes spoke.

At 4 P.M. Wessells had Wild Hog called to his office alone. "I told him I must act and that they had eaten their last meal and would have no more fuel either." As expected, Wild Hog refused to give in. He said he would do anything, including starve to death, but would not go south.

Wessells then had all the windows in the barracks prison boarded shut and every door except one sealed closed. He gave instructions that from now on every morning an interpreter was to say, "Send out your children. We will feed them." Anyone who came out of the building was not to be allowed back in. The prisoners were now sealed in without food.

Inside the freezing building, children lined up for a turn in the single shaft of late-afternoon sunlight that filtered through a crack in a west-facing window. Dull Knife argued, unsuccessfully, to let the children out in order to be fed. The young men refused, saying that if one Cheyenne must starve, they all must starve. The women took out the last of the corn they had hidden away from the times they had been forced to unpack wagons. The women tied up their belongings and made ready for an emergency.

SUNDAY, JANUARY 5, 1879

Troop strength at Robinson reached five companies, or roughly 175 men, a level considered sufficient to move the Cheyennes. General Crook ordered Wessells by telegram to make ready to move and to provide everything possible for the comfort of his troops. Wessells replied, "The Cheyenne have resolved to die before going south."

MONDAY, JANUARY 6, 1879

Bothered by the probable outcome of the impending move, and responding to Wessells's news that the Cheyennes were prepared to die, General Crook telegraphed military headquarters in Chicago that he was unwilling to let the responsibility for this case rest on the military. He demanded that the Indian Bureau send an agent to supervise the move south and stated that the military should act only as a guard for the bureau's activities.

TUESDAY, JANUARY 7, 1879

Another attempt was made to separate the women and children from the men, but the young Cheyenne warriors prevented it.

WEDNESDAY, JANUARY 8, 1879

In the morning Wessells ordered all water to be withheld from the prisoners. Hank Clifford, a local rancher who sometimes served as an interpreter, passed by the prison. Through a crack in one of the boards covering a window a Cheyenne spoke to him in Sioux. "We are all going to die tomorrow," he said. "I will not see you again."

Near noon the mixed-blood interpreter James Rowland spoke through the window of the prison to his good friend, a young Cheyenne man named Bird, and tried to convince him to come out. The interpreter said he could see to it that Bird was set free. "No," Bird said. "I will stay in here and die with the others." Rowland believed that even if there were those who wanted to go back south, they wouldn't have said so because of pride. He said that when the food was cut off the Cheyennes believed they were to be starved to death.

In the afternoon Captain Chase told Wessells that he had learned from Wild Hog that there would be an attempted escape. Wessells did not immediately respond to the news. That night, however, he made a fatal decision. "I decided to take out Wild Hog and deprive them of his advice because he was the leading spirit of it all," he said.

In the morning he would act.

THURSDAY, JANUARY 9, 1879
9 A.M.

Wessells called the commanders of all five companies of the Third Cavalry to his office in the adjutant's building next to the prison. He instructed them to be prepared for an emergency.

Wessells then ordered James Simpson and about six other officers to hide themselves in a small room off his office and to wait for his signal.

When all was ready, he sent for Wild Hog.

Fearing that he would be taken by force, Wild Hog at first refused to come at Wessells's request and answered that Wessells should come to the prison, where everyone else might see and hear what was done. Wessells replied that he wanted Wild Hog to come to his office, but he could bring Crow if he so desired. In a while Wild Hog came from the dark, cold building, followed by Crow. Outside was a lone Cheyenne woman who had just been released from the prison so she might visit with a Sioux relative. The two men stepped inside Wessells's apparently empty office. Once the two Cheyennes were in his office, and to stall for time, Wessells repeated his demand that Wild Hog agree to go south.

The tall, wide giant of a man stood silent before he spoke. "Over one hundred of my people died in the south," he said. "And we know you will starve us to death in this prison if we don't give in and go south. But I will stay in this prison forever rather than to go back south where we were dying."

At that, Wessells gave the signal. The hidden soldiers burst forth and quickly subdued Crow and slapped the handcuffs on him, but Wild Hog fought and called out for help.

When the lone Cheyenne woman outside saw what was happening she cried out the high-pitched tremolo that signaled danger. Immediately a few Cheyennes, including Wild Hog's son, broke through a window of the prison near the office. His son ran to the office door. "Get out of my way," he shouted. "I am coming in with many others." Several soldiers rushed to the side of the prison building with carbines loaded.

Just then Wild Hog produced a knife and stabbed at one of the soldiers grabbing at him. Private Thomas Ferguson's arm was caught, but the blow took effect in his sternum, opening a three-quarter-inch-long cut.

The woman outside continued to cry out, but because the others had retreated back inside the prison, Wild Hog's son stood alone at the building. When he saw that his father had finally been shackled, he too returned to the prison building.

Once he was in irons, Wild Hog stopped his struggling and fell into a sudden, deep, and morose calm. "I did not intend to hurt the soldier," he said. "I wanted to use the knife on myself." He did not look up at Wessells but spoke to the floor. "Take off these irons and I will go talk to the people and make them go south," he said.

Wessells refused and instead ordered Wild Hog to be removed about a mile from the prison building to a separate camp near the cavalry. As Wild Hog was led past the prison building Left Hand emerged and gave himself up; he, Wild Hog, and Crow were taken away from the building. The remaining Indians immediately barred doors from inside and covered any remaining cracks in the windows with cloth to conceal their movements. They could be heard tearing up the floorboards, and young men howled and shouted war cries. "Any white man who would have shown his head in the room would have met certain death," Wessells said.

10 A.M.

Wessells: "A short time after Hog was arrested, I called Dull Knife out of building. I shook his hand and told him I wanted him to come and see Hog, and I promised him he should be returned to the building unmolested. He said he could not come out. I think the young men held him to the building. The young men then shut the door as one of them pulled him in."

NOON

The Cheyennes inside the sealed prison continued to make a great ruckus, although by now not many soldiers paid it much attention. A squaw later testified that once Wild Hog was arrested, the young men decided they would break from the prison that night.

A soldier chief named Little Shield stood before the people and encouraged them. "We have given up our horses and our weapons. We have no food or water, but we will never give up and go back to that bad country. It is true we must die. We are starving to death in here, but it would be better if we died on the prairies, fighting for our lives!"

Under mostly clear skies the temperature climbed to the day's high of zero.

1 P.M.

Wessells sent word that the relatives of Crow and Wild Hog and Left Hand could go with them to the separate camp. The three shackled prisoners were escorted back to the building to collect their wives and other relatives.

4 P.M.

The building was now as quiet as a grave. The afternoon guard duty was relieved and a new one put in place. Seven armed men stood guard at the building: three at the eastern end, one each in the front and rear, and two at the west end near the adjutant's office.

Inside, the Cheyennes painted their faces and dressed in the best of their ragged clothing.

4:30 P.M.

Wild Hog's wife returned to the prison for some reason, but after she went inside she refused to come back out again.

5 P.M.

Private Michael O'Hearn was on duty guarding the south side of the building. He said the Indians had covered some windows from inside. They had torn up planks and put them up against the back windows but did so without much noise. "They would come to the cracks to look out," he said. "They had made war clubs with spikes from the floor boards in them. They gestured at me from the windows with them."

Inside the prison the Cheyennes assembled their weapons. Five rifles had been concealed for all this time and hidden under the floorboards. Eleven other weapons were reassembled from the small parts that had been distributed among the children as ornaments. Triggers, hammers, springs, screws, even cartridges had been tied to a wrist or woven into a child's hair, where they had remained unnoticed all of these weeks.

With the coming dusk, the temperature fell to around fifteen below.

6 P.M.

Wessells talked again with Dull Knife, this time speaking through the chinks between the logs of the walls of the building. Wessells urged him to save himself; if he came out Wessells would see that Dull Knife and his family had plenty to eat. Dull Knife refused. "I don't think he wanted to go south anymore than the youngest and the worst buck," Wessells said.

7 P.M.

Private Arthur Ross came off guard duty and told his relief that there had been much activity at the windows of the building. He thought the Indians had been loosening the boards covering them. He retired to the guardhouse but didn't unload his carbine as usual and instead told everyone it was loaded. He put it in a corner.

Acting Assistant Surgeon C. V. Pettys reported that Wild Hog had stabbed himself in the abdomen, but not fatally. He also said that a squaw prisoner had killed a child, saying she would kill every child in the prison.

The Cheyennes piled parfleches, saddles, blankets, and other belongings under each prison window so people could quickly climb up and out when the time came. Much would be left behind. At the west end of the building the floorboards had been torn up and the earth piled up to provide breastworks for the women and children in case the fight came inside.

Into the clear, frozen sky, the full moon had risen. Five to eight inches of snow covered the ground.

8 P.M.

At Wessells's orders, the post blacksmith took three strong chains and fastened them with staples on the outside of the prison's boarded-up windows. Both front doors were then fastened securely by screwing down iron bars across them. Wessells wanted as few ways out of the building as possible.

As the blacksmith worked on the outside, the Indians inside were heard digging and pounding.

9 P.M.

The building was quiet as Privates O'Hearn and Julius Jahnzohn were coming off their second shifts as guards. Through the tiny cracks in the building they could see figures passing back and forth in the room. O'Hearn went to the nearby guardhouse to sleep.

Because Indians hadn't used arms during the excitement over Wild Hog's arrest, most soldiers decided that their worries that weapons still existed were unfounded. Despite this, Wessells increased the 9 P.M. guard. He inspected the building himself. Everything was quiet, but he still suspected trouble.

Inside the silent building the Northern Cheyenne people went about kissing one another and whispering words of courage and endearment.

Outside the temperature had dropped to twenty-five below. Before morning, under the full crystal moon, it would reach thirty below.

9:45 P.M.

The Northern Cheyenne women, children, and old men assembled at the east end of the big room, while at west and north stood the young men with the weapons in their hands. Little Shield was at the north window, near the guardhouse, while Little Finger Nail was at the west window. Everyone waited for Little Finger Nail's shot, which would be the signal to run.

Private Frank Schmidt was patrolling the southwest corner of the building. Twenty-one men were on prison guard. Schmidt and the others around the building had been ordered to overlap one another's beats. Schmidt had just reached the end of his beat and turned when he was struck by a ball fired from Little Finger Nail's carbine. According to the medical history at Fort Robinson, the ball struck Schmidt's belt buckle, glanced, penetrated his abdomen, and exited on the right side of his spine, lodged in his overcoat. Schmidt gave a loud scream, raised his hands, and fell over backward. His intestinal cavity was full of blood. Five minutes later he was drawing an occasional breath, but there was no pulse. The ball that killed him was preserved.

Little Shield followed Little Finger Nail's first shot with his own, hitting Private Peter Hulse in the upper leg. The ball shattered Hulse's femur and escaped through the right buttock, tearing out fourteen bone fragments, each a couple of inches long. There was much blood, pain, and shock. He was later taken to the hospital, a cold water dressing was applied, and he was given a gram of morphine and some stimulants. By the next day the shock wore off and he seemed in pretty good condition, but he died two weeks later, delirious.

Corporal of the Guards Ed Pulver, also on guard duty, heard something like glass and pans falling. The main door to the prison room crashed opened as three or four shots were fired. One of the shots hit him in the upper left arm. He was about ten feet from the door when he was struck. The Indians had not yet come through the windows when Pulver was shot. He returned fire at them when they shot at him.

Little Finger Nail, Little Shield, and the other young men knocked out the window sash and jumped from the window. The others followed, first Tangle Hair and Blacksmith and Noisy Walking and the other the young men, then all of the others, pouring out into the clear, bone-cold white night.

Private Davie Tammany was walking the end of his beat when he heard the shots and a hard crash, then saw Indians jumping from a window and hollering. One shot him with a revolver; the ball struck his right arm. Tammany said the shooting then was everywhere, both from inside and outside the building. "It seemed like a half an hour until I was taken to hospital, and the firing was still going on."

When the shooting began, Private O'Hearn was sitting in the guardhouse, unable to sleep. With him were Privates Jahnzohn, James Emory, James McHale, and Arthur Ross.

Someone pushed open the door and a Cheyenne appeared, rifle in hand. He shot into the room, striking Private Emory in his right thigh four inches above the knee joint. Miraculously, the ball missed the bone, but left a large flesh wound that hit the private like the blow from a club.

With the door unsafe, Private McHale scrambled to the window of the guardhouse and started to climb out. As he did so a Cheyenne thrust a carbine through the logs of the wall near him. McHale slammed at the barrel with the butt of his pistol, deflecting the shot, but the ball split into fragments, and one, flattened to the size of a quarter, hit him in his thigh and tore a jagged, large wound through his leg, stopping five inches deep in the muscles of his thigh.

Private Ross grabbed his loaded carbine from the corner where he had left it, and he and Jahnzohn broke through the window to get out. A Cheyenne was on the guardhouse porch. Ross hit the ground and fired while Jahnzohn shot into a group of figures near the prison building.

By the time all of the other, uninjured men got out of the guardhouse, all of the Indians had escaped. Some Cheyennes later said a few women had to be run out by the young men. Dull Knife, it was said, had no gun.

Commander Wessells woke at the first shot, dressed, and ran toward the end of Company C quarters and the Cheyennes' building. He ordered the soldiers of Company C to pursue the Indians who were running toward the sawmill. "About five bucks covered the retreat," Wessells said. "These were soon killed. By mistake, I moved off to the left at the bridge, getting off on table land instead of up the creek as I ought to."

The misdirection bought the Cheyennes a few precious minutes of time.

The soldiers chased the Cheyennes into the white moonlight; it was said the Cheyennes' cold, bloody fingers froze onto the metal gun barrels.

9:50 P.M..

Lieutenant James Simpson was in the adjutant's office when he heard muffled shots. "I ran outside and saw a soldier on the ground in front of the prison building groaning. I could see the flash of firearms on the porch. The fire from Indians was too heavy for me to go anywhere."

The Cheyennes were running toward the shelter of the sawmill a few hundred yards away, near Soldier Creek. Simpson joined the other soldiers in pursuit on foot until he saw mounted soldiers and then turned to return to the post. "I had gone about a mile," he said. On his return to the post he counted nine bodies, half of them women and children.

When he heard the shooting, Sergeant Michael Lannigan jumped into his pants and boots, grabbed his rifle, and struggled to put on his belt as he ran out of a nearby building. "I got out one to two minutes after first shot," he said, "but all the Indians were all out." There was heavy crossfire in all directions and great confusion. "Soldiers followed after the Indians in no regular order," he said; "they simply ran after the Indians so that men were scattered everywhere in the brush."

Past the bridge at the creek, the Cheyennes fired a volley, and a few threw up a skirmish line. Despite the danger, many fell face first to the creek, breaking the thick ice to quench their desperate thirst in the water below. It was the first drink any of them had had in nearly thirty-six hours. Some soldiers came up from behind and shot those drinking. The Cheyennes ran in all directions; some of them broke through the ice and soaked their clothing.

Privates Jahnzohn, Ross, and O'Hearn continued to pursue the Cheyennes, often as close as thirty yards. Someone worried that the Cheyennes might have hidden additional weapons in the bushes along the creek during their weeks of captivity. Private James Payne said there was not much fire from the Cheyennes by now, but that the soldiers continued to shoot. "We could hardly see who was firing," he said. It was impossible to tell men from women or the dark moving figure of a child. "When they fell wounded they were desperate," Payne said. "They would continue to fire as long as they could lift themselves." The soldiers passed by several bodies and captured two wounded women before they saw the futility of trying to chase the Cheyennes on foot and returned to the guardhouse, where they were ordered to remain until dawn.

A group of five women was found lying under some pine trees. Among them was one of Dull Knife's daughters. She sat against the trunk of a tree, mortally wounded. Strapped to her back was a little child – not her own. Dull Knife's daughter had died trying to carry the child to safety.

9:55 P.M.
As they ran toward the sawmill and the creek, the Cheyennes were divided into small groups of about a dozen people each. They fired few shots as they ran, for behind them some of the young men had stopped and formed a line to hold off any soldiers who were following them. Five to seven of the bravest men stood in a

line and fired toward the soldiers, who scrambled now in ever increasing numbers. It was not difficult to see them, for many had come out of barracks in their white underclothing and were obvious in the light of the full moon. As the other Cheyennes tried to get away, the young men jumped and shouted as they shot, trying to draw the attention of the soldiers. They continued to dance and jump about until all of them were killed.

Some of the Cheyennes did not get even that far. Old Sitting Man broke his leg jumping from the prison window. He had suffered a gunshot wound to that same leg during the trek north, and it had never healed properly. The soldier who found him sitting near the prison building put a rifle against his head and fired. The old man was found sometime later lying near the building with the top of his skull a few feet away, his brains splattered across the snow.

10–10:30 P.M.

About a mile from the post, Major Vroom was stationed at the cavalry camp in charge of watching over Wild Hog and the eighteen other prisoners and family members who had been taken from the main prison building. As the distant sound of gunfire rose and fell, he saddled his horse and rode to the post at a gallop. Several of the soldiers under his command, including Lieutenant Chase, followed. Once there he moved up Soldier Creek until he discovered a Cheyenne trail. In a little while he came upon a large group of Cheyennes about two miles from the post, below the high, ragged bluffs just to the northwest.

He spied the main body as they were crossing a gully. Vroom said, "I thought they had gone into the ravine."

He was wrong. The Cheyennes had crossed the ravine, then had circled around a bluff and doubled back on their trail. They watched Vroom's men approach the ravine and waited.

"I had no idea there was a trail leading up into bluffs," Vroom said. He dismounted his company, and as the soldiers prepared to attack the ravine in front of them, the Cheyennes fired from the opposite direction in the shelter of some trees.

11–11:30 P.M.

Wessells had returned to the fort, gathered together about fifty men from Companies C and H, and then led them west to the bluffs, where he found Vroom and Lieutenant Chase. Vroom had dismounted his command and had charged some Cheyennes. Wessells observed that "the men had killed quite a number of Indians."

A fourteen-year-old Cheyenne boy who was with this group said another group was in the bluffs. He said that when he and several others were attacked they fell to the ground. "Just as the people dropped, the troops fired on us," he said. "A good many people were killed here." Some of the people stood up and ran through the line of Vroom's soldiers and escaped into the bluffs. The boy was among those who escaped. Once he reached the bluffs he and a few others hid in a small cave. "We could hear the women and children crying and at last the shooting stopped." Some while later he heard wagons coming to load the dead and wounded.

After this skirmish, Wessells ordered Vroom northwest up the valley of Hat Creek Road so as to cut the Cheyennes off from joining up with Red Cloud. He then sent Lieutenant Chase back to the fort with the wounded and the captured women and with orders to then take his company around the back of the bluffs north on the Sidney and Black Hills road. Another company was ordered to scout the area between the White River and the bluffs.

Meanwhile, the main group of Cheyennes retreated up toward the ridgetop through a narrow, difficult cleft in the tall bluffs along the creek.

Wessells himself took seven men along the bluffs looking for a way to get up on the ridge. He shot at three Indians, killing two of them. A recruit who had been holding the horses let them get away when the third Cheyenne ran at him. The loss of the horses forced Wessells to return to camp. "Tired, I slept 1 ½ hours," he said.

Back at the post, a soldier reported coming upon at least a dozen armed citizens. Just before meeting these, the soldier had heard shots. He found no living Cheyennes after meeting up with the citizens. He found the body of a woman with at least seven bullet holes. The soldier was convinced that the citizens had been killing wounded women and children.

FRIDAY, JANUARY 10, 1879
MIDNIGHT THROUGH 3 A.M.
Captain Joseph Lawson and a company of men moved to the east, toward Crow Butte. Along the way he found a number of chil-

dren, some alive, some dead. His men picked them up and carried them back to the post. A baby was taken to Corporal Johnson's wife to be cared for. She was shocked to find that the baby had been wrapped in a white child's clothing.

Lieutenant George Baxter was also on duty near Crow Butte and found two young boys. Shortly thereafter he found another trail and followed it. Although he found a still-burning fire, he was initially unable to find any other Cheyennes. Baxter left Private W. W. Everett and another soldier at the fire and went to the other side of the bluff.

Everett rode to within fifteen feet of a small washout and noticed a figure hidden in a tiny hole, covered with a blanket the color of clay. Everett shouted, demanding the man's surrender. The Indian threw the blanket up and fired a carbine into Everett's abdomen. The other soldier killed the Indian, and Everett died the next morning from his wound. Baxter reported that ten men had passed within twenty feet of the Indian but had failed to see him. The Indian's body was placed at the back of an ambulance, but when they got to the post the body was gone. It was never found.

About that same time a local rancher named Bronson rode to the post from his horse ranch to the south and came across the bodies of several Cheyennes "as lean as starving wolves." He claimed he identified one of Dull Knife's sons, probably Standing Bull. He was on his back with his arms extended and his face to the frigid sky. In his right hand he held an ancient knife worn down from a butcher's carving knife to a thin, feeble weapon no wider than an awl. The figure rose up and swung the blade at Bronson's leg. Bronson spurred his pony and whipped his pistol in the air, but Standing Bull fell to the ground, dead.

Meanwhile, the soldiers in the bluffs to the west had retreated to the post for blankets and fresh horses. When they returned, they struggled to find the trail of the Cheyennes.

The night had finally clouded over, and with the fading moonlight the clouds eased the bitter cold temperatures.

At 3 A.M. a correspondent for the *Chicago Tribune* filed the first wire concerning the outbreak: "Over 160 mounted cavalry are in pursuit of the Cheyenne," the report stated. "The sharp bang of carbines can be heard in the hills three miles away. It is thought not one of them will escape."

5 A.M.

Rested, Wessells returned to the bluffs where he had left Vroom and the others and distributed his command like a net over the territory. Some he sent east to Crow Butte, some north, some northwest, some even south toward the Table. Then with Vroom and Company L, he headed up the small canyon on Hat Creek Road, looking for the Cheyenne trail.

DAWN

Henry "Hank" Clifford, a rancher, lived between the post and the old agency two miles to the southeast. In the middle of the night he awoke to sporadic gunfire. From his porch he could see flashes from guns. He mounted one of his best horses and, along with a friend named Scotty, went to investigate, spending the early hours of the morning wandering among the bodies scattered like frozen, bloodied logs across the frigid earth.

At dawn Clifford and his friend met Lieutenant J. F. Cummings and a small detachment of men gathering up bodies and hauling them onto three flatbed wagons. Lieutenant Cummings, who knew that Clifford had been a regular around the post for a long time, asked him if Dull Knife was among the bodies on the wagon. Clifford said he wasn't, and that he hadn't seen Dull Knife's body in his travels, although he was anxious to find it, for Clifford valued the pipes and beadwork of the Cheyennes and knew Dull Knife's body would provide a treasure trove.

Clifford and Scotty continued to ride the area looking for bodies. "I would find seven or eight in a bunch in one place," he said, "seven or eight in another, five in another, six in another."

After several hours they stumbled on a man hidden in a hole. The man had a small girl strapped to his back. Clifford pulled out his pistol and yelled at them to lie still. The Indian said, "Friend, don't kill me, I am a Sioux." The Sioux told Clifford there were some women and children in a nearby hole. As Clifford was searching for the others, Lieutenant Cummings arrived. He had been in the area patrolling for additional bodies.

Lieutenant Cummings located a woman and three children who were "crying and frightened and too badly wounded to travel far." As Lieutenant Cummings was rounding up the Cheyennes he noticed Clifford and Scotty carried a string of scalps. Each scalp was about the size of a half dollar. Earlier Cummings had come upon the bodies of several Cheyenne women, their dresses pulled up over their heads and their naked bodies exposed and mutilated in obscene ways. Cummings believed that Clifford and his friend were the ones responsible for these atrocities.

Later Clifford claimed he had not done anything to the Cheyenne bodies. He had seen many mutilated bodies, he said, but he denied he had done any of it himself. "I was not among the citizens who scalped the bodies," Clifford said. He claimed he never got down off of his horse the entire time he was away from his ranch. "I live here and act sometimes as an interpreter," he said. "It would be very foolish for me to do such things."

6 A.M.

With four men Wessells investigated a canyon on the left of Hat Creek Road to search for Indian trails. When they found one he sent for Vroom and his soldiers. Vroom's troops followed the trail until, at the base of a large hill, they were fired upon.

Vroom positioned his entire company in the creek bottoms and opened fire at the Indians who were on the large hill near the head of a small creek. Private W. H. Good, a soldier in Vroom's Company L, was struck in the side by a shot fired from the high bluff fifty yards away. He fell from his horse. Some soldiers carried him to the creek and laid him on the ice to keep him out of further gunfire. Calm and remarkably relaxed, Good said he got an Indian last night, and this morning one got him. There was a wound the size of a fist in his intestines. A travois was made to carry him back to the fort, but he died on the way in.

The morning battle killed several horses, and Vroom worried that they might later serve as food for the Cheyennes.

At daylight Captain Lawson started west up the White River from Fort Robinson. He saw the bodies of several Indians along the way. Many of them had been scalped. He caught sight of citizens Clifford and Scotty, rummaging among the corpses on the ground, and a bit later came upon Lieutenant Cummings heading back to the fort with a wagon full of bodies.

MIDDAY

Captain Lawson continued to move up the White River until he found two faint Cheyenne trails. One led up the ice of the river. "I sent in a soldier who found a little girl of 7 or 8 who had a pack of cards and was sitting in the snow playing with them."

AFTERNOON

Wessells, Vroom, and their companies of soldiers found shelter below the high bluff, where a sizable group of Cheyennes had hidden themselves. Sporadic gunfire from both sides continued all afternoon and into the evening.

1:30 P.M.

Lieutenant Cummings was back out on his death patrol, searching for and collecting more Cheyenne bodies. Every time he filled a wagon with corpses, he would send it back to the fort. Once there, the soldiers would unload the rigid bodies near the sawmill like so much sorted lumber: the men in one row, the women and children in another.

Working to the west of the post along the main trail, Cummings rode past blankets, lariats, moccasins, and spots of frozen blood. He reached the area where at dawn he had found Clifford and Scotty and had captured the woman and three children. He decided to investigate the area further. He followed a series of meandering trails through steep and difficult terrain until he eventually came to a trail of a few bloodied bare footprints. He divided his party. "I sent Corporal Johnson and a man down a very steep and narrow ravine following the trail," he said. "I told him not to shoot or frighten Indians, except to preserve his own life."

In about fifteen minutes Cummings heard two shots, followed rapidly by a third and fourth.

Corporal Johnson had come upon a small group of Cheyennes who during the night had hidden themselves in a cave. He had called to them to surrender, but they did not answer him. An older woman started crying and attempted to get out of the cave when she was pulled back in by one of the men. Another man raised his pistol at Johnson. Both Johnson and his companion opened fire. The Cheyenne with the pistol was killed instantly. The other rolled on the ground and then raised his carbine and fired. Johnson's next shot hit the man in the head and killed him.

Cummings hurried down the trail, shouting as he went, "Don't kill them unless you have to!" He came to a cave in the face of a cliff and saw a squaw about forty years old, a young man of eighteen, a fifteen-year-old girl, and a small child. Johnson was at the mouth of the cave, examining the bodies of the two men. They were both shot through the head.

The eighteen-year-old had a knife, but he threw it into the snow as a token of surrender. By the time they returned to the main trail it was nightfall, and Cummings had to leave the bodies of the two dead Cheyennes behind.

2 P.M.

Lieutenant Chase, who was in charge of a company of soldiers hunting along the bluffs, sent his soldiers down into the valley to water their horses. While there he heard shots from up a canyon and proceeded toward them. He met some soldiers coming from that way, headed back to the post. They told him how Vroom had been ambushed, and how there was a standoff not far ahead with a larger group of Cheyennes positioned on a high ridge.

Chase and his men continued about four miles until they saw Vroom's horses in a ravine. "A man motioned me to bear left, which I ignored," Chase said. A short distance later the Cheyennes opened fire on his column from the entrenchment on top of the hill, "covering my position completely." Chase put his command under the cover of a steep bank, and then was commanded to accompany Wessells on a reconnaissance. The men nearly circled the high hill of the Cheyennes and were within 150 yards of them when the Indians fired again. "We engaged them for an hour or more until dark," he said. They halted and ate within 200 yards of the Indians.

3:30 P.M.

Having dispatched the card-playing child back to the post, Captain Lawson followed the second trail he had found leading from the White River. Shortly, he and his men came upon a Cheyenne man. The man refused to surrender and was shot dead. Lawson then followed a trail to the bluff where Vroom and Wessells had the Cheyennes nearly surrounded.

DUSK

The fourteen-year-old Cheyenne boy who the previous night had run through the line of soldiers and hidden in a cave was a few hundred yards from the high hill where all day the main body of Cheyennes had been trading sporadic gunfire with Vroom and Wessells. Just after dark, a group of cavalry came to where the boy and a few others were hidden. "There were five of us, and we had one gun and one pistol," he said. "The troops began to shoot into the holes where we were and kept shooting until all had been killed except me. I looked about and saw that every one of my friends was dead. I did not know what to do."

He waited until the soldiers stopped firing. After a bit he decided to move. "I thought I might as well go out and be killed as stay in there, and I walked out of the hole in which I had been hidden." No one fired at him, but the soldiers surrounded him and he was taken prisoner.

After ordering Vroom back to the post, Wessells stayed with his troops below the hill until after dark. Then, after a dinner on a nearby hillside, he decided to return to the fort himself. He left a small detachment behind, and most of the soldiers returned to the post. "I was willing to let the Indians get away here," he testified a week later, "because the heavy snow made travel slow." He was convinced the snow would make it easy to track the Cheyennes when they moved, and he wanted them out of the bluffs and in open land where it would be easier to shoot at them.

Later the *Chicago Tribune* reported that the Cheyennes foiled the troops and that an inadequate force had allowed them to escape from the hill.

EVENING

Cheyenne body count, filed by Second Lieutenant J. F. Cummings, Third Cavalry, Adjutant of Post:

Night of January 9 and early morning of January 10:
    14 men killed, 7 women and children killed
Died of wounds, morning of the tenth:
    4 women and children
Killed by soldiers outside post on the tenth:
    4 men, 1 woman

Lieutenant F. H. Hardie met some civilians at the post who bragged that they had killed a wounded squaw that morning.

So far a total of eighteen men had been killed, nearly all of the fighting force. No distinction was made between women and children, and their twelve deaths were counted together. Probably six were children.

The bodies of the dead Cheyennes were in rows near the sawmill. Lieutenant Edward Moseley, an assistant surgeon at Fort Robinson who had medical charge of the Cheyennes, noted in his report that dead Indians were sometimes scalped, and that he saw one man with the side of his face blown away. He reported seeing several others who had been shot after they were dead.

Four soldiers had been killed since the previous night; an equal number were wounded.

In all, the bodies of thirty Cheyennes had been found, and thirty-five Cheyennes had been recaptured. The captives were all returned to the prison building, except for the many wounded, who were spread out on tables and cots in the guardhouse. Their bloodied wounds and frozen limbs were treated by an assistant surgeon.

A count was made of the weapons retrieved from the bodies of the Cheyennes. In total there were only a handful of rifles: five Springfields (four of those had been taken from soldiers) and one Sharps rifle – a .45-caliber "Old Reliable." There was a single .39-caliber five-shot Colt revolver, a single old navy pattern Colt revolver, and one Remington revolver. Not much of an arsenal to use against a hundred heavily armed soldiers.

During the night the Cheyennes on the hills in the bluffs remained in their position.

The wire filed by the *Chicago Tribune* reported that Dull Knife was still at large and that the bodies of the Cheyennes killed were too frozen to bury.

SATURDAY, JANUARY 11, 1879

At midday a soldier on patrol saw a few civilian men on horseback and some on a buckboard driving amid bodies in the snow near the bluffs. The soldier saw them search the bodies of dead Indians and then heard one man say, "I've got a pipe! That's what I've been looking for!" A man on horseback called to the others to save him the blankets from the dead Indians.

In the morning Wessells returned to the bluffs with about seventy soldiers to find that the Cheyennes had not abandoned their easily defended position. During the day the Indians managed to shoot a horse out from under a soldier, who escaped injury. A rifle discharged when one man slammed a carbine into a saddle boot. A private named Bernard Kelly died after an operation at the post to remove the bullet from this accident. Wessells ordered the men to stand watch and fire if the Indians showed themselves. They were not again attacked by the Cheyennes, and after a long, cold day, the captain returned his men to the post.

The Cheyennes in the bluffs ate the meat from the dead horse, which was their first food in seven days. They used the untanned hide for a blanket. Sometime during the next few hours, this group of Cheyennes abandoned their strong defensive position in the high ridge and moved further north.

The *Chicago Tribune* reported that the "wretched captives" were:

> huddled together in a long narrow apartment that was their former prison. Near the door lay a woman, 60 years old, in the throws of death, unconscious, pierced 7 places by bullets. Within five feet of the woman, a little girl of 7 was combing and braiding the hair of her infant orphaned sister and singing a soft humming of an Indian lullaby. Down narrow, aisle-like space the frightfully wounded men and women, young and old, crouched or reclined without a word or groan, staring at each other with speechless melancholy and mourning, over their dead and stricken people. With hair disheveled and unkempt in token of grief, they stare.
>
> At the eastern end sits the remaining daughter of Dull Knife, who, with her grown sister killed, had been known as the Princesses at the post on account of aristocratic lineage and beauty. By her side is a little girl with big, gazelle soft eyes and bright,

sunny features. The little one has a doll made from an old bloodstained blanket. Tenderly she sways it in her arms. Just beyond them is a seriously wounded mother and her 12 year old daughter who was brought in from the hills more than 5 miles away with an infant strapped to her back that she was directed to care for on the night flight. The mother speaks to the girl, instructing.

SUNDAY, JANUARY 12, 1879

In the morning Lieutenant Chase was ordered to move toward the high bluffs where the Indians had been. Before he arrived at the bluffs he discovered a major trail leading from Hat Creek Road toward a ravine. A soldier had earlier seen a small party of four or five Indians around a small fire in the ravine. When he fired on them, they had jumped into holes that had been dug in the ground and returned the fire. Chase sent Corporal Henry P. Orr and four men from his company around the head of the ravine and toward the holes. Chase then advanced with five other men from the other side of the ravine. Orr and his men were gone only two minutes when shots were fired. Orr was shot by an Indian about twenty-five yards away. The bullet passed through his left arm, entered his chest between the fourth and fifth ribs, and tore through his lung and heart. He fell from his horse and was dead when he hit the ground. He never moved or uttered a sound.

Chase ordered his men to surround the position and not to charge, and under no circumstance to let the Cheyennes get Orr's body or weapon. That night, under cover of darkness, a soldier retrieved Orr's body and carbine.

Earlier in the day a civilian, probably Edward Cook, shot a wounded woman through the head but did not kill her.

A Sioux runner arrived at Fort Robinson from Red Cloud agency saying there was much weeping and wailing among the Sioux for the Cheyennes. The runner said the Sioux's hearts were very bad.

MONDAY, JANUARY 13, 1879

Lieutenant Chase returned to the large, main trail he had found and followed it for about five miles off Hat Creek Road until he came upon several moccasin tracks and a single, round hole in the snow near one set of prints: someone was using a cane. While Chase and his men were coming up out of a flat plain, the Cheyennes rose in a line before his men and opened fire. Chase and his men dove for cover, then sent for reinforcements. Soon Wessells, Vroom, and about ninety other soldiers arrived. Wessells immediately placed the heavy artillery into position and commenced firing on the Cheyennes.

Lieutenant George Baxter was in charge of a twelve-pound Napoleon artillery piece and fired about "40 rounds of shells and spherical cases and dropped shells where I was directed until night when the ammunition was exhausted." Baxter thought more could have been done if the cannons had been better placed. "We could have shelled them out if properly directed," he said. A later investigation determined that at least six cannon shells burst among the Cheyennes.

Wessells had an interpreter call out to the Cheyennes. He told them that if they brought out their women and children, he would protect them. In response he got a new volley of Cheyenne fire.

Wessells considered charging the Cheyennes but decided against it because this was one of their strongest defensive positions yet. "I felt certain I could get a good chance at them some later time, and thought it would be risking too much so held off." Wessells claimed he decided to let them get farther out of the hills, where he could overtake them, but others said he was panicked because the Cheyennes had reached the edge of the rich cattle country where they now would be able to get food and maybe even horses. In any event, Wessells placed soldiers to watch the Cheyennes through the night.

TUESDAY, JANUARY 14, 1879

Despite the soldiers who had been watching them, by morning the Cheyennes had vanished.

Wessells had thought to pursue them then but decided he was too poorly prepared for winter weather and ordered all of the troops back to the post. Once there he got a full hot meal and a good night's sleep. In the morning his soldiers set out again, outfitted for a week of hard winter travel.

The latest adjutant's report listed thirty-two Cheyennes killed and seventy-one captured. Counting both pistols and rifles, only fifteen guns had been found. In the five days since the Cheyennes had broken out of the prison, five soldiers had been killed and seven wounded.

The *Chicago Tribune* reported that the recaptured Indians said they had been told when they were captured in October that if they surrendered, they could stay in the north. Despite their recent ordeal, the paper said, the recaptured Cheyennes were still opposed to returning to the south.

The walkers are almost to the state park entrance. They have stopped twice for breaks along the gravel shoulder of U.S. Highway 20, the first to let a string of Nebraska National Guard trucks and tanks and jeeps rumble past, and the second – a mile from the fort – to munch on sandwiches and drink bottles of pop. Now they are walking again, and the first of them have crested a little hill and have come into view of the buildings of the fort.

I drive behind the line for a moment longer, then swing the big Olds to the left and pass the entire string of walkers in order to drive into the park ahead of them.

I park in a lot near the old parade grounds. In front of us are two small buildings. The guardhouse, where Crazy Horse was shot, and the adjutant's office, where he died, have been reconstructed at their original locations. Josie and Charlie get out of the car, and I help them set up two lawn chairs near a metal marker next to the reconstructed buildings. The marker is in three sections. On the left is a picture of the cavalry barracks as it appeared in 1874, and to the right, as it appeared just before it burned to the ground in 1900. In the center section of the sign these words are all that mark the place where so much came to pass:

Cheyenne Outbreak

149 Northern Cheyenne Indians led by Dull Knife were taken into custody by troops from Ft. Robinson on October 23, 1878. They escaped on Jan. 9, 1879. Ft. Robinson soldiers pursued the Cheyenne Indians until the last ones were killed or captured on January 23, 1879.

Some Cheyenne women pull into the parking lot in a van. They get out and begin to sing in high, wavering voices. The sun is shining on this warm June afternoon and the park is full of tourists, but all activity has stopped and everywhere people are watching. A quarter mile away, the line of walkers has entered the park.

The group of walkers gathers together as they reach the open grass of the large parade grounds. In a mass, they move slowly toward us, past the place where Crazy Horse was murdered, past the reconstructed buildings, until they reach the metal marker. There they stop. At that instant the women who had been singing fall silent and the entire park is motionless and still.

For a long moment no one speaks, and then one of the elders moves to face the group, using the metal sign as a stand. It is Andy's uncle Hubert. He speaks slowly in Cheyenne, and everywhere there are tears. Another man speaks, then another. Andy moves to the front and he too speaks in Cheyenne while we listen.

Someone motions for me and I stumble forward. I am handed a blanket, and Andy leans to tell me that blankets are a traditional gift of thanks. I mumble some words of appreciation and move to sit down, but before I am seated, I am hauled back to the front. Others are bringing me blankets, and before I return to my seat I have a pile of at least a dozen of them next to me on the ground.

Sam moves to the front. He speaks in English, Barbara on one side, Phoebe on the other, resting her hand on his shoulder. "I did this walk for my mother," Sam begins, then chokes back sobs and starts again. "I did this for my mom, my grandmother, and mostly for my great-great-grandfather Dull Knife." His words come out in quick stabs of sobbing, but no one cares: tears are everywhere.

On and on the speeches go. Josie's soft one, and, as he leans on his cane and signs as he speaks, Charlie's heartfelt and powerful one. It seems nearly everyone wants to speak. They are like survivors of a German death camp, remembering those so recently gone before.

Finally Andy's brother Vernon moves to the front.

Vernon is a few years older than Andy but looks younger. His hair is long and stylish, his body framed by toned muscles and limber arms. His jaw cuts a handsome, straight line to his chin; his eyes are clear brown stones. Among other talents, Vernon designs clothing, and he wears one of his tank top T-shirts, emblazoned with an artistic design bearing a single word: Cheyenne. When he speaks it is in clear, straight-ahead English, and his words are cutting and deep.

"That other guy, Crazy Horse, they rebuilt the building where they held him," Vernon says, pointing, "but they have never reconstructed this building. They tell us they cannot find the place where our ancestors are buried. They tell us the river has changed courses, and things are not in the same place as before." Vernon has spoken like this before: his words build slowly to a crescendo, and by the time he has finished speaking he is nearly shouting. "They are ashamed and do not want to let everyone know what they did to our grandparents and great-great-grandparents.

"Maybe it is a good thing they are too ashamed to have rebuilt this building. Maybe it is a good thing they have not looked for the burial place of our ancestors." Vernon punches at the air with a finger and jerks his thumb toward the park headquarters. "Maybe it is a good thing they have not remembered these events, because that way we will always remember to keep the story alive. That way we will continue to tell our kids and our grandkids the story of what happened here. We will tell them the story so that they might stand here a hundred years from now and a hundred years after that in order to tell the story over and over and over again. This way we will never stop telling the story of how our children and our families were massacred all because of the hatred of one people against another."

Then silence. Vernon's words echo across the quiet park, and he steps aside. The speeches have ended.

As the group drifts over to some nearby picnic grounds, I inspect the area where the building that held the Cheyennes once stood. Blue posts have been driven into the ground to mark the four corners. I step off the dimensions. The foundation is thirty-three steps long, eighteen wide. The grass in the area of the rectangle is a darker green than the emerald, mowed grass of the surrounding parade grounds.

29. Dances with Wolves

After the speeches, the large group of descendants drift to some neighboring picnic tables, where for the better part of the afternoon, everyone eats and laughs and talks, fifty yards from where their ancestors had perished. A handful of children play and run about, while women in scarves and men in blue jeans carry on and catch up on things.

I linger near Sam or Andy, or join conversations where I can. Just as the first young ones start to raid the two tables piled high with pots of bubbling stew, plates of hamburgers, mountains of salads, and numberless hot dogs, I am sitting with Vernon. He is explaining how the Cheyennes believe the spirit doesn't rest until one's body is buried, whole, and at the correct place. He watches the kids scrambling for the food. "Instead of being buried here where they died, many of those killed here were eventually buried in Montana," he says. "Some people believe those spirits are wandering around. Maybe those spirits can rest now because of what happened today." Although his words are indignant, he is careful to treat me with kindness and respect. He voice rises with anger when he speaks of how there is not even a monument to the Cheyennes who had died at Fort Robinson.

I join the procession at the food tables, and every time I empty my plate a half dozen people lead me back to the mounds of food for more. I sit with Andy and Sam, but our conversation is cut off by those who come up to us with congratulations or questions. We answer them while catching one another's eyes. Each of us knows it will be some time before we will meet again.

As if by a silent sign, once the food finally disappears, people come together beneath a large picnic shelter. Before long everyone is gathered there. They sit around at the tables, on the floor, or on the grass. A silence falls. Andy's sister Rubie stands. "Some Cheyenne have been working to put the story of our people's journey from Oklahoma on film," she says. "It was thought maybe I would read a bit from the movie script we're writing." She holds a large ringed binder, then flips it open. "This is from after the breakout," she says and then begins to read.

It is a scene where Dull Knife's daughter Trail Woman is killed while trying to save the infant she is carrying on her back. Rubie's words form a picture that all of us gathered here can see. It is the story of the death of a single woman, but we realize how strongly we all cling to the fragile flame of life. When Rubie puts the script down the only sound is of several people quietly crying. Slowly people begin to move about again, and again conversation resumes. One by one people walk away. Most stop to say final words to me. I walk with Rubie, her mother, Josie, and her father and sister to their car. Last words simply come when they come. Josie stands before me and speaks quietly in Cheyenne. Without warning she takes the shawl from her shoulders and hands it to me. "No . . ." I stammer, but she holds a finger to her lips to silence me. Then she is in the car and they are gone.

Andy's car had been parked right behind them. I turn to him.

"Yeah," he says, "walking farther north would be good to do."

"I'll let you know how far I get," I say.

"Okay," he says. We embrace and then he too is gone.

I look around. All the others have disappeared, drifted away like smoke from a campfire. The odd collection of Montana cars and trucks have all gone. I walk around, looking for Sam.

Barbara's car is parked next to where I had set my backpack. Phoebe and Barbara and Sam wait at a table. Phoebe smiles her wide, encompassing smile. Barbara speaks as I walk up. "So, we're talking that we'd like to walk the trek maybe again next year," she says. "Bring others to see it." In a short while we stand. I hug Phoebe and Barbara.

Sam sits at the table, his lip a strong accent to his firmly set jaw. He is looking for words, but words are not needed. We embrace, and then these friends too are gone.

Suddenly all is normal. My backpack sits on the ground, a hundred yards from the site of the breakout. The sun shines on a busy state park in July. A dad, with his small child strapped safely in a bike seat, pedals up to the breakout site. They both wear bright helmets and light clothing. He stops to read the historical marker, then pauses a moment, looking for the safest bike route to ride back out across the smooth lawn of green.

The early Sunday morning dawn is deceptively cool. I make a standard breakfast of hot oatmeal and boiled coffee, take down my tent, and then pack up my backpack. I leave my gifts of blankets and Josie's shawl in a shed at the state park where I can pick them up as I pass back through here when my brother comes to drive me back to Lincoln at the end of my hike.

I tighten the laces of my boots, stretch, and then hoist the pack onto my shoulders. I walk north, past the park's northern boundary, near the fenced field of a friendly burro, across open land of pronghorn and rock, moving my tiny steps forward.

Onward on deserted roads, on faint paths over vague hills, toward chalk cliffs and white mounds. The Red Cloud Hills marking the park boundary linger all day along the southwestern horizon. All day I walk toward a moonscape of bare pinkish-tan hills, streaked with ghostly lines of ash that fell from a distant, prehistoric volcano, which in one instantaneous moment of the violent past, stopped rhinoceros and camels in their tracks and then buried their bones under blankets of lung-choking ash in these badlands of Nebraska.

An hour before sunset I reach my night's camp. I am at Toadstool Park, a geologist's dream. The land here seems to have been twisted into a nightmare of strange, beastly shapes, whittled and carved by the wind and the rain. At the base of the landscape of balancing rocks and serpentlike boulders is Cottonwood Creek, where Crazy Horse and his fifteen hundred people camped when they came to surrender at Camp Robinson the summer before the Northern Cheyennes were to escape Indian Territory. There is no one here, not even the ghost of Crazy Horse. I set up my camp with nothing but the wind for company. After my meal, I sit on my comfortable camp chair and look about. Far away I see a speck of dust on the bleak horizon. Though it is too far away to see or hear, I know it is a car. I watch it disappear below hills and then reappear closer. It is coming here. Ten minutes later a car with California plates pulls in. A solitary camper emerges and busies about, set-

ting up his camp at one of the four remaining tent sites that constitute this tiny campground.

He sets up his one-man tent in an instant, and I watch him power
up a stove not dissimilar to my own. Good camping equipment, I
reflect. I wave. He waves back. He sets a pot on the stove, rises, and
hesitantly comes toward me. At first I think he is an Indian but realize instead he is Japanese. He is dressed in tight-fitting black
pants, a fitted blue jacket, and sandals over ridged white socks.

"Hi," I say and rise from my chair.

He bows slightly, then speaks. "You camp?"

I am confused. "Excuse me?"

He puts his fingers to his lips, and thinks. "Um," he starts again,
struggling with the words. "This. Camp. You no car?"

"No," I say. "I don't have a car."

He smiles, tips his head. "Why don't have car?"

I begin to explain, but he knows very little English. "Walk," I repeat. He shakes his head, brow wrinkled in confusion. I mimic the
action with my fingers.

"Hmmmph!" he says. "You *walk*. Here?" There is a pause.
"From where walk here?"

I try to explain, but his knowledge of U.S. geography is limited.
We trace the location of my starting point in Oklahoma by deter-
mining which states he does know. There are five: California, Arizona, New Mexico, Colorado, Nebraska. With a limited English
vocabulary and no sense of the interior of the United States, somehow this young man had found his way to this isolated camp in the
Nebraska badlands. He looks at me again with a furrowed brow.
"Why walk? Here?"

I laugh. This ought to be something to try and explain. "Indians," I begin. He shakes his head vigorously. "Indians? You understand: *Indians*?"

"Yes," he says, "Yes. Indians."

"How do you know *Indians*?"

He looks at me. "How . . ."

"Yes. Indians? You? Understand?"

"Ahhh . . ." He does not pause now, for he knows these words.
"*Dances with Wolves*," he says.

"The movie," I clarify. "*Dances with Wolves*?"

He nods. "Movie. *Dances with Wolves*. Very popular. Japan." He looks back to his camp, then to me again. "You eat?"

"I've eaten, yes," I say.

"You sit? I eat?" He is pointing back to his stove.

"Sure," I say. "I will sit with you as you eat."

As we walk to his campsite, he repeats my words, trying to master the English. "I will sit with you as you eat."

As he prepares a meal of instant miso soup, we talk. Kazuya is his name. Three simple syllables just like that: "Ka Zu Ya," he repeats for my feeble memory. Just shy of his twenty-sixth birthday, Kazuya has been in the United States for three weeks. He lost his Japanese-English dictionary somewhere in Arizona and has struggled with finding the right words ever since. Thankfully we have nothing but time and will work out our communications.

He has traveled the world – to Australia and the Middle East – but likes the United States the best of all places.

"Why?" I have to ask.

By gesturing toward the twisted barren rock shapes that stand like ghouls in the twilight around us, he patiently explains that he prefers the most barren landscapes of the world. Still, it does not fully explain why a tourist from Japan would travel halfway around the world and drive fifteen hundred miles in a rented car to come to a pile of twisted rocks at the end of a fifteen-mile dead-end road in the most isolated part of Nebraska, all simply because of a love for barren landscapes.

"Why here?" I ask, pointing to the ground at our feet.

"South Dakota?" he asks.

"Nebraska," I say. "This is Nebraska."

I have not understood. "You know South Dakota?" he asks.

"Yes."

He smiles. "I go South Dakota."

All right then: I find it hard to understand why he would come all the way from Japan to go to Dakota. "Why South Dakota?" I ask.

He is infinitely patient with me. "*Dances with Wolves*," he repeats.

I remember reading somewhere that movies are our nation's leading export. Kazuya has been influenced by the popular movie about the Sioux Indians so much that he has structured his vacation in order to see its setting in the grasslands of the American West – more precisely, the grasslands of South Dakota. Until he came here today, his favorite spot in the United States had been White Sands National Monument. "Very good place," he says motioning to the waterless, wasted badlands all about us. He will love South Dakota.

The motion picture show was how I first came to know about history. However simplistic the movies' Technicolor version of who was hero, who was villain, from war to westerns the screen at the ornate downtown theater taught me lessons of the past. Movies opened doors to my imagination and set my dreams afoot.

It suddenly makes a kind of perfect sense to me: the movie's luxurious scenes of the prairie were so beautiful that *Dances with Wolves* naturally would attract a young adventurer like my new friend.

Kazuya starts to speak, then stops. This hesitation is different; he knows the words, but not the etiquette. "I walk South Dakota?"

It takes a moment for me to understand. "You want to walk with me to South Dakota?"

He nods and smiles broadly. "I *want* to walk to South Dakota *with* you," he repeats, then raises his hands. "Is okay? I walk South Dakota?"

Although I had anticipated being alone as I crossed into my last state, I am not disappointed. From the beginning my journey has been one of an absolute acceptance of circumstances. This is what the day has brought me. I accept it and wait to see what happens next. "It is okay to walk with me to South Dakota," I say.

We have gotten a not-so-early start. Kazuya is in excellent physical shape, and I have trouble keeping his pace. We pass Sugar Loaf Butte, walking over mostly long, rolling hills with the ridge lands to the south and west nearly invisible now. Some of the creeks we crossed have had water, but I suspect it is only because of the damp spring and that normally they are dry. After a tedious twelve miles we rest at Long Branch Creek, amid a little rare shade provided by two cottonwood trees. We have passed several abandoned ranchsteads that date from the early twentieth century. They are monuments to the government's final attempt to secure the interior by enticing people to settle in the empty places that still remained on the map. At the turn of the century a new homesteading law provided two full sections of land rather than the old 160 acres previously offered to anyone who was willing to scratch out a life in these remaining empty places. The legislation was sponsored by a Nebraska congressman named Moses P. Kinkaid, and thousands of his "Kinkaiders," as the last wave of homesteaders came to be known, came to the barren places like these badlands to find a home. The bulk of them gave up the waterless wasteland of their alkali dirt farms within a generation, and it is their empty houses we have been hiking past. Most appear to have been abandoned long ago, but the house near where we now sit has only recently been emptied. The white paint is still bright, and none of the glass in the windows has been shot out. In twelve miles we have passed a dozen abandoned ranches but only a single occupied one.

After our break we rise and walk again. The only movement caused by humankind are the occasional coal trains that race through on immaculate railbeds of bright steel and crushed stone. Two or three times an hour they come alive with the deep-chest rumble of a half dozen enormous engines. Behind them slide 110 identical black monster hopper cars, each filled with a massive mound of black coal. Once the violence of the roaring engines has passed, the whir of the hopper car wheels is of metallic wings on gigantic dragonflies. The coal is bound for power plants and factories in the Midwest – 110 cars full of coal, every thirty minutes of every day. Most of the coal that races past in these countless trainloads comes from open mines immediately adjacent to the Northern Cheyennes' Montana reservation. Andy told me the power companies have had their eye on the reservation coal for a long, long time. After the coal train has whirred past, the only remaining sound is of a windmill creaking water up from the depths of the earth to spill out for a small handful of cattle dotting the hillside to our left. A bit beyond the cattle there is another movement: a pronghorn spies us. I point.

"Is dangerous?" Kazuya asks.

"No," I say. "Not dangerous." All morning he has been pointing to birds and lizards and plants and asking, "Is dangerous?" frightened by what he does not know of the land, just as I would be –

have been – when alone in an unknown place. An hour ago we saw a rattlesnake, which gave me an opportunity to bob my head in exaggerated nods. "Yes! Is dangerous!" I said. "Is dangerous!" Kazuya took a picture of the snake. Worries about the grizzly bears of Yellowstone, where he plans to camp in a few days, have left him sleepless many nights.

We walk on into dry land in the full heat of summer sun and talk. We have been talking a lot, really, considering how complete is my lack of Japanese and how limited is his English. Many of my questions confuse him. Words like "sooner," "later," "before," and "after" he does not know, and I must seek compromise words; but words like "massacre," "buffalo," and "idea" he understands completely.

He has survived a 6.0 earthquake; he wants to travel around the world on a motorcycle; he is going back to Australia so he can explore the outback for a year. He works as a massage therapist in a hospital in Japan. His mother works very hard at some job I don't quite understand, and his father is an acupuncturist. He was very good at gymnastics in high school, he tells me. Two years ago he ran in the Tokyo marathon after training for three months. He wants to learn how to rock-climb. He wants to go to Outward Bound in Minnesota.

Just before the South Dakota border we both stop when a sound like a metallic wind fills the air. A blue solitary fighter jet screams the air alive a few hundred yards above the ground. The sleek capsules of bombs and missiles hooked to the undersides of its wings make it look like some metal insect heavy with eggs.

I ask him if the people in Japan of his generation talk much about Hiroshima or Nagasaki.

"Yes," he says. "In Japan we talk sometimes. Many people . . ." he searches for a word that might encompass what he needs to say, "many people *know* about Hiroshima and Nagasaki." Before coming to Nebraska he had visited the site of the very first atomic bomb blast, in a remote desert in New Mexico. He pauses, then, "Very bad history," he says.

Very bad history. So lengthy is the record of wars and killing that even the unspeakable horror of a hundred thousand fiery deaths rapidly fades before the span. Hiroshima and Nagasaki,

Buchenwald and Auschwitz, lost to the past. Very bad history. On and on such forgetfulness goes, until our memories blur at the sheer expanse of the horror: Somalia, Cambodia, Korea, Tibet. Very bad history. Belfast, Jerusalem, Beirut. Beijing, Santiago, Chiapas.

"You know about Oklahoma City?" I ask Kazuya.

He has heard. "Very bad," he says. "Many die."

So a new name is added, a name now connected to all of the countless others by the common thread of horror and destruction we have wrought upon one another. In time it too will fade from the world's memory.

The tragic story of the Northern Cheyennes' race to their homeland has all but disappeared from that memory. The names and the numbers of those who were killed are now insignificant; lives that were once lived are now nearly forgotten, nearly wiped from memory. Dull Knife and Little Wolf and all of the other Northern Cheyennes wanted to create some small place where their children could live in defiance of humankind's enormous, immeasurable history of war and killing. It is not important that the weight of horror makes such a perfect place impossible; the significance of their trek is that they were willing to die trying to create it: the endless irony of preserving life by exerting an unflinching will to sacrifice it.

From the land of Hiroshima and Nagasaki, my new friend Kazuya has been lured to the land of *Dances with Wolves,* the land of the Great Sioux Wars. Here he has found a man who has walked in the footsteps of a few people who once, long ago, fought a brief and nameless war for their homeland. A tiny, forgotten war, but one as great and as senseless as any that has ever been fought.

The fighter jet's roar has faded and is forgotten.

When we reach the "Welcome to South Dakota" sign on a paved highway, it is the hottest part of this broiling day. Kazuya takes our self-portrait using a lightweight tripod. He has decided to turn around and return to his car, but my maps show that the town of Ardmore is only a couple of miles further. "Wait until we reach the town," I say pointing to the tiny speck on the map. "I'll buy you a Coke in Ardmore."

"Coca-Cola!" Kazuya says.

What we find when we reach Ardmore, however, is, in Kazuya's words, "a ghost town." It is a very recent one, apparently, since the half dozen empty buildings on the one-block-long main street look relatively tidy. They still retain all of their window glass, and although a foot-high jungle of grass grows where there once was a sidewalk, the bright and colorful poster of Mr. Zip flashes in the abandoned post office as if it could have been placed there yesterday. There are as many as ten houses, but apparently all are empty. It is a ghost town, all right, probably killed by the effort to hammer a life from the hard soil of the prairie. There will be no bottle of Coca-Cola in Ardmore.

We lean against the locked doors of a shed marked "Volunteer Fire Department." We eat an orange and some peanuts and then doze off for twenty minutes. When we awake it is time for Kazuya to turn back. He rummages in his pack for a pen and small notebook. He scribbles on a sheet of paper and then tears it out and hands it to me.

"Japanese words," he says.

There is a column of Japanese symbols with their English translation next to them: sun, moon, star, I read, then realize my friend has written a kind of haiku:

sun, moon, star,
sky, wind, rain,
walk,
love, thank you, good-bye

I dig into my pack until I find my can of pepper spray. "Here," I say, handing it to him. With pantomime and single-word sentences, I get him to understand the function of my gift. "For bears," I say. "Yellowstone bears." Kazuya beams. He feels more secure about the dangers of the America he has yet to face.

We stand and stretch and put on our packs. We walk to the abandoned intersection. To my left above the flat horizon is the rising dark line that marks the magnificent Black Hills; to Kazuya's right is the grassland of Nebraska and his car.

"Have a good journey," I say. He smiles. We shake hands, then turn away.

Across the street the sliding door of a garage rattles, then moves. We jump back. From the shadow inside an older man wheels out a ghost of a lawnmower. He is as startled to see us as we are to discover him.

He motions us inside the cool garage. "You're from Japan," he barks at Kazuya. "I can tell. I've been to Japan twenty-two times in my life. Yes, sir, twenty-two times – working for Uncle Sam, the armed services, you see, after the big war." Kazuya would probably appreciate it if he were able to understand the man's garbled, non-stop speech. "Oh, hell, yes, I've been all over your country. Know it pretty damn well – like the back of my hand."

"Like back of hand?" Kazuya says.

"So you're traveling these parts of the U. S. of A.? You Japs like to visit our country, huh? Oh, hell, there's things you've got to see while you're here," the man says and then rattles off a list of obscure sights. "And Custard," he pronounces it just like that, "and Custard Monument – where he was killt." He does not even consider for a second that Kazuya might not have heard of it. "You've got to go there." Kazuya's face is lost in confusion.

The man may be Ardmore's only resident, and what happens next makes me believe he might be some ghostly resident at that.

"Hell, you boys look hot. How about a can of pop?" He steps further into the shadows. Against a far wall near a workbench of ancient, greasy tools and rags he opens a small refrigerator.

When Kazuya and I are once more outside on the hot pavement, we say a final good-bye and walk away. A block later I turn around. When I last see Kazuya, he is walking back toward the south, sipping a Coke.

30. Coming to See Bear Butte

Sturgis, South Dakota, sits too far north of the main tourist traps to worry about outward appearances. It is at the edge of the end of this world, off of the Interstate by a good three miles, a good thirty from the golden glimmer of the slot machines of Deadwood, and a hundred twisting miles by highway from the Winnebagos parading up the steep road to Mount Rushmore.

On Sturgis's dusty, cracking streets there is not a single place to buy an ice cream cone, nor a single tourist gift shop, nor a museum, nor a neon-blazing post card shop. If you like your food fast and your stops quick, Sturgis is not the place for you. Even so, the town does have its own peculiar attractions. For one thing, it is the Harley-Davidson capital of the United States, and bikers in leather and beads and beards and bouffants stream through the village every day of the year. For another, no other town in the country has as many tattoo shops per capita as Sturgis. In this town of five thousand the phone book lists eleven places where a person can be tattooed, including a shop above the liquor store and one in the back room of the Road Kill Cafe.

Sturgis is the last outpost in the shallow Bear Butte Valley, north of the Black Hills. A couple of miles east of town State Highway 34 climbs out of the grassy valley, zips by the veterans hospital and parade grounds at Fort Meade, then shoots east into the empty sage and wheat of the western Dakotas. It is sixty miles along this featureless road until you hit the first town – Union Center, population forty-five – and seventy-five miles to White Owl, population ten. Beyond White Owl the road turns to dirt and eventually peters out on the stark bluffs above a deserted Missouri River.

Here, just on the edge of this emptiness, and just beyond the busy and beautiful Black Hills, a conical mountain pops up out of the barren drylands a few miles north of the highway. For the past twenty years the mountain has been a seldom-visited South Dakota state park, but for a thousand years before that it had been the center of the universe for nearly every single tribe of humans to have lived on the Great Plains.

At sunset on this dry July day I turn north onto the narrow asphalt road. The road drops down a hill, climbs back up past patches of wildflowers and yucca, and rises to a small crest exposing a full view of Bear Butte: the holy mountain.

The road to the visitor's center is closed, so I turn to the other side of the highway to camp on the shore of tiny Bear Butte Lake. There is no one else at the camp, and as I walk in a couple of mule deer hop through the short grass and slide down into a draw. In the near distance, the mountain's bulk creates the skyline: a dark, tree-covered stump of stone framed on one side by a nearly perpendicular wall of rock half its height.

Just after dusk a big green Ford truck enters the campground, slowly circles toward the tent, and stops. A park ranger unfolds himself from the cab. Soon we are leaning against the front hood of the Ford and talking. He is a seasonal worker, a full-time undergraduate student at a local college studying the effects of polluted groundwater on invertebrates. His voice is slow, serious, low, nearly monotone, but in an easy, natural way. He is a native of the area, a Cheyenne River Sioux. He nods off to the south-southwest to the nearby Black Hills, where tomorrow he is bound for a conference on the effects of large-scale gold mining on groundwater.

There haven't been many campers this season, he tells me, sipping the cold water I have offered him, probably because it was first too wet and now too hot. "But there are never too many tourists who find this place," he says. Soon he is talking about the mountain he has been hired to watch. "The ancient ones camped at the flat base of the mountain as early as 1000 AD," he says. "They drew pictures of animals with the legs of humans, and strange faces of men on the necks of great birds." He points across two miles of prairie to a place at the base of the mountain. "It was there that the Kiowas got the kidney of a sacred bear," he says, and his arm swings again, toward the slab of vertical rock. "And it was there that the Arapaho got medicine to heal the sick." His arm sweeps again. "It was there, near that notch on the mountain, that the Apache got a medicine that saved their horses."

As the night cautiously comes over us like a thief, we lean

deeper into the truck, and he tells me the Sioux legend of how the mountain came to be here. It seems that long ago some boys went out to gather food against their mother's wishes. When they had wandered a long distance from camp, a great bear appeared and began to chase them. As they ran, they prayed for help. Soon they heard a voice that told them to climb up on a tree stump. The boys scrambled up the stump and the bear clawed at them. The tree stump began to rise up into the air, and as it did, the giant bear continued to try to get the boys but could not reach them. "You can still see that stump with the bear's claw marks," he says. "Today it is called Devil's Tower. The boys flew off to become the morning and evening stars, while the bear grumbled off to the east and went to sleep. He sleeps still, and you can see him there: Bear Butte."

The young ranger finishes the story and looks out toward the red strip of sky on the dark western horizon. He pauses only a moment before he adds: "To the Cheyenne this is the most holy of places. To them the mountain is known as Noahvose."

"Ah, yes," I say. "The very first day of my hike I met a young man who told me this." I pause a moment remembering back nearly two months to the day I had met Cecil Black. I say, "He told me *Noahvose* means 'teaching hill' or 'place where people were taught.'"

"That's right," the ranger says. "That's because here – at Noahvose – the holiest of Cheyenne men, Sweet Medicine, came face to face with God. After that, Sweet Medicine was very powerful," he says. "For one thing, he was a shape shifter." He looks again out into the distant sky a moment before explaining.

Sweet Medicine apparently had the power to assume the shapes of different animals and plants, or even rocks. If he was being chased by the enemy, the ranger explains, he could shift his shape into a coyote or a magpie or a rabbit. He may have been born an ordinary man, but after his visit here Sweet Medicine gained his supernatural powers and became the one who brought to the Cheyennes the wisdom of God's message.

"Once, when Sweet Medicine was being chased by warriors, he made a fire near a cliff. The warriors surrounded him, and then they ran into the bushes saying, 'We have Sweet Medicine, kill him,'" the ranger says. "A coyote ran out of the bushes and the warriors said, 'Why, a coyote was in there too?'" After that they looked everywhere for Sweet Medicine, but they could not find him. "Another time other warriors found him in a similar place, but when they attacked the place where Sweet Medicine was hiding, a rabbit hopped out of the bushes. Sweet Medicine was gone."

The crickets are singing in the buffalo grass and the Milky Way is pouring across the sky when he finishes the stories. "Sweet Medicine was gone for a long while, and what happened then is not known by the Cheyenne, but when he finally reappeared, he told the people he had been called to this place, to Noahvose, by a powerful dream," the young ranger says. He stands upright and stretches. "Like Sweet Medicine there are many who have been called to this place by dreams."

He tells me that a week ago the state park was the site of a demonstration by two hundred Indians who were protesting the desecration of a sacred place by "fake" mystics. The demonstrators, who were organized by the American Indian Movement and were watched carefully by dozens of state police troopers, claimed that the fake mystics are selling sacred ceremonies to rich whites who defile Bear Butte with their crystals and their chanting.

He shows the most emotion of the evening when he purses his lips, blows softly, and says: "I won't say what I think, but I've never seen a single one of those agitators from AIM come here for a sweat or for prayer. People come here to pray," he says; "it doesn't matter what color skin they have, or what they believe. People come here to pray and seek visions. How can that be bad?"

The only complaint he has is that people have been pulling sage out for gifts, instead of cutting it off. Because of this, most of the sage has disappeared from the park grounds.

"For gifts?" I ask.

He nods. "Yes," he says, "you have to give something of value in exchange for what the mountain will give you." He moves to the cab of the truck. "I'll let you get on with setting up your camp," he says. He nods again, climbs back into his rig, and drives off.

In the morning while it is still dark, I set off walking from the campground toward the butte. A white-tailed deer scampers off just in front of me, the snowy flag of its tail bright against the dark

sky. Everywhere in the faint light there are golden western mead-
owlarks and kingbirds. I pass the reddish skin of a dead bull snake
near the side of the road. I reach the state highway, then turn up
the entrance road to the visitor's center. The butte seems impossibly large and abrupt now, a sudden presence on an otherwise rolling landscape of low hills. Even turned away from it, I can feel its
massiveness at my back, as if the mountain were a cloak and the
endless prairies some cold winter's night.

Shortly after passing the entrance gate I cross a cattle guard
and a sign that reads: "Buffalo are dangerous and unpredictable –
stay in your vehicle," although nothing is said about what to do if
you have no vehicle. I spy a small herd a quarter mile off and keep
checking and double-checking the distance between us. The road
is doubling back toward them, and soon they are quite close. I suddenly realize that they have taken an active notice of me, and just
as I decide which is the dominant bull, an unseen giant jumps to
his feet, snorts, and eyes me. This creature towers a good foot over
all of the other bison, a shaggy black rock of fur and muscle
framed by a pair of long, curved horns that glimmer in the coming
dawn's light. I immediately look away, not to tempt him into mis-
taking my beard for that of a rival. I try to recall what I'd recently
read about the warning signs of an enraged bull bison – head
down, pawing the ground, blowing – but he simply watches me,
and despite my having plotted escape routes up sign posts and
trees, I soon cross another cattle guard and am safe. The bull continues to watch me, an unmoving and stern statue on the golden
grass plains.

The road swings past the deserted visitor's center, and it is not
yet dawn as I begin to climb the steeper, narrower road east and up
toward the base of the butte. The air has grown noticeably calm
and quiet, in part owing to the increase in vegetation: the pine,
chokecherry, alder, and cottonwood that grow along the low areas
at the flank of the mountain where the road now clings. But the se-
renity is due to more than just the additional plants; there is a kind
of respectful silence all about me that makes the sound of my hiking boots on the asphalt reverberate like gunshots.

I stop walking and take a deep breath. Last night the ranger
had said everyone who comes here to pray goes through purifica-

tions and sweats, and although I don't know the first thing about such ceremonies, I decide I am going to take the mountain seriously and respect this strange, sacred place as best as I know how. While the long and sacred tradition of Native American worship is not a part of my culture, and I shudder at the thought of pretending to be something I am not, I *am* schooled in prayer, and I do have a working knowledge of worship. I take another deep breath and then sit down at the edge of a sharp ravine that drops back toward the visitor's center to try and clear my mind.

I can't pretend that a few minutes of quiet contemplation will purify much of what is soiled in me, but at least my own spirit might calm a bit and more readily accept what the mountain might offer. So I sit, and breathe, and listen. I breathe, and listen. I listen:

Quiet, predawn sounds of insects.

Light breeze in leaves.

Breath.

On a mountain just to be. Motiveless, I think, and for a few fleeting moments can even believe it.

When the rabbit appears from behind me and comes toward me, I am most curious how I am not startled, how I nearly expect to be this closely watched. The rabbit comes close enough for me to count its whiskers, then comes closer yet and settles within an inch of my knee. I am swept over by the way this moment will seem to me in the future: perhaps even composing these lines then – and the instant ceases to be "now," and the rabbit startles at the sudden recognition of danger and is gone. I look in front of me to the spot where he has disappeared. There is a wild sunflower growing there. With my knife I reach out and cut it and tuck the flower into my shirt pocket.

"You have to give something of value," the ranger had said, "in exchange for what the mountain will give you."

I stand and move on. Long pieces of colorful cloth are tied to the branches of a tree along the side of the narrow road. Soon there are others: some on branches of trees, some tied to single sticks driven into the ground. They are prayer flags. The cloth is tied to a place where it will flap in the wind and serve as a benediction to the great spirit – a benediction that will continue long after the worshiper has left. There are many colors, although blues, whites, reds, and yellows are the most common. Like candles in a cathedral, the colored flags are everywhere on the hillside of this natural chapel. I soon recognize other offerings, medicine bundles and sage bundles: small cloth pouches tucked into the nooks of trees or tied to branches.

Just before the road ends and the skinny trail into the mountain begins, there is a ledge. I peer over it down into a remote valley. In it is one sweat lodge, the uncovered stick frames for several additional lodges, and sticks piled for the construction of still more. This is the place where the purification ceremonies are held, and the location of last week's protest by AIM, but in the coming dawn of this July morning the valley is deserted.

The trail leads to the east, around this valley, along a low shoulder of the butte, and toward the towering rock wall that frames the mountain. I pass the still-obvious circle of stones that is the tepee ring of an ancient ceremonial tepee and beyond it the point of rocks where Crazy Horse had his greatest vision. The words of the Sioux holy man Black Elk are mounted on a sign: "It does not matter where the body of Crazy Horse is, but where his spirit is, that place is holy."

Suddenly the path curves toward the cleft between the butte and the rock wall and seems to vanish straight into the side of the mountain. Instead, invisible until I am nearly upon it, the path enters an impossibly narrow canyon as if through a secret door.

I have entered an immense room between the bulk of the sacred mountain and the towering slab of rock wall. Between them, and below me, is a steep canyon, narrow enough that I could toss a rock across it. In the east, slicing through a cleft in the stone, the sun has begun to rise.

Here in this canyon quiet is everywhere. A kind of quietness not of sound but of the stilling of the machinations of what we know. The shell I wear drops away in this hush. The skeleton of time rots away in such a silence: you do not think of the past, the future, or even of yourself here and now. There is nothing, really, nothing but this narrow, green canyon, the steaming black wall of rock before me, the trees, the red earth, and the arrow point of yellow sunrise.

It is then, just then, that it happens. Suddenly the light of thousands of shimmering stars fills the narrow canyon. Everywhere in the still air are diamonds of light, miniature golden suns gleaming and glowing in the green and red air. I fall back and gasp for breath, staggering at the sight. I finally seek out a single soaring orb to discover that the dawn's light has caught on thousands of dragonflies, whose whirling flat wings have made the light of the narrow canyon move and dance and shimmer. The vision is even more powerful now that I have seen the dragonflies, for the light is alive with them. Despite it all, despite the world's ills and my own unpurified soul, there is grace in the universe. There is a grace, and for a moment on the Teaching Place – Noahvose – I am allowed to see this miracle for what it is: a canyon full of burning lights of a thousand tiny suns on the wings of star blue dragonflies.

The sacred Cheyenne Sweet Medicine had traveled deep into the Black Hills, past the Badlands, until he came at last to a towering tepee, this place, Noahvose.

A very old woman sat inside the giant tepee of this mountain. "Come in, my grandson," she had said to Sweet Medicine. "Why did you not come sooner? Your people are hungry and in trouble. I will help them. You must come to this place whenever you need time to decide what is to be done." And then she told Sweet Medicine a great many things, about the time of the buffalo, and the time of the horse, and of corn, and of the end of the Cheyenne way of life.

She reached over to Sweet Medicine and untied the feather he had in his hair and threw it into the fire. She painted him with red paint and painted the sun and the moon in yellow, then from the ashes she drew out a red feather and tied it to his hair.

She said: "There is a time coming when many things will change. Strangers will appear among you. Their ways are powerful. They clip their hair short and their skin is light colored. There will be so many of these people that you cannot stand before them. Follow nothing these men do. Keep your own ways.

"But at last you will not remember. Your ways will change. You will leave your religion for something new. You will take after the strangers' ways and forget the good things by which you have lived and in the end you will become worse than crazy. They will tear up the earth and at last you will do it with them."

But the old woman who lived inside the great tepee of Noah-vose gave Sweet Medicine strength to help him keep his faith. She gave him the gift of a creed:

"You must take these four laws back to the people," she said as he rose to leave. "There are only four laws to follow for a good life:

"Never kill another Cheyenne.

"Never marry too young.

"Always respect others.

"Always take pride in the purity and health of all things."

And, truth be told, thinking of those words, I can't help but reflect on my own failures to follow a purer path.

The angle of the sun has changed and the vision of dragonflies evaporates. The canyon is now in the bright white light of morning. Using a piece of yellow tent ribbon from my pocket, I remove the sunflower from my shirt and tie it to the short branch of a nearby pine. The branch points directly into the canyon at the rock wall opposite.

For the rest of the hike, across the shoulder of the sacred mountain and back down to the visitor's center, I see each prayer flag, medicine bundle, tobacco offering, tree, stone, and rock cairn as reminders of a spirit I had become so distant from: the spirit that is everywhere: in rocks and trees, in sunflowers and rabbits, in dragonflies and buffalo, in air, in earth, in us.

31. The Holy Cost

I have turned around. I am returning back to Nebraska, where I have made arrangements for my brother to pick me up. I don't mind retracing my route, and there's one final place I have yet to visit: the site where the last of the Fort Robinson escapees fought their final battle. The dome of sun, clouds, and stars that watched Little Wolf's half of the Northern Cheyennes leave the security of their hidden valley to move north again today just as impassively watches my last day of walking. The earth that holds the dust of those tracked down from Fort Robinson and slaughtered patiently waits for the dust of my bones as well.

Little Wolf's people must have gotten word of the tragedy that befell their comrades at Fort Robinson, for soon thereafter they tried to create a diversion. On the very day when the long-sought "final battle" with Dull Knife's Cheyennes was being raged – a bloody massacre in a shallow pit forty miles north of the fort – Little Wolf's people were on the move. A ranch just over the South Dakota line had been surrounded, and the two men there gave supplies to the half dozen armed Cheyenne warriors who had appeared. A day or two later the last civilian killed in a long season of death met his fate in South Dakota when he fired on two of Little Wolf's Cheyennes who had approached him. He killed one of the Cheyennes; the other Cheyenne returned fire and shot him dead. As they moved further north, along the east side of the Black Hills, Little Wolf's people took beef from ranches. A soldier later reported that Little Wolf's band had then stopped a train. The crew was unharmed. The Cheyennes took food.

Later still, while on a raid along the Bismarck–Black Hills road, a young Cheyenne was given an order by Black Crane, a chief with Little Wolf's band. The young man defiantly said he would do things his own way. Black Crane said to obey or be whipped. "No one ever strikes me," the young man said. "I will kill anyone who does." Black Crane struck at him, and the two men came to blows. An old man tried to stop the fighting, but the young Cheyenne pulled out a pistol and shot the old man through the arm. The young man then shot Black Crane through the heart, killing him instantly.

The young man had violated one of Sweet Medicine's commandments and, even in this desperate time, had to face the punishment. As was the Cheyenne way, the young man's stock was taken from him and his family of seven given only one horse. They were banished from the tribe and set adrift on the prairie to survive as best they could. These eight drifters – three men, four women, and a child – were later captured after opening fire on a company of troops and killing a soldier.

By late February Little Wolf's people made it to the Yellowstone River, their long-sought homeland. They had remained invisible and undetected while thousands of troops from Kansas to the Canadian border continued to search for them. A week of temperatures hovering near thirty below was broken by a warm Chinook wind. Travel became difficult as water rose and ice broke free, making it impossible to cross many rivers.

On March 11 Sioux scouts under the command of a second lieutenant from Fort Keogh were fifty miles up the Powder when they spied a few lone Cheyenne men hunting. The scouts rode back to tell the news to their commander, W. P. Clark. Clark moved rapidly north, crossing the high ground at night and camping in hidden valleys so as not to alarm the Cheyennes, but he searched in vain for Little Wolf's village. The rain that had come in buckets following the Chinook turned back to snow, obliterating tracks.

A week later, frustrated by the army's lack of response to his requests for an interpreter, Clark hired one at his own expense. The Seminole interpreter, Wolf Voice, agreed to search for the Cheyennes but did not want them to be harmed. "To shoot at these people," he said, "would be like shooting the children in my own lodge."

Meanwhile, on Box Elder Creek two of Clark's Sioux scouts had been betrayed when a small fire they had built for coffee accidentally set fire to the prairie. Little Wolf's men captured the scouts and brought them to camp. The scouts claimed they were Sioux from Sitting Bull's camp in Canada, but the Cheyennes weren't fooled. One scout managed to slip away, and Little Wolf let the other go, telling him, "I know who you are, and everybody knows who I am. Go tell the soldiers we are here."

If any more evidence was needed about Little Wolf's extraordinary strategic abilities, the place he chose to negotiate the end of the long flight should be enough to prove his genius. On March 24 Wolf Voice and two of Clark's scouts came on day-old tracks of horses and followed them until the tracks split in a dozen different directions. Each track then disappeared over a wide shelf of hard rock. The trackers were delayed for several hours until they at last discovered the main trail again. Before nightfall they stopped, hoping to discover Little Wolf's location by spotting a campfire. After dark Wolf Voice came upon three horses. As he stood there, a man wrapped in a white sheet walked by. Wolf Voice followed this man a little way and came upon the group of small lodges, absolutely concealed in the clumps of bushes. He shouted out, "I am Cheyenne!" and immediately the camp came to life. Wolf Voice was taken to Little Wolf. He told Little Wolf that Clark, a man they knew and trusted from their previous life in Montana, was near and wanted to talk.

In the morning Little Wolf and his camp rode a little way until they met Clark and his soldiers. The soldiers deployed in a skirmish line. The army packers dove for the bushes. The Cheyenne women and children hid high up among the rocks.

Clark and Little Wolf met on horseback. "Friend," Clark said. "You know me. I am the one you call 'White Hat.' I have prayed to God that I would be the one to find you."

Little Wolf recognized Clark and believed him to be an honest man. "We do not want to fight," Little Wolf said. He said that since leaving the Sand Hills they had fired only after being fired upon. "But you are the first who has come to talk before fighting." Because of what happened to Dull Knife's people, Little Wolf said, they would not give up their weapons. "The wind has torn at them for so long our hearts will soon fall down," Little Wolf said. Because he trusted Clark, however, they would stay near him.

The two sides camped together for several days. To establish trust, Clark did not initially try to confiscate Little Wolf's weapons and instead let the Cheyennes use them to hunt. He gave the people food and blankets and offered help to the sick and wounded.

Over the next few days he assured Little Wolf of his good intentions. A great deal of confidence and good feeling had begun to be established between the two.

After a few days they talked again. "In the two years since I last saw you," Little Wolf said. "We have been to the south and suffered. Many died there of a disease we have no name for. We want to live here in the land of our birth."

Clark said he would do what he could to see to it that the Cheyennes remain in the north and not be taken south again. He asked that the Cheyennes give up their weapons.

"Because of our friendship," Little Wolf said, "we will do what you say."

At 11 A.M. on April 1, 1879, Little Wolf's band of 114 – 33 men, 43 women, and 38 children, reached Fort Keogh, Montana. They had 240 horses and a mere thirty weapons. It was reported that soldiers at the fort cried when they saw the destitute condition of some of the Cheyennes.

"I know these Cheyenne very well," Clark telegraphed the commander at the Department of the Dakotas when he reached the fort. "I have no fears of treachery or an attempted escape. They are weary with constant fighting and want a home in this country where they were born and reared." He said the Cheyennes should be allowed to remain north, where they would become trusted friends and allies.

As a result of the publicity generated by the massacre at Fort Robinson, the U.S. Congress authorized a committee to investigate the conditions surrounding the removal of the Northern Cheyennes to Indian Territory. The committee examined witnesses and wrote up hundreds of pages documenting the errors of the initial removal. The committee recommended that the Northern Cheyennes be allowed to stay in the north. As a result, Little Wolf's people stayed near Fort Keogh and were later joined there by those recaptured after the Fort Robinson breakout. This small band of survivors were the first to resettle in what would eventually become the Northern Cheyenne reservation.

The army did not find Dull Knife's body among those killed during the outbreak, nor among the twenty-four slaughtered in the shallow pit in the final battle. Of the 149 prisoners held at Fort Robinson only a small group, possibly as few as seven and not more than seventeen, survived capture or slaughter. Among these was Dull Knife.

Andy, Sam, and I spent many hours talking about exactly which route Dull Knife might have taken up this creek bed or that valley. We were in confident agreement on some routes, and at other times each of us believed his own version of the path northward was the true one. It may be fitting then that no one knows the exact route that Dull Knife took to escape the horror of Fort Robinson to make it to the safety of the Sioux reservation.

Most of his family was gone. Of his eleven children, five had been killed in battles fought during the two short years since the Little Bighorn. One son and two daughters had been killed during the breakout from Fort Robinson. Two wives were dead.

After the breakout, Dull Knife and a small group of others avoided capture by hiding in a dirt cave for several horrible sub-zero days. When the Chinook wind came to break the weeks of bitter cold, they moved northward. Once at the Sioux reservation the small group managed to blend in without detection until, some weeks later, word seeped back to the army that Dull Knife was among the Red Cloud Agency Sioux. By then the tide had finally swung in the old wise one's favor. Permission was granted for Dull Knife to remain on the Pine Ridge Reservation for the time being.

Of the Northern Cheyenne people who had been with Dull Knife at Fort Robinson, troops recaptured over fifty before the killing stopped. After the final battle, as many as sixty-five others were dead. In spring, most of the recaptured ones joined Dull Knife at Pine Ridge. During the summer months another fifty Cheyennes appeared at Pine Ridge to join Dull Knife's people. These were probably relatives from Little Wolf's band, who were by then at Fort Keogh, and a few lone families who had slipped out of Indian Territory on their own during the summer. In November all of these Cheyennes were granted permission to join Little Wolf's people at Fort Keogh, where they formed the nucleus of the present-day reservation.

Dull Knife died near the Tongue River in 1883. His tombstone in the cemetery at Lame Deer marks an empty grave. In the Chey-

enne way, his physical remains were placed on a remote mountain-
top at the center of the Montana homeland so many died trying to
create.

Wild Hog and the others who were to stand trial for the deaths
of the Kansas pioneers had been imprisoned separately at Fort
Robinson when the breakout came. On the morning of January
31, after the killing was finished, the recaptured survivors were led
past Wild Hog's prison on their way to Pine Ridge. Just as the line
walked past the place where Wild Hog was being held, Wild Hog's
wife cried out, grabbed a pair of scissors, and stabbed at her husband. She then tried to drive the blades into her own heart before
she was subdued. A reporter described the scene afterward. In the
room was Wild Hog's daughter. She had been shot through the
neck at the final battle and had been brought back to be cared for
by her family. "Lying head to head with her was the wounded
chief, his daughter sleeping like a besotted drunk, her face close to
the burning fire in the middle of the flimsy habitation." Wild Hog
breathed heavily through the morphine given him. His wife sat
near the entrance, wild and terrified.

When he was partially recovered, Wild Hog and six other men
were taken to Kansas for trial. They were transported from Fort
Leavenworth to Dodge City by train under the supervision of Ford
County sheriff Bat Masterson. At Leavenworth the train platform
was crammed with hundreds of people who wanted to see the captives. Masterson had to fistfight a path through the throngs to get
the prisoners onto the train. When the train stopped at Topeka a
crowd of one thousand waited to catch a glimpse of what the local
paper called the "real live wild Indians." The prisoners were not
allowed to use a knife or fork for fear they would use the utensils
as weapons. The paper reported the "savages . . . convey the fare
to their mouths with dirty fingers." At every station along the way
mobs were waiting. When the prisoners finally arrived at Dodge
City, the paper there reported that Dodge City crowds were less
curious to see captive Indians as they were to get "close enough to
sight one with a rifle or a six-shooter."

After a trial that lasted until October, the charges were dis-
missed because of lack of evidence. These men and their families,
a total of twenty Cheyennes, returned to Indian Territory.

The tragedy of Wild Hog, Dull Knife, and Little Wolf did little to change the minds of men in power. At the very same time these Northern Cheyennes had been escaping northward, 186 additional Northern Cheyennes under the leadership of Little Chief were being taken from Montana to Indian Territory. General Nelson Miles himself promised Little Chief that if they went south and did not like it, they could return north. Little Chief took the word of the white soldier chief and agreed to let his people be taken south. When Little Chief's people stopped at Bear Butte on their journey to Indian Territory there was a total eclipse of the sun. The occurrence of such an event at such a holy place foretold evil times, and many cried in terror at the blackened sky.

Like the other Northern Cheyennes, soon after arriving in Indian Territory many of Little Chief's people became sick. His grown son died within weeks of their arrival. Little Chief immediately expressed his dislike for Indian Territory and requested that they be allowed to return north as Miles had promised. "A great many are sick and some have died," he said. "I have been sick much of the time I have been down here, homesick and heartsick in every way. I have been thinking of the native country, and the good home I had up there, where I was never hungry. It makes me feel sick when I think about that, and I cannot help thinking about that."

By this time Little Chief had learned of the outbreak at Fort Robinson and the massacre in the pit at the final battle, and he insisted that his people not leave Indian Territory unless allowed to do so by the government. At one point he even held back at rifle point some of his young warriors who were trying to organize an escape. Over the next four years Little Chief did everything he could to return peacefully to his homeland. He repeatedly requested adequate food and supplies and traveled frequently to Washington DC to plead his case. In August 1879 a congressional committee arrived in Indian Territory to hear his complaints. He patiently outlined the many facts: how, despite assurances to the contrary, their horses had been taken from them, how a single beef was often the only food given for a week to feed thirty-five people, how the cornmeal had made people sick, how many had died since their arrival, and how they so longed to return to the land that God had given them. The committee took pages of notes and then disappeared back to Washington.

Finally in 1881 the commissioner of Indian affairs allowed 250 Northern Cheyennes, including those of Little Chief's band, to leave Indian Territory, but they were still not allowed to return to Montana. Instead, the Cheyennes were permitted to go only as far as Pine Ridge, where they were to forced to live with the Sioux.

While with the Sioux, Little Chief continued to argue that his people should be allowed to return to Montana. They had never caused any problems, he reminded officials; although the government's promises had been broken over and over, they had done everything that was asked of them.

Finally, in 1891, after ten years on the Sioux reservation, Little Chief agreed to abandon one of the most sacred of Cheyenne rituals, the sundance, and agreed not to allow his people to join in on the Ghost Dance movement, which was then sweeping through the reservation system. Because of these concessions, Little Chief's people were finally allowed to join the rest of the Northern Cheyennes. It had been a twelve-year separation.

Little Chief died in 1908 at the Northern Cheyenne reservation.

For two months I have been walking over empty land, so at first, when I come upon the ghost town of Montrose, Nebraska – nothing but an unused church and a run-down shed – I am not bothered by the haunted remnants of human history. With a historian's curiosity, I note the high hill that rises opposite the church. The hill served as a local fortification for settlers when fears of a Sioux uprising came that cold week in 1890 when troops massacred so many at Wounded Knee. At the base of the hill, just across the dusty road from the church, is a stone monument announcing the spot where, two weeks after the Battle of the Little Bighorn, Buffalo Bill Cody claimed he killed an Indian and took "the first scalp for Custer." The story of Cody's heroic battle to kill the man was possibly the result of Cody's own bad pride once again getting the best of him. He may have scalped an Indian who had been killed by others, then later bragged he had killed the man in a hand-to-hand battle.

This abandoned place, with Cody's monument, the church bereaved of parishioners, a grass-choked cemetery, and the fortress hill, suddenly begins to spook me. It has the peculiar feeling of a place forever altered by human dealings. Despite the time that has passed, this landscape will never be fully without the taint of its human history. I can't put a name to it; it is just that something lingers here. I hurry away from these vague remnants of hopes that have died and climb up a road headed away.

It is a great and high ridge road that rides the knife blade of a divide between two valleys and provides me a spectacular view to the south and below, where Squaw Creek parallels my route. Beyond Squaw Creek are the undulating golden hills of Oglala National Grasslands. To the north the country is broken into smaller hills, and the creek that lies in this direction is further distant, tumbling down from the northern ridges into a series of twisted loops like a string suddenly unwound. This is Antelope Creek, the one the Cheyennes called "River Where the Crazy Man Jumped off the Bank," the place where the last of them were killed at the final battle.

Just before the road drops down into the valley, I see a dozen pronghorn antelope in a single herd. They are beautiful animals; their legs move as if in a stiff, powerful march, loaded on tight springs. I watch as they cross a slope in a long, loose line, then they disappear over a rise.

I climb down off the ridge and head north on a road that descends into the Antelope Creek Valley. The first ranch I see for the day is the place I am headed. A small, tidy house is set back a little way from the road. I walk down the drive past a dingolike cow dog who is wagging her tail and fawning before me. I step inside a small fenced yard and shut the gate before she can follow me. She watches me a moment, then returns to a shady spot, circles twice, and flops down into the dust. Inside the tiny fenced area near the house is a tidy, trim lawn, and pretty flowers to mark the space. A collection of old tools has been mounted on the fence near the back door to create a frontier work of art.

A moment after I knock on the door it springs open. A round, carefree face peers up at me. "Hi," the boy says. Behind him, in the kitchen, are spread the fixings for a peanut butter sandwich. "I'm Max, who are you?" He considers my answer, then swings the door

wide. "Come on in, I'll get my mom." He scampers off into the
bright interior of the house. The kitchen has an organized, busy
messiness to it. Near an empty lunchbox on the counter is an orderly pile of paperwork and the opened jar of peanut butter. On
the kitchen table are a pair of work gloves, wire cutters, pliers, a
half-filled cup of coffee, and a plate with Max's half-eaten peanut
butter sandwich. A pair of boots are in a corner as if they have only
recently been removed, and empty grocery bags are neatly folded
in a pile on the floor.

"This is the guy," Max says as he reenters the kitchen.

"Hi," I say. "Your son let me in, I hope you don't mind."

"Not at all." Max's mom is a young woman with pretty blond
hair and an easy, attractive smile. "Are you lost?"

I laugh. "No, I don't think so," I say. "I'm looking for the site of
a battle with Cheyenne Indians."

"Oh," she says, "oh, yes, this is the place. Sure you can see the
site. There's no problem." She extends her hand. "My name is
Holly."

Holly Federle and her husband, Andy, have raised registered
Herefords on this ranch for the past eleven years. Before that she
lived in Lusk, Wyoming. "That's home," she says definitively, wist-
fully, longingly. "But it takes a lot of land out there to raise a beef."
She uses the word in the singular instead of "cattle" or "cow." "It
takes a lot of land out there to raise a beef, and the land here is
much better than back at home; at least it is in most years. Besides," she says and pauses, "this land is where Max has been
raised. It's the place he knows as home." Max has abandoned his
sandwich and stands about near his mom, peering up at me. "My
husband should be here any second. He knows much more about
the site than I do. It's just out there," she says, pointing through
the kitchen's eastern window. "You see that point of land? Well,
that's the place, right above the creek."

As I study the bright landscape and finally pick out the distant
low bump she refers to, her husband arrives. A thin, angular man
walks into the kitchen, takes the three of us in in an instant, strips
off a pair of work gloves, and offers his hand. "I'm Andy Federle,"
he says. His face relaxes into a friendly grin as he speaks. In spite
of his work as a rancher, Andy dresses neatly. A worn but clean

dress shirt has come partially untucked from his slender fitted blue jeans. Even though it is his own kitchen, he had removed his cap as soon as he stepped foot inside.

After a bit of talk we turn our attention to the battle site. He clearly has respect for the significant place where so many died. His reverence is not that of a boastful owner but of a dedicated caretaker who has been granted the privilege of watching over a sacred place for a short while. "We try to keep it undisturbed. I'd like to be able to make it a place where people can come and visit," Andy says.

As he leads us out of the house the dog rises up and circles us. Max stops to scratch his ears. We go east on a private path to the north of Antelope Creek. "Back in the 1930s and before, the creek used to have water in it all the time," Andy says. Like most ranchers, Andy uses the status of creeks as a benchmark for history – when this or that creek had water, when it was dry, whether it froze that winter of '74 when everything else for miles froze, when it was highest, or lowest – using water as a witness to history's vagaries.

Three hundred yards from the house, we leave the path to cross an unmarked valley filled with grass. We have angled a ways away from the creek and have to walk quite a distance before we see the winding path of the dry stream again. "A while back the Historical Society came out and dug here to make sure it was the place," he says. "They found a lot of gunshells and some beads. They said it was the final battle site, and then they covered everything back up again."

We cross a steep, grassy ravine and then climb up onto a roughly level piece of land bordered on one side by the ravine, on another by a bend in the creek, and nearly surrounded elsewhere by the steep slope of dry ravines that feed the creek. Andy stops. "This is it," he says. "This is where it happened." The only reason this place is not an isolated island standing by itself is a narrow strip of land that, if followed, would lead to the higher hills to the north. It is as if the creek below has sculpted a flat finger of land to curl about. A few weedy cottonwoods grow below us along the creek. Beyond them and across the creek, a wide, flat plain, ideal for camping, spreads out below abrupt and significantly higher hills that spring up to the south.

For ten days after the breakout a group of around thirty-two Cheyennes had been closely followed by troops from Fort Robinson. Traveling on foot and using the topography of hills, cliffs, and caves to their advantage, they had managed to elude the soldiers a half dozen times, most recently just two nights before they stopped here on Antelope Creek, when they slipped out of a strong position in the bluffs of Crow Ridge and crossed the stage road, suddenly changing directions. Instead of moving north, they headed almost due east, more directly toward the Sioux reservation.

Captain Wessells, in command of the troops in pursuit, had come across the Cheyennes' trail late in the afternoon of January 20, 1879. He had followed the trail east until the day grew dark. Because the hostiles were close, he ordered an early start the following morning. At the same time, other troops were to the north, following the feeder streams down out of the hills toward Antelope Creek. About noon Wessells's scouts discovered the Cheyennes hidden in a buffalo wallow on top of this small rise above the creek.

"Here's the pit," Andy Federle says, pointing. Just at the edge of the finger of land where a steep bank falls down to the creek is an oblong dip in the ground, ten or twelve feet wide and perhaps thirty feet in length. It is only large enough to hold three or four large picnic tables. I hesitate, then step into the pit. It is not very deep but would have provided slightly better protection because of the frozen dirt the Cheyennes had hastily thrown up around the edges. In all but one corner of the pit I can get a clear view of the higher ground around me. It would have been a good position if I was attacked from the west or south, for people might have been able to slip up into the hills behind us, but if soldiers surrounded this place, as they did that day, this tight space would offer scant protection.

Messengers from the four different companies converging on the Cheyennes rode back and forth as Wessells coordinated his plan of attack. The soldiers coming from the north spread out in a tight semicircular line and approached the finger of land on foot.

Three or four Cheyennes popped up in the near distance and

fired on the advancing troops, hitting the Sioux scout Woman's Dress. The troops retreated a distance. Soldiers exchanged fire with the Indians from a distance of 125 yards, patiently waiting for the other companies to arrive. Wessells knew he had the Cheyennes trapped.

By noon all four companies, 152 men in total, were deployed around the position of the Cheyennes. In the buffalo wallow were the remnants from the massacre at Fort Robinson: seventeen males old enough to hold one of the few weapons, and fifteen women and children.

From the bottom of the pit I discover that you would have to stand up and look out in order to fire with any accuracy, which, of course, would leave you open to return fire. Conversely, in order to get a good shot into the pit, soldiers would have to have approached from close in and shoot down into the wallow. I climb out again and study the terrain. Of all the sites I have seen during my hike, this one is the poorest defensive position. Unlike the others, I cannot see beyond a half mile. It is certainly not like the expansive view at most of the other strongholds the Cheyennes chose. Perhaps these thirty-two survivors missed the strategic leadership of men like Little Wolf and Wild Hog. In any event, I am distracted enough scrambling around to ignore for a moment the overwhelming sorrow that is everywhere here.

Once the final siege began, it would be all over in twenty minutes. From his command position just out of range of the Cheyenne fire, but high enough to afford a view of the area, Wessells said, "Enough. We have lost too much just waiting for the Indians. We must charge their position." He set up a company on a hillside that provided a clear shot at anyone who rose up above the lip of the pit and instructed the soldiers there to keep the Indians down. He then sent Company A, under the command of Lieutenant Chase, along Antelope Creek toward the Cheyennes.

Despite some fire from the Cheyennes, Company A managed to snake its way along the steep banks of the creek until it was in the ravine directly below the pit. Another company covered the Cheyennes' retreat to the north, and another held the hillside on the opposite bank. When all was in place Lieutenant Chase gave the prearranged signal: a yell to his soldiers to attack. The men from

Company A scrambled up the embankment, firing as they went. At twelve yards, during heavy firing, three of Chase's men were killed. His soldiers fell back to reload, but by now all four companies were charging the pit, firing a half dozen volleys, falling back, and then charging again.

From where I stand in the buffalo wallow everything is remarkably near. The steep bank that sheltered the soldiers at the edge of the pit is so abrupt that the illusion is of an unbroken landscape to the gentle slope of the creek bed in the near distance. To someone in the pit the countless soldiers would have appeared as if rising suddenly from the earth itself.

When the soldiers closed in from all sides, the firing was so close that there was fear they would shoot across and hit one another. After the initial volley the smoke from the weapons was so thick that Wessells had to call a temporary halt in order to let the air clear: no one could see.

During this lull some Cheyennes began singing a death song. Wessells called out in Sioux for the Indians to surrender. He was answered with a gunshot. Then there followed another intensive attack from the soldiers. When the shooting stopped this time, there was nothing but silence from the pit.

Captain Wessells and Lieutenant Chase decided to climb up to see what was left. "It was difficult to find men to approach the pit," Chase later said. "But finally I found a few trusted men." Side by side Chase and Wessells led the men around to the very edge of the pit with pistols cocked and ready. "I saw an Indian with a pistol rise above level of crest," Chase said. Both officers fired, and Wessells was slightly wounded with a shot to the head. Chase dragged him back down the slope. On seeing Wessells wounded, one of the other officers shouted, "Give it to 'em boys. Don't leave a one of them."

Three Cheyennes jumped up from pit and rushed at the troops. One had an empty pistol and the other two held knives. One sprang to jump down the embankment but was shot by dozens of soldiers. The other two never cleared the edge of the pit.

The soldiers charged the wallow. One soldier estimated that over three hundred shots were fired in rapid succession before the order was given to cease firing. The edges of the pit were riddled bare with bullets.

Chase later said that when the smoke cleared away from this final charge, the little cup that held the remnants of the Northern Cheyennes "was in a singular and horrible appearance." Bodies littered the ground "like bags filled with sand." He ordered a detail into the pit to pass out the bodies. Huddled in the furthest corner, the only place where there had been any protection from the rain of death, were the survivors: five women and two children. They had dug into the embankment in the frozen ground to gain a little more protection. One, a girl named Blanche, was recognized. She had been taught to write her name while imprisoned. As the survivors were being led out, two fourteen-year-old girls were found alive, covered with dust and blood, under the bodies of the slain.

A man was found still alive, although his wound was mortal. An officer asked him in Sioux if there was anything he could do. The Cheyenne said he only wished to be left in the pit to die with the others. In a few moments he passed away.

One of the children, a boy about Max's age, had been wounded. Some claimed he had been the one to shoot Wessells. The boy died on the way back to Fort Robinson.

One of the wounded women was Big Antelope's wife. When her husband was mortally wounded, she had crawled across the bodies in the pit to be with him. As she did so, a shot had hit her. She was still able to reach her dying husband. "Let us die here together, at least," he had said. Big Antelope's body was found in the pit. It had several gunshot wounds as well as stabs in the chest from a knife. His wife died the next day in the prison room at Fort Robinson.

The bodies were laid down side by side and counted by Lieutenant John Baxter Jr. To Baxter the bodies looked like "horrid phantoms or defaced mummies." Some of them were stripped, while some had clothing of blankets or pants or overcoats, or simply wore bed coverings. In the center of the pit was a good stock of dried beef from cattle recently killed. It formed a pile three feet high and two feet wide.

The medical officer roamed about the pit, taking notes. He wrote: "The great proportion of fatal wounds is remarkable and their concentration on the trunk of the body shows a deliberation and skill in [the soldiers'] handling the improved breechloading arms."

The Northern Cheyennes had run out of ammunition early in the fight. They had been using cartridges that they had reloaded themselves from a small supply of powder, bullet molds, and reloading caps. To conserve the supply, they had loaded many cartridges with less than a full load of powder. Wessells had been hit by a bullet loaded in this fashion. Instead of penetrating his head, the weak charge simply stopped, and he suffered only a small concussion. Despite trying to make every shot count, the Cheyennes had exhausted their ammunition. Wessells had been hit by one of the last Cheyenne shots. When the final rain of bullets came from the 150 soldiers, the Cheyennes who were still living had no ammunition for their guns. Amid the bodies, the troops found unloaded rifles stuck around the edges of the pit to give the illusion that living men still held them.

After they had been counted, the bodies of the Cheyennes were placed back in the pit, and the next day a detachment was sent out from the fort to bury their remains somewhere in the vicinity of the final battle. The long voyage of the Northern Cheyennes had ended.

I sprinkle the last of some tobacco leaves into the pit, more concerned with understanding than with praying. I am still distracted by the geography of this place: trying to see the way the troops attacked, to imagine how thirty-two Cheyennes might have arranged themselves in this shallow hole. I step out of the pit and walk a bit away in order to look over the steep bank where the soldiers hid between volleys. Here is where they must have stood to reload, there is where they must have climbed to the pit, over there is where some stood to get a good shot. My figuring and figuring speeds to a frenetic pace until, exhausted at last, I can no longer deny what is inescapable and I finally turn to face the horror that is everywhere here.

They died here in blood. Children. Men. Women died here. Families perished. I take a long, slow breath. I choke with a wordless, thick sorrow. My tears come. I turn around.

Young Max has climbed down into the pit. He stoops to the ground and clips off a sprig of grass between his fingers. He places the stem in his mouth and looks out across the green and golden covering of this beautiful earth. The emerald shine of grass, the cold dome of blue, suddenly transforms the youthful face into an ancient one. He gazes beyond all of this, beyond these hills, this sky, this suffering, this and all time, beyond. Max looks down to the ground near his feet. With the tip of his finger he begins to draw an aimless pattern in the dust.

Notes

Part 1: Kit Fox Drums

CHAPTER 1: THE LEAVING

Several months after the Oklahoma City tragedy an additional body was identified, raising the death count by one.

CHAPTER 2: BLACK KETTLES

The events leading up to the escape of the Cheyennes are from C. E. Campbell, "Down among Red Men," *Collections of the Kansas State Historical Society, 1919–1922*, vol.17 (1928): 623–91.

The information regarding the conditions in Indian Territory is from "Testimony Taken by a Select Committee of the Senate Concerning the Removal of the Northern Cheyenne Indians," Senate, *Report No.708*, 46th Cong., 2d session, 1880; and the testimony of Old Crow and Wild Hog in Military Division of the Missouri, *Proceedings of Board of Officers*, 1879, Special File, War Records, National Archives.

Many of the details of the events immediately preceding the Cheyennes' escape are from *Report of the Secretary of War*, vol.1, *Report of the General of the Army*, 1878, National Archives.

The numbers and names of the Cheyennes gone north are from Agent John D. Miles to commissioner of Indian affairs, September 10 and November 18, 1878, in the records of the Bureau of Indian Affairs, Office of Indian Affairs, *Letters Received*, and from the unpublished manuscript of Marla Sawyer and Alan Boye, "Names of the Cheyenne Indians on the 1878 Exodus."

General Pope was quoted in the *Denver Tribune*, October, 19, 1878, denying he had neglected to command the officers at Fort Reno to adequately watch over the Cheyennes given rumors of their imminent escape. He said he had "no authority or right to interfere with them until they had left the reservation." He also claimed that the army was not well equipped to chase the Cheyennes once they escaped, since there was not a single company of cavalry in Kansas, and many of his cavalry units had been transferred to the other areas. Pope said that the Indians left because there had been no real hunting at the reservation and that the government had not kept its promise to issue adequate supplies.

"Children were brained and hacked . . ." is from John Mooney, "The Cheyenne Indians," *American Anthropological Associations Memoirs*, vol. 1, part 6 (Lancaster PA, 1905–6).

Roman Nose State Park was named after Henry Roman Nose, a returned Pennsylvania's Carlisle School student and later a council chief, who was allotted the land in 1892, when he was about twenty-five years old. This was not the Roman Nose who was killed at the Battle of Beecher's Island in 1868. For information on the great warrior Roman Nose see John H. Monnett, *The Battle of Beecher Island and the Indian War of 1867–1869* (Niwot: University Press of Colorado, 1994).

CHAPTER 3: OH KOM HA KA

For an excellent introduction to the stories of Black Kettle and Roman Nose, as well as Dull Knife and Little Wolf and other important Cheyenne leaders, see Stan Hoig, *The Peace Chiefs of the Cheyennes* (Norman: University of Oklahoma Press, 1980).

For more information on the horse-stealing incident see John D. McDermott, *The History of Fort Casper and the Upper Platte Crossing* (Lander WY: Frontier Crossroads, 1993), 12–13. Another account is in George Bird Grinnell, *The Fighting Cheyenne* (New York: Scribners, 1915).

"He was never afraid . . ." is from Thomas B. Marquis, *A Warrior Who Fought Custer* (Minneapolis: Midwest, 1931), reprinted as *Wooden Leg: A Warrior Who Fought Custer* (Lincoln: University of Nebraska Press, 1957, 1962), 17.

For a good summary of Cheyenne tribal organization see E. Adamson Hoebel, *The Cheyennes: Indians of the Great Plains* (New York: Holt, 1960); Karl N. Llewellyn and E. Adamson Hoebel, *The Cheyenne Way* (Norman: University of Oklahoma Press, 1941); and George Bird Grinnell, *The Cheyenne Indians*, 2 vols. (New Haven CT: Yale University Press, 1928; reprint, Lincoln: University of Nebraska Press, 1972).

According to Grinnell and Mari Sandoz, Little Wolf was the only man who was allowed to retain his chieftainship in a warrior society once he had became an Old Man Chief.

Little Wolf's remarks in Indian Territory are from Senate, *Report No. 708*; Campbell, "Down among Red Men"; Marquis, *Wooden Leg*; and Grinnell, *The Fighting Cheyenne*.

The information about the sign language book is from Mark H. Brown and W. R. Felton, *The Frontier Years* (New York: Holt, 1953), 41. The book *The Indian Sign Language* was published in 1885 in Philadelphia.

The newspaper quote about the killing is from the *Yellowstone Journal*, Miles City MT, December 18, 1880.

The best accounts of the life of Little Wolf are to be found in Grinnell, *Fighting Cheyenne*; John Stands In Timber and Margot Liberty, *Cheyenne Memories* (New Haven CT: Yale University Press, 1967); Gary L. Roberts, "The Shame of Little Wolf," *Montana: The Magazine of Western History* 28, no.3 (summer 1978): 37; Thomas B. Marquis, "Little Wolf: First Chieftain of That Appellation Was Later Ostracized by Tribe," *Billings Gazette*, April 17, 1932; and Marquis, *Wooden Leg*. Also see Little Wolf Papers, Special File, Military Division of the Missouri, Records of the U.S. Army Commands, records group 393, National Archives.

CHAPTER 4: KIT FOX DRUMS
The wolf attack is quoted in Tom McHugh, *The Time of the Buffalo* (New York: Knopf, 1972), 224.

Part 2: Morning Star

For information in this part, I am indebted to David Wilson for his help as well as his excellent manuscript "Morning Star's Burden: Cheyenne Chieftainship and the Dull Knife Battle," and to Andrew Sooktis for use of his thorough and superb genealogical studies of the Dull Knife family tree.

CHAPTER 6: MORNING STAR
Morning Star's birth date is conjecture based on ages given at other times; Grinnell says he died in 1883 (*Fighting Cheyenne*, 427), while other sources give an 1881 date (see for example Llewellyn and Hoebel, *Cheyenne Way*, 215).

Information on Morning Star's life is from George Bent, "Forty Years with the Cheyenne," *The Frontier* 6 (1905–6): 38–51; George E. Hyde, *Life of George Bent* (Norman: University of Oklahoma Press, 1968); Stands In Timber and Liberty, *Cheyenne Memories*; and Marquis, *Wooden Leg.* See also Campbell, "Down among Red Men"; Senate, *Report No.708*; Edgar B. Bronson, *Reminiscences of a Ranchman* (New York: McClure, 1908); "Liquidation of Dull Knife," *Nebraska History* 22 (1941): 109–10; and other works of George Bird Grinnell.

For details on the Fetterman fight see George S. Hyde, *Red Cloud's Folk* (Norman: University of Oklahoma Press, 1937); and Grinnell, *Fighting Cheyenne.*

Dull Knife's first appearance in written records is in *Report of the Commissioner of Indian Affairs, 1856*, 638–54, National Archives.

Grinnell was taken to the site of the Fetterman fight by the eyewitness; see *Fighting Cheyenne*, 234.

That Sherman was removed from the commission is from Hoig, *Peace Chiefs of the Cheyenne*, 127.

For the text of this treaty see *United States Statutes at Large* 15:655.

"His face to the sky . . ." is from Billy Garnett, a Sioux interpreter present at the battle. The quote is from Nebraska State Historical Society, "Survey Notes, William Garnett at Cane Creek, SD, 1907," Eli Seavey Ricker Collection.

An especially good source for information on the Dull Knife battle is Sherry L. Smith, *Sagebrush Soldier: Private William Earl Smith's View of the Sioux War of 1876* (Norman: University of Oklahoma Press, 1989). See also Homer W. Wheeler, *Buffalo Days* (New York: Macmillian, 1925), John Bourke, *John MacKenzie's Last Fight with the Cheyenne* (1890; reprint, Bellevue NE: Old Army Press, 1970), as well as his *On the Border with Crook* (Scribners, 1891; reprint, Lincoln: University of Nebraska Press, 1971). See also Jerome A. Greene, *Lakota and Cheyenne: Indian Views of the Great Sioux War, 1876–1877* (Norman: University of Oklahoma Press, 1994), chapter 9; and Grinnell, *Fighting Cheyenne.*

For an excellent summary of the events leading to the removal of the Cheyenne from the north, see Orlan J. Svingen, *The Northern Cheyenne Indian Reservation, 1877–1900* (Niwot: University Press of Colorado, 1990). See also Marquis, *Wooden Leg*; Grinnell, *Fighting Cheyenne*; Senate, *Report No.708*; and Ramon S. Powers, "Why the Cheyenne Left Indian Territory in 1878: A Cultural Analysis," *Kansas Quarterly* 3 (fall 1971): 72–81.

The recommendation to send the Cheyennes to Indian Territory is from Sheridan to Sherman, May 15, 1877 (telegram), Assistant Adjunct General, Office of Adjunct General, *Letters Received, 1877–1891*, records group 94, National Archives.

Porcupine Bull, a Southern Cheyenne, is quoted in Grinnell, *Cheyenne Indians* 1:288.

CHAPTER 9: TURKEY SPRINGS

"Have struck trail . . ." is from *Report of the Secretary of War*, vol. 1, *Report of the General of the Army, 1878*, National Archives.

The map can be found in *Records of the War Department, United States Army Commands, Dept. of the Missouri, Letters Received*, enclosure of 6193-3-1878, National Archives.

The quote from the court-martial is from *Army and Navy Journal* 17 (July 12, 1879): 884. Rendlebrock and another officer were questioned about their conduct at Turkey Springs. Shortly thereafter Rendlebrock was arrested on February 1, 1879. He was taken to Camp Supply, where a general court-martial was convened to hear his case. The court found him guilty and sentenced him to dismissal from military service. Later, President Rutherford B. Hayes pardoned Rendlebrock because of his age and long years of service.

For an excellent summary of the military's activities in pursuit of the Cheyennes in Oklahoma see Peter M. Wright, "The Pursuit of Dull Knife from Fort Reno in 1878–1879" *Chronicles of Oklahoma* 46, no. 2 (summer 1968): 141–54. See also *Record of Engagements with Hostile Indians: The Military Division of Missouri, 1868–1882*, facsimile ed. (Bellevue NE: Old Army Press, 1969).

Part 3: Ghosts

CHAPTER 12: HENRY FORD AND MR. GOODNIGHT

The *New York Times* quote appeared in the September 19, 1878 edition. The *Nebraska State Journal* also published their account on September 19, 1878. The *Russell KS Reformer* report appeared February 4, 1898.

The unnamed cowboy's report of Cheyenne activities comes from Senate, *Report No. 708*.

CHAPTER 13: THE SPEECH OF THE WOLVES

Dull Knife was married to Goes to Get a Drink when he took a captive woman, known as Pawnee Woman, or Pawnee Wife, as his second wife. As was the custom, after the death of Goes to Get a Drink, Dull Knife married her sister Slow Woman (also known as Short Woman and Short One), so that when they left Oklahoma, both of these wives, Slow Woman and Pawnee Woman, were with him.

The story of Dull Knife's wife's being killed by a horse is found in Mari Sandoz, *Cheyenne Autumn* (New York: McIntosh & Otis, 1953), and is apparently based on information provided by a Cheyenne interpreter, Ben Clarke. A Cheyenne woman and her sixteen-year-old son had been captured in northern Kansas shortly after the Cheyennes had passed through the area. The woman had told Clarke that "Dull Knife's wife" had been killed while the Cheyennes were camped and one of the horses had jumped on her. Apparently based on evidence from informants she contacted, Sandoz's version has Short Woman killed by the horse as the Cheyennes are preparing to flee pursuing troops (see *Cheyenne Autumn*, 128–29, and material in the Mari Sandoz Collection, Special Collections, University of Nebraska Library).

The current version is based on my collection of Cheyenne oral history, which also supports the idea that one of Dull Knife's two wives was killed by a horse during the exodus. However, many of these accounts claim it was Pawnee Woman who died, and some versions place the incident after the Fort Robinson escape. On February 11, 1879, the *Chicago Tribune* reported that Dull knife "and his wife and son" were at Pine Ridge. A woman identified only as "Dull Knife's widow" is mentioned in Llewellyn and Hoebel, *Cheyenne Way*, 215.

Part 4: The Rattlesnake Way

CHAPTER 16: PUNISHED WOMAN

The quote from General Pope is from the *Denver Tribune*, October 19, 1878.

Part 5: Depredations

CHAPTER 20: DEPREDATIONS ON THE SAPPA

The most convincing discussion of the Battle of Cheyenne Hole and the best argument that the military did not riot nor cause a massacre can be found in G. Derek West, "The Battle of Sappa Creek, 1875," in *Kansas Historical Society Quarterly* 34, no.2 (summer 1968): 150–78. Information on the various accounts of the Battle of Cheyenne Hole is also from the following sources: Campbell, "Down among Red Men"; see also *Kansas Historical Society Collections* 10 (1907–8) and 12 (1911–12); Wheeler, *Buffalo Days*; Austin Henely, "Report of Operations of Detachment under His Command on the Scout from Fort Wallace and of Engagement with the Cheyenne on North Fork Sappa Creek on the 23rd Instant," from *Annual Reports: Division of the Missouri*, AGO and reprinted in George Nellans, *Authentic Accounts of Massacre of Indians, Rawlins County, Kansas, 1875, and Cheyenne Indian Raid in Western Kansas, Sept. 30, 1878* (n.p., 1958); William D. Street, "Cheyenne Indian Massacre on the Middle Fork of the Sappa," *Kansas Historical Society Collection* 10 (1907–8): 368; Wright, "Pursuit of Dull Knife"; National Archives, *Report of the Secretary of War 1875*, vol. 1; *Rocky Mountain News*, April 25, 1875.

Mari Sandoz's version is based in part on the information provided to her by means of correspondences from H. D. Wimer during 1949, which includes Wimer's account of "John Koontz who came to Kansas in 1879 and settled on the land in Raulins [*sic*] Co. where the Cheyenne were massacred" (Letter to Sandoz, November 15, 1949, Mari Sandoz Collection, Special Collections, University of Nebraska). Her story of why no one was willing to talk is apparently based on a version of events from "Written by F. M. Lockard, 1910" (from materials in the Mari Sandoz Collection, Special Collections, University of Nebraska).

Information regarding the depredations on the Sappa in 1878 was gathered from the following diverse and often obscure sources. I am graciously indebted to many people for providing these, but especially to Rosalie Seeman, the County Clerk of Thomas County, Kansas, and Fonda Farr, Director of the Last Indian Raid Museum, Oberlin, Kansas: John S. Bird, "Prairies and Pioneers" (n.d., n.p.); George W. Martin, *Indian Raid of 1878: The Report of Commission Appointed in Pursuance of the Provisions of Senate Joint Resolution No. 1, Relating to Losses Sustained by Citizens of Kansas by the Invasion of Indians during the Year 1878* (Topeka: Kansas Publishing House, 1879); *Kansas State Historical Society Collections* 9 (1905–6) and 11 (1909–10); Craig Miller, *West of Wichita, 1865–1890* (Lawrence: University Press of Kansas, 1972); E. S. Sutton, "More about Dull Knife Raid by the Constable of Atwood, 1901" and "The Indian Boy," in *Tepees to Soddies* (n.d., n.p.); Mrs. Henry M. Anthony, "Early NW Kansas Reminiscences," *Seldon KS Advocate* (n.d.); *Record of Engagements with Hostile Indians: The Military*

Division of the Missouri, facsimile ed. (Bellevue NE: Old Army Press, 1969); Pearl Toothaker, *History of Sheridan County, Kansas* (n.p., 1961); Fred Wallsmith, "Kansas' Last Indian Raid," *Kanhistique,* October 1978, 12–13; Captain William G. Wedemeyer to Post Adjutant Fort Wallace, Kansas, October 26, 1878, "Copy of Official Report of Lives Lost and Property Destroyed and Stolen in Indian Raid of 1878 through Decatur County and Rawlins County, Kansas," reprint in Nellans, *Authentic Accounts.*

Additional information was drawn from the following newspapers: *Colby (KS) Citizen Patriot,* various dates; *Herndon (KS) Nonpareil,* November 16, 1933; "The Last Indian Raid in Kansas," *Kansas Sentinel,* March 14, 1929; *Oberlin (KS) Herald,* various dates; *Wichita (KS) Sunday Eagle,* October 17, 1920: Fred Hinkle, *Soldier Creek.*

The following manuscript sources were also consulted: H. D. Colvin, "Dull Knife's Raid"; "The William Laing Story," photocopy of unpublished manuscript prepared by the Last Indian Raid Museum, Oberlin, Kansas; letter from Pat LeMoine and Lloyd LeMoine to Last Indian Raid Museum, Oberlin, Kansas, July 12, 1988; Rose Rosicky, "A History of Czechs in Nebraska" and "The Last Indian Raid." These last two items, as well as valuable additional information, were provided by Rosalie Seeman, County Clerk of Thomas County, Kansas. The other items can be found at the Last Indian Raid Museum.

Part 6: In the Time of the Buffalo

CHAPTER 22: IN THE TIME OF THE BUFFALO

For much of the information about the bison, the size of the herds, its range, and various other information in this chapter I am indebted to Tom McHugh's masterpiece *The Time of the Buffalo* (New York: Knopf, 1972), a thorough, entertaining, and impeccably written account of the role of this mighty animal in American history. Additional source material is from Ed Park, *The World of the Bison* (Philadelphia: Lippincott, 1969).

For more information on Doc Carver see Alan Boye, *The Complete Roadside Guide to Nebraska* (St. Johnsbury VT: Saltillo, 1992); Federal Writers Project, *Nebraska: A Guide to the Cornhusker State* (New York: Viking, 1934); and Ed Russell, *The Lives and Legends of Buffalo Bill* (Norman: University of Oklahoma Press, 1960).

The Cody quotes are from Russell, *Lives and Legends of Buffalo Bill*. See also *Where the Buffalo Roamed: Stories of Early Days in Buffalo County* (Shenandoah IA: World, n.d.).

A. T. Andreas, *History of the State of Nebraska* (Evansville IN: Unigraphic, 1975); and *Compendium of Historical Reminiscence and Biography of Western Nebraska* (Chicago: n.p., 1909).

The information about the 1883 discovery of the South Dakota herd is from Ed Park, *World of the Bison*.

The information on grasses is from Ann Bleed and Charles Flowerday, eds., *An Atlas of the Sand Hills* (Lincoln: Conservation and Survey Division, Institute of Agriculture and Natural Resources, University of Nebraska, 1989); Lauren Brown, *Grasses: An Identification Guide* (Boston: Houghton Mifflin, 1979); J. E. Waver, *Native Vegetation of Nebraska* (Lincoln: University of Nebraska Press, 1965); and Robert C. Lommasson, *Nebraska Wild Flowers* (Lincoln: University of Nebraska Press, 1973).

Part 7: Sand Hills Sundays and Others

CHAPTER 23: WHITE TAIL

The true extent and importance of violence on the frontier will perhaps never emerge from what twentieth-century movies and television has portrayed as truth. Nevertheless, recent scholarship has often focused on trying to determine the nature and magnitude of violence on the frontier by using contemporary accounts such as diaries, newspapers, and court records. Two useful works that take such a look at the violence of Kansas and Nebraska during the Cheyenne exodus are Nyle H. Miller and Joseph W. Snell, *Great Gunfighters of the Kansas Cowtowns, 1867–1886* (Lincoln: University of Nebraska Press, 1967); and Wayne C. Lee, *Wild Towns of Nebraska* (Caldwell ID: Caxton, 1988).

Recent scholarship has also revised and justly reestablished the important role women played in settling the frontier. Combatting the Hollywood image of dutiful, passive, and frightened women cowering in covered wagons led by John Wayne types, a more accurate portrait is emerging of strong women who bore the brunt of childrearing and house chores, as well as doing much of the "man's work" of hunting, building, farming, and riding. An excellent example of this kind of work is Mike Helm's presentation of interviews with pioneer women that were conducted by an Oregon newspaperman from 1900 until the 1920s. See Mike Helm, ed., *The Lockley Files: Conversations with Pioneer Women* (Eugene OR: Rainy Day, 1981).

The best source for information on the Sand Hills is Bleed and Flowerday, *An Atlas of the Sand Hills*.

John Stands In Timber says the split of the groups occurred after they crossed the North Platte (Stands In Timber and Liberty, *Cheyenne Memories*, 234–35). Grinnell says it was there or at least near the Platte, but neither of these important sources say much about *why* the separation took place. Grinnell claims that Little Wolf wanted to keep moving northward with caution, but Dull Knife believed that because they were in the north again, nothing bad would happen. He also claims that the split did not happen all at once, but that small groups of Dull Knife's band split off over the course of several days and then regrouped north of the Platte (*Fighting Cheyenne*, 409–10).

The movements of troops and Indians are based on reports in the *Omaha Herald*, October 19, 1878, and correspondences found in Assistant Adjunct General, Office of Adjunct General, *Letters Received, 1877–1891*, records group 94, National Archives.

For another description of this special place, see "The Lady White Tail" in John Janovy's beautiful masterpiece, *Keith County Journal* (New York: St. Martin's, 1978).

CHAPTER 24: WALKING

The official report of the "Mormon Cow Incident" can be found in LeRoy R. Hafen and Ann W. Hafen, eds., *Powder River Campaigns and Sawyer's Expedition of 1865: A Documentary Account Comprising Official Reports, Diaries, Contemporary Newspaper Accounts, and Personal Narratives* (Glendale CA: Arthur H. Clark, 1961), 60–63. As always, the superb writings of Robert M. Utley are also an excellent source. See his *Frontiersmen in Blue: The United States Army and the Indian, 1848–1865* (Lincoln: University of Nebraska Press, 1981).

One of the best accounts of Ishi is Theodora Kroeber, *Ishi: The Last of His Tribe* (New York: Parnassus, 1964).

CHAPTER 25: GOOD REPORTING

Red Cloud is quoted in the *Chicago Times*, October 13, 1878; Carlton's brief summary of this meeting can be found in Bureau of Indian Affairs, Central Superintendency, *Letters Sent, 1875–1880*, National Archives. Quotes and information about Thornburgh are taken from various articles found in Thornburgh's scrapbook at the Colorado Historical Society.

CHAPTER 26: A TABLE COMMUNITY

According to the historian John McDermott, the soldier was probably Captain Henry Wessells, commander at Fort Robinson, who later claimed he had teased Dull Knife about marrying his daughter (private correspondence).

Part 8: All Is But a Beginning

CHAPTER 27: WITNESS TREE

Information on the capture of Dull Knife comes from Grinnell, *Fighting Cheyenne*, 414–16; Stands In Timber and Liberty, *Cheyenne Memories*, 232–37; *New York Times*; and *Annual Report of the Commission of Indian Affairs, 1878; Records of the War Department, Department of the Platte, Letters Sent; Report of the Secretary of War, 1878*; and *Office of the Adjunct General, Letters Received*, all in National Archives. See also Senate, *Report 708*. The official investigation into the events at Fort Robinson are an important source of information as well: Military Division of the Missouri, *Proceedings of Board of Officers*, 1879, Special File, War Records, National Archives.

CHAPTER 28: FORT ROBINSON

A wide variety of sources were used to gather the information in this chapter. General sources included conversations with Josie Sooktis, and Military Division of the Missouri, *Proceedings of Board of Officers*. I was also guided by comments in correspondence with the historian John McDermott.

Sources by month:

October: Testimony of Baxter, Chase, and Carlton in Military Division of the Missouri, *Proceedings of Board of Officers*; *Records of the War Department, Department of the Platte, Letters Sent*; *Report of the Secretary of War, 1878*; Office of the Adjunct General, *Letters Received 1877–1891*; and U.S. Army Continental Commands, *Letters Received*, records group 393, all in National Archives; *Chicago Times*; Grinnel, *Fighting Cheyenne*.

November: Military Division of the Missouri, *Proceedings of Board of Officers* (see especially the testimony of Cummings); *Annual Report of Commissioner of Indian Affairs, 1879*; Ricker interviews, Nebraska State Historical Society; *Omaha Herald*; *Chicago Times*; Hugh Lenox Scott, *Some Memories of a Soldier* (New York: Century, 1928). Many quotes from the military personnel in this section were taken from correspondences found in Assistant Adjunct General, Office of Adjunct General, *Letters Received, 1877–1891*; U.S. Army Continental Commands, *Letters Received*, records group 393, National Archives; and Grinnell, *Fighting Cheyenne*.

December: Bronson, *Reminiscences of a Ranchman*; Hoig, *Peace Chiefs of the Cheyenne*; Grinnell, *Fighting Cheyenne*; United States Army Continental Commands, *Letters Received*; Military Division of the Missouri, *Proceedings of Board of Officers*; Assistant Adjunct General, Office of Adjunct General, *Letters Received, 1877–1891*.

January: Military Division of the Missouri, *Proceedings of Board of Officers*, especially Schuyler Report of Crook, forwarded to Sheridan; interview with John Shangrau, Garnett Book, "The Medical History of Ft. Robinson," all in Eli Seavey Ricker Collection, Nebraska State Historical Society; *Chicago Tribune*; *New York Times*; *Omaha Herald*.

CHAPTER 30: COMING TO SEE BEAR BUTTE

The best descriptions of Cheyenne beliefs are to be found in Grinnell, *Cheyenne Indians*; Stands In Timber and Liberty, *Cheyenne Memories*; and the works of Peter J. Powell, including *Sweet Medicine: The Continuing Role of the Sacred Arrows, the Sun Dance and the Sacred Buffalo Hat in Northern Cheyenne History*, 2 vols. (Norman: University of Oklahoma Press, 1969), and *People of the Sacred Mountain: A History of the Northern Cheyenne Chiefs and Warrior Societies, 1830–1879* 2 vols. (1969–74; reprint, New York: Harper, 1980).

CHAPTER 31: THE HOLY COST

For information concerning the events leading to the formation of the Northern Cheyenne reservation see Svingen, *Northern Cheyenne Indian Reservation*.

The information that Dull Knife is actually buried in the hills of the reservation was told to me by Josie Sooktis.

The movements of Little Wolf are determined from reports in the *New York Times*; Bureau of Indian Affairs, Office of Indian Affairs, *Letters Received*; Grinnel, *Fighting Cheyenne*; and Little Wolf Papers, records group 393, National Archives.

Dull Knife's movements after his escape are based on information from Grinnell, *Fighting Cheyenne*; *Chicago Tribune*; *Omaha Herald*; oral history; and from Bureau of Indian Affairs, Office of Indian Affairs, *Letters Received*.

Grinnell says that Dull Knife died in 1883 (*Fighting Cheyenne*, 427), while other sources give an 1881 date (see for example Llewellyn and Hoebel, *Cheyenne Way*, 215).

Information about the actions of Wild Hog is from Assistant Adjunct General, Office of Adjunct General, *Letters Received, 1877–1891*; *Chicago Tribune*; Interview with John Shangrau, Eli Seavey Ricker Collection, Nebraska State Historical Society; Military Division of the Missouri, *Proceedings of Board of Officers*; Bureau of Indian Affairs, Office of Indian Affairs, *Letters Received*; and Miller and Snell, *Great Gunfighters of the Kansas Cowtowns*.

The story of Little Chief can be found in Hoig, *Peace Chiefs of the Cheyenne*.

For other views of the battle involving Buffalo Bill, see Russell, *Lives and Legends of Buffalo Bill*.

Information about the final battle can be found in Assistant Adjunct General, Office of Adjunct General, *Letters Received, 1877–1891*; Military Division of the Missouri, *Proceedings of Board of Officers*; Bureau of Indian Affairs, Office of Indian Affairs, *Letters Received*; *Chicago Tribune*; Interview with John Shangrau and "The Medical History of Ft. Robinson," in the Eli Seavey Ricker Collection, Nebraska State Historical Society; *Chicago Tribune*; *Omaha Herald*; and Grinnell, *Fighting Cheyenne*.